·THE·
SCOTS
·CELLAR

·THE·
SCOTS
·CELLAR·

its traditions and lore

F. MARIAN McNEILL

LOCHAR PUBLISHING · MOFFAT · SCOTLAND

A catalogue record for this book is available from the British Library.

ISBN 0-948403-68-3

CONTENTS

The Cellar

Convivial Life

Recipes

INTRODUCTION

The Scots Cellar has been designed as a companion and complement to an earlier work, *The Scots Kitchen*. It differs, however, in plan. In the *Kitchen* my main object was to preserve the recipes for our national and regional dishes, many of which were in danger of falling into undeserved oblivion, and the short chapters in which I attempted to throw some sidelights on Scottish social and domestic history are merely introductory. In this volume, however, the emphasis is reversed, the recipes being only a supplement to the major part of the book, which is concerned with the social and convivial life of the Scots and their delight in hospitality, together with the part played therein by their indigenous drinks, ale and whisky, and the wines imported throughout the centuries from their old ally, France.

There are many good people, I know, who regard whisky as an intrinsically evil thing; but many more, I feel sure, are in agreement with what I contend in the chapter under that heading —a chapter which, incidentally, I cannot claim to be much more than an annotated anthology—that it is the abuse of whisky, or indulgence in some spurious concoction sold under that name, that has played such havoc in many homes and communities. As Neil Gunn wisely comments, 'Perfect knowledge and appreciation beget natural temperance.'

The marked convivial disposition of the Scot has found expression in an astonishing output of song and verse. Hardly any poet or writer of note, not to mention those of little or no note, has failed to make his contribution; and it is significant that virtually all of them, whether poet, peer or peasant, man of letters, man of law or working man, turn instinctively to the old Scots tongue, which remains to the Lowland Scot (as does Gaelic to the Highlander) the language of the heart.

A word about the recipes. In the ordinary way, the Scot prefers his drink, whether ale, wine or whisky, straight from the cask or the bottle, and the Highlander, at least, dilutes his whisky, if he dilutes it at all, with cold spring water. (Notable exceptions are toddy and Atholl brose.) Nevertheless we have a number of traditional drinks that are well worth preserving, and their recipes will be found within. I include also a number of whisky cocktails, which appear to be growing in popularity south of the Grampians (we trans-Grampians are still a bit snooty about them), although I cannot guarantee that they were all invented in Scotland, or even by Scots. There are also a number of drinks based on our good Scotch ale. Lastly, there is a fairly complete collection of recipes for country wines, in which our women used to excel, and which have a growing number of devotees today.

Times have greatly changed, and few of us can afford nowadays to entertain as freely as we used to; but, 'contented wi' little and canty wi' mair', we can still guard the convivial flame and still take delight in entertaining the stranger in our midst. Long may we do so!

F. MARIAN McNEILL

Edinburgh, June 1956

ACKNOWLEDGMENTS

I have to thank the following authors, owners of copyright and publishers for giving permission to include poems and prose passages in this book:

The Executors of Douglas Ainslie for a poem from *Chosen Poems*; Ivor Brown and Collins, Sons & Co. for passages from *Summer in Scotland*; Robert Browning (Scotus) for a poem published in *Glasgow University Magazine* (1905-6); Sir Robert Bruce Lockhart and Putnam & Co. for passages from *Scotch*; John Carswell and Routledge & Kegan Paul for passages from *The Scots Weekend* by Catherine and Donald Carswell; B. Feldman & Co. and Harms Inc. for 'Just a wee deoch-an-doris' by Sir Harry Lauder; Ian Finlay and Chatto & Windus for a passage from *Scotland*; Dr George Fletcher (Caurnie) for a poem published in *Glasgow University Magazine* (1905-6); Francis, Day & Hunter and Leeds Music Corporation for 'I belong to Glasgow' by Will Fyffe; Neil M. Gunn and Routledge & Kegan Paul for passages from *Whisky and Scotland*; the Executors of Hugh Haliburton (James Logie Robertson) and Blackwood

& Sons for a poem from *Horace in Homespun*; the Executors of Violet Jacob and Oliver & Boyd for one of her *Scottish Poems*; Michael Joyce and Longmans Green & Co. for a passage from *Edinburgh: the Golden Age*; the Kennedy-Fraser Trust and Boosey & Co. for part of Marjory Kennedy-Fraser's English version of *Kisimul's Galley*; H. D. F. Kitto and Penguin Books for a passage from *The Greeks*; Eric Linklater and Jonathan Cape for passages from *White-maa's Saga* and *The Lion and the Unicorn*; Hugh MacDiarmid (C. M. Grieve) and Blackwood & Sons for part of *A Drunk Man Looks at the Thistle*; Moray McLaren and Douglas & Foulis for passages from *The Capital of Scotland*; Moray McLaren and Hollis & Carter for passages from *A small Stir*; the late Kenneth MacLeod for his *Rune of Hospitality*; Mrs Rona Mavor and Hollis & Carter for a passage by James Bridie from *A Small Stir*; Augustus Muir for a passage from *Scottish Portrait*; the Executors of Charles Murray and Constable & Co. for a poem from *In the Country Places*; the Executors of Will Ogilvie for six lines from *A Braw Scots Nicht*; Dr John Oliver and *The Scotsman* for a passage from an article published on 3rd April 1954; George Scott-Moncrieff and B. T. Batsford for a passage from *Edinburgh*; the Executors of George Saintsbury and Macmillan & Co. for passages from *Notes on a Cellar-Book*; P. Morton Shand and Jonathan Cape for passages from *A Book of Food*; Marie Stuart and Robert Hale for a passage from *Old Edinburgh Taverns*; the Executors of William Soutar and Andrew Dakers for two of his *Collected Poems*; and H. Harvey Wood and Nelson & Sons for passages from 'Literature in Scotland' in *Scotland* edited by Dr H. W. Meikle. The Rt. Hon. Walter Elliot, M.P. (Parvus) for a poem published in *Glasgow University Magazine* and *University Verses* (1910-27).

I have also to thank R. Macdonald Robertson for the legend regarding the origin of Atholl brose, which he picked up in a gamekeeper's cottage in Glen Tilt; Mrs Catherine MacLennan of Port Appin, a foremost authority on country wines, for her valuable advice on this subject; Tommy P. Beaton, J. Marshall Robb and the Drambuie Liqueur Co. for eight Drambuie recipes published in *Scotch Whisky* (W. & R. Chambers); and William Younger & Co., brewers, Edinburgh, for a number of recipes from *Father William's Gazette*.

To
Neil Gunn
John McIntyre
Pat MacLaren
and
Duncan McNeill
(my brother)
FOUR HIGHLAND HOSTS
and in memory of
W. G. Burn-Murdoch
A PRINCE OF EDINBURGH HOSTS

THE CELLAR

1: *Ale and Beer*

FROM the earliest times people everywhere have contrived to make some sort of stimulating beverage from whatever materials lay to hand, whether grapes, grain, flowers, fruit, roots, herbs or honey. In Scotland the earliest drink we hear of is ale—not the kind of ale we drink today, but heather ale, the secret of which has long been assumed irretrievably lost. (The legend of heather ale and the surviving traditions will be found on pages 207-209.) When the navigator Pytheas visited the land that was to become Scotland, he found that the Picts were skilled in brewing a potent drink, and it has been suggested that the Scots were lured from Eire to Alba by the fame of its heather ale, as the Romans are alleged to have been lured to Britain by the fame of its oyster-beds. 'Indeed, as wars go,' comments Mr Morton Shand on the Roman invasion, 'the pretext seems to have been both respectable and logical.'[1] Some of these primitive Pictish 'breweries' have survived in Galloway. They are pear-shaped enclosures about sixteen feet in length by eight at their greatest breadth, with a side wall about three feet in height, and are situated on southern hill slopes near clear, swift-running streams.

About the twelfth or thirteenth century the German method of brewing was introduced into Scotland, and, like mead in England, the indigenous drink was gradually superseded by ale derived from malted barley. In Galloway, however, which appears to have been its stronghold, and in the remoter parts of the High-lands and Islands, heather ale continued to be brewed up to

1. *Book of Food.*

In Kinross, the browst which the gudewife of Lochrin produced from a peck of malt is thus commemorated:

> Twenty pints o strong ale,
> Twenty pints o sma',
> Twenty pints o hinky-pinky,
> Twenty pints o plooman's drinkie,
> Twenty pints o splitter-splatter,
> And twenty pints was waur nor water.

An anecdote concerning the misadventure of an ale-wife in the town of Forfar and the whimsical legal decision resulting therefrom has a place all its own in the annals of Scots Law. It is related by Sir Walter Scott in a note to *Waverley*:

'When the landlord of an inn presented his guests with *deoch an doruis*, that is, the drink at the door, or the stirrup-cup, the draught was not charged in the reckoning. On this point a learned bailie of the town of Forfar pronounced a very sound judgment.

'A, an ale-wife in Forfar, had brewed her "peck of malt", and set the liquor out-of-doors to cool; the cow of B, a neighbour of A, chanced to come by, and seeing the good beverage, was allured to taste it, and finally to drink it up. When A came to take in her liquor she found her tub empty, and from the cow's staggering and staring, so as to betray her intemperance, she easily divined the mode in which her "browst" had disappeared. To take vengeance on Crummie's ribs with a stick was her first effort. The roaring of the cow brought B, her master, who remonstrated with his angry neighbour, and received in reply a demand for the value of the ale which Crummie had drunk up. B refused payment, and was conveyed before C, the bailie, or sitting magistrate. He heard the case patiently and then demanded of the plaintiff A whether the cow had sat down to her potation or taken it standing? The plaintiff answered, she had not seen the deed committed but she supposed the cow drank the ale while standing on her feet, adding that had she been near she would have made her use them to some purpose. The bailie, on this admission, solemnly adjudged the cow's drink to be *deoch an doruis*—a stirrup-cup, for which no charge could be made without violating the ancient hospitality of Scotland.'

In Scots legal phraseology, the defendant was assoilzied (freed from the charge).

'Do as the cow o Forfar did: tak' a staunin' (standing) drink' has become a proverbial saying.

In 1600, by which time Holyrood had become a royal residence and the Abbey had been abandoned, an enterprising citizen, by name John Blair, took over the monks' maltings and sold his beer to the Palace, where it proved extremely popular with both King and courtiers. The brewery he founded still flourishes, under another name, at the foot of the Royal Mile. With the introduction of commercialized brewing, breweries now famous far beyond these islands sprang up, centring upon Edinburgh, Alloa and Glasgow.[1] By the eighteenth century, the ales of Edinburgh had won a very high reputation. One of the most popular was Bell's Beer, which was sent over a great part of Europe and even as far as the East Indies. Foreign visitors were invariably delighted with the quality of the ale, and the exiled French royalties who took refuge in Edinburgh in 1831 called the liquor 'Scottish Burgundy'.

In point of fact, Edinburgh owes much of her reputation for good ale to a freak of Nature in the form of a 'structural trough' —a sort of underground lake—which runs beneath and beyond the Royal Mile from Fountainbridge to Arthur's Seat. It is this water that feeds the breweries, which are established all along the line of the trough. The water contains a high percentage of gypsum, and it is this invaluable mineral element that constitutes the 'magic' which has imparted to Edinburgh ales their distinctive quality down the centuries.

In the mid-nineteenth century an offshoot of this geological phenomenon was discovered at Craigmillar, to the south-east of the city, and in consequence more breweries sprang up in that locality.

Trough water differs as much from tap water as does the proverbial cheese from chalk. Tap water is used by the Edinburgh brewers for one purpose only—to wash bottles.

The well sunk by monks of Holyrood eight hundred years ago is still in use; but instead of being pumped by a sweating lay-brother and carried by hand to the primitive mash-tub, the water

---

1. Edinburgh, with twenty-three breweries which contribute from ten to fifteen million pounds a year to the Customs fund, produces two-thirds of the beer exported from Scotland and is the second largest brewing centre in Great Britain.

is conveyed in a steady stream by a pulsating power-pump to the vats—huge vessels of burnished copper—where white-coated men, surrounded with gauges and graphs and all the other paraphernalia of modern science suited to their trade, watch over the first tumultuous ferment and direct each stage of the brewing process until at last the casks are piled on to the great transport lorries and set out on their journey by road, rail or sea to all parts of the world.

'The Scots,' writes Donald Carswell in *The Scots Week-end*, 'unlike the English, make no boast of their brewing. They have no need; for, as a Spanish poet said of good wine, "it is its own best testimonial". That the great English beers are supreme of their kind is indisputable, but on the other hand there is an unconscionable amount of bad beer in England, and by bad we mean inherently bad. In this sense there is no bad beer in Scotland, though you may get beer that has been ill kept or ill drawn, or you may get no beer at all at the moment when you most want it. The great brewers recognize the quality of Scotch beer and take their Scotch trade seriously. Hence the bottled Bass or Allsop you drink, when you can get it, in Glasgow or Edinburgh, is a more heartening drink than any contained in bottles bearing the same labels in London or Manchester. How else could they compete with our MacEwans, our Ushers, and our Youngers? Edinburgh and Alloa provide the bulk of our native beers of the true mouth-gripping and gullet-soothing properties, and to Dalkeith belongs the invention of green beer, which additionally soothes the eye. Glasgow manufactures a special light lager of which even Germans speak with a reverence verging upon awe and not unmixed with envy. But there is no home market for it. If you want to taste it you must ship yourself somewhere east of Suez. At the other end of the scale, there is what represents the "yill" or "tippeny" of our ancestors, the so-called "sweet" or "Scotch" ale. It is a noble liquor, ideal for cold weather, especially when mulled. But remember that it is the same drink that Willie brewed and Rab and Allan came to pree, and is therefore not to be trifled with.

'. . . The practice of lacing (ale and beer) with strong waters is an ancient but it is not an honourable one. It is a mode of drinking suitable only for navvies, ironmoulders, and Carlylean heroes.'

2: *Whisky*

The Origin of Whisky

'Round the southern corner of the dun there was a field of barley all ripened by the sun. In a small wind it echoed faintly the sound of the ocean; at night it sighed and rustled as the earth-mother thought things over, not without a little anxiety. It was cut and harvested and a sheaf offered in thanksgiving; flailed and winnowed; until the ears of grain remained in a heap of gold: the bread of life.

'In simple ways the grain was prepared and ground and set to ferment; the fermented liquor was then boiled, and as the steam came off it was by happy chance condensed against some cold surface.

'And lo! this condensation of steam from the yellowish-green fermented gruel is clear as crystal. It is purer than any water from any well. When cold, it is colder to the fingers than ice.

'A marvellous transformation! A perfect water. But in the mouth—what is this? The gums tingle, the throat burns, down into the belly fire passes, and thence outward to the finger-tips, to the feet, and finally to the head. . . . Clearly it was not water he had drunk: it was life.'

Thus Neil Gunn visualizes the genesis of our great national drink.

It is generally accepted that whisky or *uisgebeatha*,[1] to give it its ancient Gaelic name, originated in Scotland and Ireland, but in which first no one can definitely say. According to an Irish legend mentioned by Mr Gunn, the Irish learned the art of distillation from St Patrick, whose birthplace is thought to be Dumbarton on the Clyde; but, he adds, the two countries were so closely linked in ancient times that the drink may well have appeared more or less spontaneously in both.

1. *Uisgebeatha* (pron. ooshku-bey-a), *water* of life. *Uisge* was corrupted first into *usky* and finally into *whisky*.

B

History

'The history of malt whisky lies shrouded in the mists of the Celtic dawn', writes Sir Robert Bruce Lockhart. 'Some authorities hold that cereals and spirits were the secrets of long life and that the Celts simplified the recipe by combining the two in whisky. . . . It is a fact that for centuries a spirit distilled from a fermented barley mash has been made all over the Highlands where Nature still supplies the essential ingredients for its distillation: home-grown barley for the malt, the pure air of the mountains, the unpolluted water of the hill burns, the rich dark peat of the moor, and, in the opinion of some experts, the granite rocks from which the water springs.'

By the fifteenth century the manufacture of whisky was well established in the Highlands and its fame had penetrated to the Lowlands, even to the Court. We learn from the Exchequer Rolls that James IV had his *aqua vitae* distilled from barley by a friar. During the first half of the seventeenth century the popularity of whisky grew steadily in the Lowlands, particularly in the West, and along the Highland line distilleries sprang up to meet the demands of the Glasgow taverns. In the Highlands, the distilleries, which were much smaller than those in the south, aimed mainly at supplying local needs; but probably the finest whiskies were those distilled by the Highland chiefs for use in their own households.

The first mention of a famous whisky occurs in 1690. This is 'Ferintosh', which was already widely noted for its quality when the 'ancient brewery of aquavity in Cromarty', the property of Forbes of Culloden (the Whig jurist and statesman who broke the rising of the 'Forty-five), was sacked by marauding Jacobite Highlanders and 'all whiskie pits destroyed'. In compensation, the Government passed a special act of Parliament farming out to Culloden and his successors the yearly excise of the lands of Ferintosh. Soon, it is computed, as much whisky was distilled there as in all the rest of Scotland where the duty on malt was enforced, and the family made enormous profits. In spite of jealous complaints, it was not until 1784 that the owner was bought out. Burns commemorated the event in the well-known lines:

Thee, Ferintosh! O sadly lost!
Scotland laments frae coast to coast!
Now colic grips and barkin' hoast
May kill us a,
For loyal Forbes's chartered boast
Is ta'en awa!

During the greater part of the eighteenth century whisky remained an unfashionable drink in the lowlands, pride of place being given to claret and brandy. This is quite understandable, for the cheap popular whisky of the period was the rawest and nastiest of its kind. 'Whisky, in those days,' writes Dr John Strang, 'being chiefly drawn from the large, flat-bottomed stills of Kilbagie, Kennetpans and Lochrin, was only fitted for the most vulgar and fire-loving palates; but when a little of the real mountain dew, from Glenlivet or Arran, could be obtained, which was a matter of difficulty and danger, it was sure to be presented to guests with as sparing a hand as the finest *Maraschino di Zara* is now offered by some laced lacquey . . . at the close of a first-class repast.'[1]

After the Union of the Parliaments in 1707, the Scottish whisky industry was plagued and badgered by political intrigue and oppressive measures. One of the first grievances was the imposition, in 1713, of a tax on malt—a staple of the utmost importance in the interior economy of Scotland—which was forced upon the country in face of the strenuous opposition of the Scottish members. Another date of gloomy memory is that of Culloden (1746). The Highlands were now opened up to the Lowlands, and whisky flowed south in a stream of ever-increasing volume. The Westminster Government, however, were set on pursuing a vindictive policy towards the Highlanders, 'loyal' and 'disloyal' alike (actually only a minority of the clans were 'out' in the 'Forty-five'), and among the numerous harsh measures imposed was a ban on the small stills and an increase in the duty on whisky. Coming at a time when the first demands for Scotch whisky were arriving from England, these were bitterly resented.

But as Burns asserts, 'Freedom and whisky gang thegither', and in defiance of the law private stills sprang up everywhere—notably in Glenlivet, a district favoured by its inaccessibility. An

1. *Glasgow and Her Clubs.*

army of gaugers, sometimes supported by the military, was let loose in the land, but in spite of all they could do, an immense illicit distilling industry was carried on in the bothies at practically every farm. Sir Robert Bruce Lockhart, whose maternal (Macgregor) forebears were distillers in Glenlivet, tells us how the smugglers, 'sturdy, determined, and embittered by injustice, loaded their whisky on hill ponies and led them skilfully by secret tracks to the rich markets of the Lowlands'.

Smuggling, as Sir Robert reminds us, had its humours.

'On one occasion, a smuggler was cautioned by a gauger in a friendly manner. Both were Highlanders.

'"Sandy," said the gauger, "you and me are weel acquent, and ye ken I'm a man o my word. Weel, I'm tellin' ye for yer ain gude ye're gaun too far, and I hae my orders. From now on I'm on yer trail."

'"Thanks," said Sandy. "Ye'll admit my word is as gude as yer ain. Weel, I'll gi'e ye a chance. On Friday I'll bring in a firkin o whisky under yer very eyes, and it'll be on the north road between Beauly and Inverness between nine a.m. and five p.m."

'. . . By the Friday the gauger had gathered a strong band of excise officers and police to watch the road. From nine in the morning onwards there was a steady stream of traffic. First came carts with hay. Each cart was searched. Then came carts with turnips followed by carts with sheep, and, later, carts with wool. All were examined with infinite care, but no whisky was found. Later came a funeral cortege which held up the queue of carts for some time until a dray with a load of oats made a sudden dash to pass the procession.

'"Stop that dray!" called the head gauger. The dray was searched in vain.

'The queue of carts continued until five in the evening, when the gauger and his weary men were glad to call a halt.

'Later in the evening, gauger and smuggler met to compare notes, and the gauger took Sandy to task.

'"It's no the playin' o a trick on me that I mind," he said. "It's the fact that ye broke your pledged word. Man, I trusted ye."

'"I kept my word," said Sandy, "and the whisky's in Inverness now."

'"Ye brought the whisky along the north road between nine and five? Have ye any witnesses?"

'"Aye," said Sandy, "there's yersel'. Man, ye took aff yer hat to it!"'

'Now dawned the heroic age of whisky' (I quote Aeneas Macdonald), 'when it was hunted upon the mountains with a price on its head as if it were a Stuart prince, when loyal and courageous men sheltered it in their humble cabins, when its lore was kept alive in secret like the tenets of a proscribed and persecuted religion. If whisky has not degenerated wholly into a vile thing in which no person of taste and discernment can possibly take an interest it is because its tradition was preserved by men whose names an ungrateful posterity has forgotten, during years when the brutal and jealous Hanoverian Government sought to suppress in the Highlands this last relic of the ancient Gaelic civilization.'

To the Highlanders, the duty on whisky was as unreasonable as the game laws; as clearly a violation of God's providence. Distilling had always been carried on as a sideline to farming, the surplus grain being mashed, fermented, and fed into the spirit still. Without this supplement to their earnings, many crofters would have been hard put to it to pay their rent.

'Old men all over the north and west of Scotland have told me stories of their early boyhood,' writes Neil Gunn. 'Bolshen was a crofter, and the farmers and crofters in his neighbourhood sent him barley and received back whisky, just as they sent oats to the mill and received back meal. There was no real sense of guilt in this transaction. . . . If the sensitive were troubled at all, it was by the guilt of evasion, not of moral wrong. Most of them were decent, God-fearing men and women, who would have been shocked and grief-stricken at any son who would have stolen a penny.

'This may be difficult to grasp by one who does not understand the background from which such thought and action naturally emerged. To the poor Scot, deriving from the ancient Gaelic social life, ideas of property and ownership of certain fruits of earth and sea were radically different from those of a poor Anglo-Saxon deriving from feudalism: so much so that it was a difference not merely in conscious idea but in blood impulse.'

In the same writer's *Young Art and Old Hector*, the ethics of smuggling are discussed in the smuggler's cave.

'"Haven't I proved you the very fount and origin of law-breaking and all that's wrong?" demanded Red Dougal. "Law-breaking, yes," said Old Hector. "But wrong is a difficult word. ... For, you see, laws are necessary, and to break them is wrong. Yet a law can be wrong. ... This is our own native drink, made in this land from time immemorial. We were the first makers, as you have just said. For untold centuries we had it as our cordial in life, distilled from the barley grown round our doors. In these times, because it was free, it was never abused. That is known. Deceit and abuse and drunkenness came in with the tax, for the folk had to evade the tax because they were poor. ... We do not make this drink to profit by it at the expense of the tax," proceeded Old Hector. "We do not sell it. Just as Donul does not sell a salmon he takes out of the river. Nor would we even make it thus for ourselves if we could afford to buy it. But we cannot buy it. We are too poor. The men who have made the law have taken our drink from us, and have not left us where-with to buy it. Yet they can buy it, because they are rich. I have the feeling that that is not just. I do not grudge them their riches and all it can buy for them."

'"And do you think," said Dougal, lifting his head, "that the Sheriff in his court will listen to your fine reasons?"

'"I have no foolish notions about that," replied Old Hector. "But I am a man whose eightieth birthday is not so far distant, and I had to decide for myself whether my reasons might meet with understanding in a Court higher than the Sheriff's." '

Even the Highland ministers declined to stand on the side of law and order, for they, too, drew a sharp distinction between offences against harsh and unjust man-made laws and those against the unchanging moral law.

It was Alexander, Duke of Gordon, who at last persuaded the Government to see reason. Himself one of the principal land-owners in Glenlivet, 'he told the house bluntly that the High-landers were born distillers, whisky was their beverage from time immemorial, they would have it and sell it too, when tempted by high duties. But if the legislature would pass an act making it possible to manufacture whisky as good as the smuggled product on payment of a reasonable duty, he and his brother proprietors in the Highlands would use their best endeavours to put down smuggling and encourage legal distilling.'

Thus it came about that in 1823 an act of capital importance in the whisky industry was passed, sanctioning legal distilling at the 'reasonable duty' the Duke had advised. The small private stills were made illegal, but although this put an end to whisky-making in the home, it encouraged enterprising individuals to undertake the manufacture of good whisky on a much larger scale, and many distilleries were set up in those areas where natural conditions were most favourable to production. The materials and, in principle, the methods employed were substantially the same.

The first licensed distillery in Glenlivet was opened by George Smith, a remarkable man—farmer, architect, scholar and (hitherto) illicit distiller and smuggler. Smith's Glenlivet was reputed 'a great whisky'.

The next outstanding event was the invention, in or about 1830, of the patent still, which revolutionized the manufacture of whisky and led to its vastly increased consumption throughout the English-speaking world. The patent still contrived to extract alcohol from a variety of sources, and as it was also independent of geographical locality, it had the advantage of relative cheapness—but at a price.

'The product of the pot still',[1] writes Neil Gunn, 'contains the oils and aromatic substances that give true whisky its body and flavour. The product of the patent still is almost pure alcohol, flavourless, and is mainly used for industrial and scientific purposes. . . . Now a patent still produces alcohol much more cheaply than a pot still and in vastly greater quantities. If, therefore, one can put upon the market a bottle of this patent still spirit, reduced with water to the usual retail strength and coloured nicely with caramel, a bigger profit would be obtained from its sale than from the sale of a bottle of pure pot still whisky. It is the aim of every commercial concern to make as big a profit as possible.

'When the Highland and Irish distillers of the real *uisgebeatha* saw what was happening they became alarmed. This trade of theirs that they had been conscientiously building up for generations was facing disaster, for of course the patent spirit (or "silent" spirit as it was called) was being alluringly labelled as fine old matured Scotch whisky. . . . It does seem hard on Scotland that one of her most distinctive products should be thus imitated

1. The pot still is a large copper vessel used in the distillation of whisky.

throughout the world. The commercial loss, taking everything that is wrongly labelled "Scotch" into account, must be enormous; but, as I suggest, it is surely more enormous that so fine and indeed so noble a spirit should be so vilely treated.'

Since the invention of the patent still, door after door has been opened to commercial vandalism. The Highland distillers, who scorned the unscrupulous manufacturing methods of their rivals, protested that the new patent still spirit was 'Scotch'd spirit', not whisky.

Another blow was delivered by the Royal Commission on Whisky of 1908-9, which defined whisky as a spirit obtained by distillation from a mash of cereal grain, saccharified by the diastase of malt.

'[This] reckless extension of the term whisky has had the gravest consequences for the prestige of the industry,' writes Aeneas Macdonald. 'It has tended to deprive whisky of the special character it had built up during centuries of careful and pious labour and research. The tasteless distillate of grain, made at one process in a patent still, is equally entitled to call itself whisky as the exquisite, pot still whisky dried above a peat fire. It is only right to say that the definition was made in defiance of the best opinion of the distilling industry. . . . At the same time it is to be deplored that the opposition of serious-minded, cultivated whisky-drinkers to the pretensions of the Whisky Commission was not stronger. . . . The evil having been done, it is necessary to instruct the whisky public, especially young and inexperienced drinkers, in the true facts of the case, so that, as far as possible, "whisky by the grace of the Royal Commission" may be left to those who ask for nothing more from their beverage than a "kick". But the children of light will continue to demand of their Scotch whisky that it should be distilled in Scotland by means of pot stills, from mashing materials consisting of malted barley and nothing else, dried in kilns by peat or other fuel according to the locality; and of Irish that it should be pot still, from malted barley either alone or with unmalted barley, oats, rye, or other indigenous cereal.'

But in the enjoyment of most of the good things in life the 'children of light' form a small minority. As with vintage wines, so with pot still whiskies—few possess both the palate and the purse to enjoy them; and today blends form by far the greater proportion of the whisky sales.

Blending

Blending on a large scale began between 1860 and 1870.

'Crude as the first mixings may have been,' writes Sir Robert Bruce Lockhart, 'blending today has become a fine art, for whiskies are like the breeding of pedigree stock. Like must be mated with like, and only time and the most careful selection can ensure a happy creation.'

The pot still whisky used in all Highland distilleries consists of three stages—germination, fermentation and distillation. The process completed, the whisky is filled into casks and stored in one of the large bonded warehouses attached to every distillery, where it is left to mature over a period of years. The wooden casks, being permeable, allow air and oxygen to pass within, and any undesirable products in the young whisky to pass without. It is from the cask, too, that the whisky, which when first distilled is as clear as water from the well, abstracts its golden colour. Sherry casks give the best result, but as the shades vary, they are brought to uniformity by adding a solution of caramelised sugar.

After maturing, the whiskies, of which no two are exactly alike, however strong their family resemblance, are removed to the blending warehouses. These are situated chiefly in the larger towns—Perth, Edinburgh, Glasgow and Kilmarnock. Here they are skillfully blended to produce a whisky that remains identical from year to year. The number of brands thus produced is legion. There are about a hundred main varieties on the home market, and many more are exported. Some brands are sold only locally or to private clubs.

Actually, many pot still whiskies are never sold in their pure state, but are reserved exclusively for blending with patent still spirit. The proportion of pure malt and grain varies, but there is rarely more than forty per cent malt to sixty per cent grain, and often much less. As a rule the whiskies, once blended, are left another twelve months to 'marry' before they are bottled. Formulas are, of course, carefully guarded secrets.

For the export trade, it is necessary to prepare the blends to suit the climatic conditions—lighter for India and warmer climates, heavier for Scandinavia and colder climates, and somewhat stronger for the United States than for the home market.

Although, like all art, the distilling of whisky is founded on science, it remains an art and not a science. It is not the chemist, but the expert blender and the connoisseur who can judge the character, quality and bouquet of whisky, and their discrimination is based entirely on sensitiveness of nose and palate.

Taxation

In 1707 the Board of Excise was set up. Up to 1742, the duty was 3d. and 6d. per proof gallon, but thereafter it fluctuated considerably. By 1826, it was fixed at 2s. 10d. per proof gallon; by 1914, at the outbreak of war, it stood at 14s. 9d. Later increases have brought it up to the unprecedented figure of 210s. 10d., representing 24s. 7d. per bottle, or the equivalent of a purchase tax of five hundred per cent.

Once upon a time it was as natural for a Highlander to make whisky as for a Frenchman to make wine. Distilling was a rural craft in which nearly everyone was skilled, and in every home from croft to castle there stood the immemorial crock of whisky, until the Government's covetous hand reached out from London to grasp it. And still, in the mid-twentieth century, Westminster retains its heavy-handed, blundering policy in dealing with this national asset. Money from the ever-growing world sales of whisky pours into the Exchequer,[1] but the Highlander's crock is empty. Taxation has put his native beverage completely beyond his reach.

Hear what some of our connoisseurs of whisky have to say about it:

Ivor Brown: 'It is a monstrous injustice that the Banffshire farmer who has toiled at his harvest in the barley-field, the Banff-shire ghillie who has served the shooting-tenant beside the salmon-river or on the moors above the barley, and the Banffshire distillery worker who kindles the pear, dries the grain, and tends the mash-tub and the still beside the river whose water he bewitches with his craft, are all denied the cheap and general enjoyment of the homely miracle they have made'; and again, 'The British Treasury first taxes "Scotch" as if it were a vice and then battens on it as liquid gold.'[2]

1. In 1953, for example, the sum amounted to some thirty-three million pounds, most of it in dollars.   2. *Summer in Scotland.*

Neil Gunn: 'The discrimination against whisky is so manifestly unjust that it does have the appearance of being deliberately vindictive.... No country behaves in this manner to a native product. The whole idea of a tariff is to protect the home article against the foreign. In every other country they so protect and foster their native drinks. But in this country we deliberately lure the foreigner to destroy Scotch whisky'; and he points out that 'People in the South of England make their own cider and consume it without paying a farthing of duty, yet if charged on the same alcoholic content basis as whisky they would be obliged to pay 6s. 5d. a gallon. Again beer, the national beverage of England, is taxed just about half the whisky rate.'[1]

Eric Linklater: 'The tax on whisky is manifestly a stupid tax. It appears also to be a malevolent tax. One cannot believe it would continue at its present monstrous figure if distilling were an English industry—or should one call it an art? Some little time ago the tax on beer, which is predominantly an English product, was considerably reduced, with resulting benefit to the English brewers and hop-growers.'[2]

And a final word from *Sir Robert Bruce Lockhart*: 'No one wants to see Scotland a drunken country, but surely it is for Scots themselves to decide how much [whisky] they shall drink and how much they shall pay for it. No other race understands better the virtues of moderation.... The English are ripe in political wisdom, but they do not seem to understand that whisky is part of the Scottish heritage, and that if they continue to tamper with it, they will cause trouble for themselves. For high taxation produces much the same consequences as prohibition, and these are excess, bad liquor, and the evasion of the tax by illegal distilling.'[3]

Geography

Good whiskies are made in other countries than Scotland and Ireland—notably in the United States and Canada, where their manufacture was introduced by British, especially Scottish settlers —but the richly flavoured malt whisky of the Scottish Highlands

1. *Whisky and Scotland.*   2. *The Lion and the Unicorn.*   3. *Scotch.*

is not only supreme: it is inimitable.[1] This unique quality we owe, apart from the inherited skill of the distillers, to our much-maligned climate, for which, indeed, it has been claimed as a heaven-sent compensation. To the geographical basis of the supremacy of Highland malts there are four main contributory factors—air, water, peat and barley.

Air. The quality of whisky is definitely affected by the coolness of the climate as well as by the purity and humidity of the atmosphere. Many of our distilleries are situated within, or almost within sight of the sea. 'The great belts of wood and heath which are characteristic of the Banffshire and Morayshire uplands clean the winds which sweep across them and impart some of their own purity to the whiskies of hallowed name that are distilled there.'[2]

Water. Purity is of the utmost importance. Abundance of spring and burn water, crystal-clear and, as far as may be, flavour-less, has determined the location of many a distillery. 'Each distillery recites the praises of its own water supply. Highland Park, the well-known Orkney distillery, obtains its water from two hidden springs. "It never sees the light from source to mash dam." The Glenlivet distillery relies upon the finest and purest water upon earth, which tumbles down the mountainside for twelve hundred feet, and glides through the district in the sparkling stream of Livet.... The best and most productive whisky district in the world is served by waters flowing from the hillsides of the Cairngorms and their sister outposts of the Grampians in Banff and Moray.'[3]

Peat. It is the drying of the malt by means of a fragrant peat fire that gives Highland whisky its distinctive smoky flavour. The proximity of a peat-bog is therefore essential to a Highland malt distillery.

'Good whisky is very fastidious in its tastes and demands a peat which is wholly free from mineral impregnations.... The famous Faemussach Moss, with its inexhaustible peat deposits, con-

---

1. 'The Japs came to this country years ago, copied our plant, and even employed some of our Deeside personnel. They produced an imitation of Deeside whisky, not good, but drinkable.'—S. H. Hastie: *From Burn to Bottle.*
'The process of preparing sovietsky visky is complex and long.' Leaflet issued by Gastronom No. 1, Moscow. Quoted in *The Observer* (Sayings of the Week), April 18, 1954. 2. Aeneas Macdonald. 3. Id.

tributes something to the distinctive flavour of Glenlivet whisky.'[1]

Barley. Although a good deal of imported barley is used nowadays, and it is admittedly difficult to detect any marked difference from the home product, 'Personally I am persuaded,' writes Neil Gunn, 'that the home communicates a soft maturing excellence which the foreign never has to the same degree. This, I admit, is very difficult to test with certainty, for surely there is no product under the sun that can be so affected in its processes as pot still whisky or is so sensitive to influences altogether beyond the chemist to isolate and weigh.' And, speaking again of the Glenlivet distillery, Aeneas Macdonald tells us that it has obtained its barley for generations from the same farms lying in the deep fertile fields of the Laighs of Banff and Moray. 'In this', he adds, 'it accords with the practice of the makers of most of the classic whiskies. An inherited skill in raising barley for distillation—for a great deal depends on the degree to which the grain has been allowed to ripen before cutting, and on its garnering and threshing —accounts for the long and close association between farm and distillery which is so common in the north. And of course locally grown barley, even where it is not superior to the imported grain, helps to preserve the traditional character of the spirit made from it.'

A survey of our Scottish distilleries shows that they tend to concentrate in one or other of those circumscribed areas which centuries of experience have proved to possess all these natural conditions.

There are four main types of malt whisky: the Highland malts, the Islay malts, the Campbeltown malts and the Lowland malts.

The whiskies produced in the Isle of Islay and the burgh of Campbeltown in Kintyre are not mere local variations of those produced in the main Highland area. 'They are indigenous and inimitable types which have a definite place and function in the orchestra of whisky,' writes Aeneas Macdonald. Campbeltowns he describes as the 'double basses' in the orchestra—'potent, full-bodied, pungent whiskies'—and although their flavour is not to everyone's liking, yet the orchestra would be irredeemably impoverished without them. Islay whiskies, again, are the 'violoncellos, somewhat less heavy and powerful of flavour than Campbeltowns, yet perfectly equipped after their insular fashion, round

1. Aeneas Macdonald.

and well-proportioned. . . . They give breadth and fulness to the harmony, but they do not drown the voices of the less capacious instruments.'

But the most favoured district, the home of the finest 'violins', lies in the eastern Highlands.

'The best malt whisky', writes Sir Robert Bruce Lockhart, 'is produced in the belt of land bounded on the west by the river Ness and on the east by the river Deveron. Here Nature has been generous in her gifts. The land, cold and hard in winter but in summer warm to eye and heart, slopes down from the granite of the Blue Mountains (the Cairngorms) through peat and heather moor to the rich farm lands which lie to the Moray Firth and which grow the life-giving barley. It is peopled by a race which retains to this day the graces and natural manners of the High-lander. Wondrously beautiful are the summer evenings when sky and setting sun weave a kaleidoscopic pattern of light and shade on hill and glen, until night in the form of a low white bank of cloud steals slowly like a wraith over the tops of Cairngorm and Braeriach. . . . There is magic, too, in the rivers which water it: the wild Findhorn, the noble Deveron, the lordly Spey with its numerous tributaries including the ice-clear Aven into which runs the world-famous Livet. Who shall say which is dearest to his heart, when each stream has its local lovers?'[1]

Intemperance

It must be confessed with shame that from the middle of the eighteenth to the end of the nineteenth century, Scottish social life was indelibly stained with the vice of drunkenness. It was not whisky, however, but claret that the well-to-do classes habitually drank to excess; but it was whisky, or rather the raw, fiery tipple which passed as such, that the working-classes in the industrial areas indulged in to their detriment. These unfortunate people

1. One fine summer evening, some years ago, the present writer visited the wife of an estate-worker at Gordon Castle, Fochabers, whose cottage was delightfully situated on the banks of the Spey. She herself came from a district much higher up the river, beyond Ballindalloch—a district watered by the Spey's two best-known tributaries. She was seated with her knitting just outside the cottage door. 'I like to sit here,' she remarked; 'I sometimes think I hear the voices of the Livet and the Aven in the river. They make a chord.'

had been forced by economic pressure to leave the country districts in a continuous stream and seek work in the cities, where new industries were springing up, with their train of slums, the breeding grounds of vice and disease. Many of the incomers miraculously contrived to preserve the decent traditions in which they had been reared, but many more—particularly the temperamental Celts—were driven by horror and despair to seek in alcohol an escape, however temporary, from the poverty, wretchedness and squalor of their surroundings.

'One wonders', comments Neil Gunn, 'why those who were (and still are) repelled abhorrently by whisky were not infinitely more repelled by the social conditions which let whisky act so revealingly. One would think that whisky had been the *cause* of the state of the poor, that it had built the slums and ensured the poverty, that it was the whole monstrous creator of that economic hell. . . . One may readily have patience with the women who, being realists, condemned the drunken horrors they saw. But with the so-called social and temperance reformers, as with the religious and political rulers, patience is less easy, for it is natural to expect that they would have made some effort to see through the effect to the cause, and once having seen, to have become the people's impassioned leaders against the savagery of a system that produced such appalling results.

'But not only did they support the social order (many seeing in it the righteous handiwork of a God who had called each to his appointed place), but were themselves of the owning or governing class who hunted and persecuted brutally such "friends of the people" as, haunted by humanity's vision of liberty and fraternity, dared raise a voice in the people's favour.

' . . . In our story it [social intemperance] is only a phase, however, and its worst excesses are lessening in precise correspondence with the improvement in the social order.'

Drunkenness has been, too, the ruin of many of our brightest intellects.

'As an enemy,' writes Sir Robert Bruce Lockhart, 'there is no Scot who does not know its dangers, and almost no Scottish family without its whisky skeletons. They rattle in my own cupboard, and I myself have been near enough to destruction to respect whisky, to fear it, and to continue to drink it.'

So profound an impression have the annals of drunkenness

made on the Scottish mind that countless people still shudder at the very name of whisky. The impassioned advocacy of total abstinence was the natural reaction of ordinary decent folk to the drunken horrors of the old industrial life. Even the most temperate of whisky drinkers were apt to be looked on askance, and were sometimes obliged to resort to subterfuge to safeguard their reputation.

This situation had its humours. The story is told of a minister in a rural parish who, when out walking a day or two after his return from the General Assembly in Edinburgh was accosted by one of his parishioners.

'I've just been up at the station, sir, and I see there's a wooden box lying there addressed to yoursel'.'

'Quite so, Tammas, quite so. Just a few books I was buying when I was in Edinburgh.'

'Aye. Imphm. Ah weel, sir, I wadna be owre lang. They're leakin'.'

The man who chooses to be a total abstainer is to be respected. In some cases it is a wise precaution, even an imperative duty, to abstain; but the man who would thrust total abstinence on everybody else is misguided. He errs in equating total abstinence with temperance and in refusing to learn the lesson of experience—that prohibition tends to encourage the very evils it seeks to destroy.

When George Scott-Moncrieff was visiting the Island of Lewis between the Wars, 'a very shrewd citizen put it to me', he writes, 'that the trouble with Stornoway is that there is too big a gap between those who drink too much and those who don't drink at all, in short, not enough true temperance.'

This applies not only to Stornoway, but to Scotland as a whole. In this respect, the Scots have something to learn from the Greeks. 'The doctrine of the Mean is characteristically Greek, but it should not tempt us to think that the Greek was one who was hardly aware of the passions, a safe, anaesthetic, middle-of-the-road man. On the contrary, he valued the Mean so highly because he was prone to the extremes. . . . He sought control and balance because he needed them. . . . When he spoke of the Mean, the thought of the tuned string was never very far from his mind. The Mean did not imply the absence of tension and lack of passion, but the correct tension that gives out the true and clear note.'[1]

1. H. D. F. Kitto: *The Greeks.*

The Preein' O't

Whisky-tasting, like wine-tasting or tea-tasting, is an art which takes years of study before it can be mastered.

R. H. Bruce Lockhart

These generous whiskies [the single ones], with their individual flavours, recall the world of hills and glens, of raging elements, of shelter, of divine ease. The perfect moment of their reception is after bodily stress—or mental stress, if the body be sound. The essential oils that wind in the glass then uncurl their long fingers in lingering benediction and the whole works of creation are made manifest. At such a moment the basest man would bless his enemy.

Neil Gunn

There are two things that a Highlander likes naked, and one is malt whisky.

Old Saying

I am told that it is now no use saying that there are only two correct ways to drink whisky: neat and in small quantity as a liqueur after a meal . . . or diluted with plain water. The world asks for whisky and soda, and the syphon destroys the work of the still. No more effectual way of ruining the flavour of a good whisky could have been imagined than this one of drowning it in a fizzy solution of carbonic acid gas.

Aeneas Macdonald

If you would truly enjoy whisky, lay to heart these simple precepts:

1. Failing a 'single' whisky from a classic still—and unless you are in its native district you may find such hard to come by—get a good blend. That is not difficult. Every good-class wine merchant in Scotland has one. Take your choice and stick to it.

2. Have nothing to do with a whisky that has not a cast-iron guarantee of being at least five years old. About ten years of age whisky reaches perfection. After fifteen it deteriorates.

3. Don't be misled by the prescription 'liqueur whisky'. There is, strictly speaking, no such thing. The term is used to suggest, without actually saying so, that the whisky in question is above ordinary strength. It may be, or on the other hand it may not. If you must have a Scottish liqueur there is Drambuie, which some people prefer to Benedictine.

4. On no account contaminate good whisky with soda or any other mineral water. If you must dilute it, plain water—spring water if possible—is best, as Pindar observes.

5. Lastly, don't let your appreciation get the better of your discretion. It is often said that good whisky never did anybody any harm, but the statement requires some qualification. *Est modus in rebus*, or, to quote a bit of wisdom overheard in an Angus tavern: 'Moderation, sir, aye moderation is my rule. Nine or ten is reasonable refreshment, but aifter that it's apt to degenerate intae drinkin'.'
Donald Carswell in The Scots Week-end

Mr Ivor Brown defends the use of soda-water, at least by city-dwellers: 'Most urban water supplies are now chlorinated for necessary purposes of safety. The highly chlorinated water originally drawn from sluggish rivers, such as Londoners obtain whether they like it or not, is so remote from the natural water of the mountain spring that to substitute good soda-water (and some soda-waters are paltry) is not only to obtain a liveliness in the glass but to escape a flavour of chemical that destroys the natural tang of the whisky.'
Summer in Scotland

Take a small wine-glass, preferably one with a generous belly and a narrow rim, let him [the taster] warm it slightly with his hand and then pour in a little of the whisky. Having assisted the process of evaporation with a gentle rocking motion of the glass, let him sniff the vapour at the rim. It should be mild and yet potent, round and 'warm', with no trace of the objectionable acridity of raw spirit. Then he should take a sip—only a drop or two—and allow it to remain in his mouth for a few moments. There ought to be no harshness in the liquor's assault on his palate: 'kick' only indicates a young or badly mannered spirit. It should be gentle,[1] with nothing of that 'mineral' taste about it which causes all but hardened and careless drinkers to shudder a little and contract the facial muscles; and it ought to have a smooth, elusive and varied flavour in which it is very difficult to distinguish a dominant constituent. Having performed this operation, the experimenter should add some water to the remainder of the spirit and drink thoughtfully; it will be found better to use soft water for diluting, but it is a refinement which the beginner can spare himself.
Aeneas Macdonald

1. 'The gentle kiss of the barley.' From a whisky advertisement.

There is one way to have a whisky that is better than merely good, a whisky that is always uniform, a whisky with merits that can be propagated: and that is to keep a cask. The tap must be half-way down, so that you know when to refill; thus the goodness of the original spirit is infused into all that you may subsequently add, while the addition gives useful strength to the body of the old. A friend of mine[1] was given by his father a large sherry cask filled with a great whisky, and for over half a century it has been regularly replenished with spirits as good as he could procure, the result being a drink that no guest of his can fail to remember.   Augustus Muir: *Scottish Portrait*

Tributes to Whisky

This great, potent and princely drink.   Aeneas Macdonald

This warlock liquor that came to him (the Englishman) out of the mists.   Id.

This swift and fiery spirit ... belongs to the alchemist's den and to the long nights shot with cold, flickering beams; it is compact of Druid spells and Sabbaths (of the witches and the Calvinists); its graces are not shameless, Latin, and abundant, but have a sovereign austerity, whether the desert's or the north wind's; there are flavours in it, insinuating and remote, from mountain torrents and the scanty soil on moorland rocks and slanting, rare sun-shafts.   Id.

Scotch whisky is a mystery, a magic of locality.... The ancient Greeks imagine spirits of the tree and the brook, the Dryads and the Naiads, elements made persons, forces with a fairy status. In Scotland there are, in the same way, animations of the burn and the river: furthermore each separate distillery has its own daemon and creates a unique effluence.... The genius of [the barley-bree] is so volatile that it cannot be captured out of Scotland: and inside Scotland, inside one glen, it is again so

1. The late Mr William Roughead, the well-known writer on crime.

capricious that neighbouring distilleries evoke distinct qualities of their own.

... Whatever the explanation may be, all this subtlety of the craft working upon the curious diversities of nature now matters little enough. The 'single' whiskies are swept away to be blended into the multiples. The blends can still have character, but to the champions of the malt it is a kind of massacre and sacrilege.

Ivor Brown

Whisky—even inferior whisky—has a potency and a directness in the encounter which proclaims its sublime rank. It does not linger to toy with the senses, it does not seep through the body to the brain; it communicates through no intermediary with the core of a man, with the roots of his consciousness; it speaks from deep to deep. This quality of spiritual insistency derives from the physical nature of the liquid. Whisky is a re-incarnation; it is made by a sublimation of coarse and heavy barley malt; the spirit leaves that earthly body, disappears, and by a lovely metapsychosis returns in the form of a liquid exquisitely pure and impersonal. And thence whisky acquires that lightness and power which is so dangerous to the unwary, and so delightful to those who use it with reverence and propriety.   Aeneas Macdonald

Throughout the ages whisky has been an integral part of the Celtic civilization.... It was the natural drink of a poor people who, however poor they might be, had never known servitude, and to whom, in the absence of other luxuries, it was indeed the water of life which gave inspiration to their songs and strength to their bodies. It was a noble spirit, a symbol of independence, to be approached with reverence, and, in spite of the changes wrought by blending, the Celts have communicated something of this reverence to the whole Scottish nation.   R. H. Bruce Lockhart

'In spite of Kipling's eulogy of the soothing and soporific qualities of beer and denunciation of the inflammatory effects of whisky, I cannot believe that the change (from whisky to beer) has benefited the Highlands. Each country has the drink that nature intended for it. Wine is the drink of the Mediterranean countries. Beer is the Englishman's tipple.... Vodka, akvavit and whisky are the national drinks of Russia, Scandinavia and Scotland, and who will deny that Scotch whisky, as the only one

which demands a connoisseur's palate, is the purest and noblest
of the three? Id.

Some say that whisky is a Protestant drink, but it is rather a
rationalistic, metaphysical and dialectical drink. It stimulates
speculation and nourishes lucidity. Aeneas Macdonald

Whisky has made us what we are. It goes with our climate
and with our nature. It rekindles old fires in us, our hatred of
cant and privilege, our conviviality, our sense of nationhood, and,
above all, our love of Scotland. It is our release from materialism,
and I often think that without it we should have been so irritatingly
efficient that a worse persecution than the Hebrews ever suffered
would have been our inevitable fate. R. H. Bruce Lockhart

The ruddy complexion, nimbleness and strength of these people
is not owing to water-drinking but to the *aqua vitae*, a malt spirit
which is commonly used in that country.
An Exciseman writing in 1736

Edie Ochiltree: 'Ay, ay—it's easy for your honour, and the like
o you gentlefolks to say sae, that hae stouth and routh [abundance]
and fire and fending, and meat and claith, and sit dry and canny
by the fireside—but an [*if*] ye wanted fire, and meat, and dry
claise [*clothes*], and were deein' o cauld, and had a sair heart, whilk
[*which*] is warst ava [*of all*], wi' jist tippence in your pouch,
wadna ye be glad to buy a dram wi't, to be eilding [*fuel*] and
claise and a supper and heart's ease into the bargain, till the morn's
morning?' Sir Walter Scott: *The Antiquary*

This is smart stuff.
John Keats (when visiting Scotland and tasting whisky for the first time)

Note: 'Smart, taken as brisk, keen, challenging, is exactly the right word.'—
Ivor Brown

This autumn [1822] King George IV visited Scotland. The
whole country went mad. Everybody strained every point to
get to Edinburgh to receive him. Sir Walter Scott and the Town
Council were overwhelming themselves with the preparations.

My mother did not feel well enough for the bustle, neither was I
at all fit for it, so we stayed at home with Aunt Mary. My father,
my sisters, and William, with lace, feathers, pearls, the old
landeau, the old horses, and the old liveries, all went to add to the
show, which they said was delightful.... One incident con-
nected with this time made me very cross. Lord Conyngham,
the Chamberlain, was looking everywhere for pure Glenlivet
whisky; the King drank nothing else. It was not to be had out
of the Highlands. My father sent word to me—I was the cellarer
—to empty my pet bin, where was whisky long in wood, long
in uncorked bottles, mild as milk, and the true contraband *goût*
in it. Much as I grudged this treasure it made our fortunes afterwards, showing on what trifles great events depend. The whisky,
and fifty brace of ptarmigan all shot by one man, went up to
Holyrood House, and were graciously received and made much
of, and a reminder of this attention at a proper moment by the
gentlemanly Chamberlain ensured to my father the Indian
Judgeship.

> Elizabeth Grant of Rothiemurchus: *Memoirs of a Highland Lady*

Isle of Skye.

Today, in the cellar, Cameron came on a treasure we had long
forgotten—the little four-gallon brass-bound keg which we used
to call the Colonel's Bottle.... It had filled his flask for forest,
moor and stream; was the only cordial spirit he cared for at the
table. 'There is not a harsh word or a headache in a hogshead of
it,' he would say at the age of over eighty.

There is a limit to the maturing period of whisky, as of wines;
bottle it in its teens and it will keep as fresh as the dawn for half
a century.... In my bottled whisky (of the same brand) is all the
distinctive character of the Colonel's keg—the same *blas*, as we
say in the Gaelic; the same fragrant tang he used to describe as
the breath of barley and bog-myrtle. Unless you 'drown the
miller' altogether, that essential, seductive quality comes through
any water you may add to it.

A blithe drink! The cordial for companionship!

> Alan Breck MacNeill

When my cellar, if not exactly my cellar-book, was started, I
had recently returned from a two years' sojourn in the North of

Scotland, where, it is needless to say, I had become something of a judge in whisky; and the loss of the unblended product, direct from the Morayshire distilleries, was a real privation. . . . It was then difficult to get any other (than blended whisky) in London; a personal friend, himself a distiller, who allowed me to have some of his ware 'neat', begged me not to mention the fact, as he was under a sort of contract only to supply the big middlemen.

George Saintsbury: *Notes on a Cellar-Book*

(Regarding the respective merits of Irish and Scotch), 'For my own part, I am as impartial as an Englishman should be, and can afford to be in this instance, between *the* Two. Indeed, I used, while it was still possible for persons not millionaires or miners to do so, to drink one at lunch and the other at dinner, completing the *Quis separabit* with English gin at night. But I think it must be allowed that the "Scotch Drink" has more numerous and more delicate varieties of character than the Irish.' Id.

The notion that we can possibly develop a palate for whisky is guaranteed to produce a smile of derision in any company except that of a few Scottish lairds, farmers, gamekeepers and bailies, relics of a vanished age of gold when the vintages of the north had their students and lovers. . . . While a high standard of culture was still to be found in a Caledonia less stern and wild than today and whisky still held its place in the cellars of the gentry and of men of letters, who selected it with as much care and knowledge as they gave to the stocking of their cellars with claret, whisky retained its place as one of the higher delights of mankind.

Aeneas Macdonald

A fine pot still whisky is as noble a product of Scotland as any burgundy or champagne is of France. Patent still whisky is no more a true whisky than, at the opposite extreme, is any of those cheap juices of the grape heavily fortified by raw spirit which we import from the ends of the earth a true wine. . . . Each pot still might very well carry as proud a name as any one of the vineyards of France. The aim should be quality above all else, a perfect matured spirit, whose aroma and flavour would be distinctive without ever being harsh, whose essential oils would impart a gently growing warmth throughout the body, a delicate excitement and a fine clarity to the brain. . . . Whisky can be coarse and aggressive, but, perfectly conceived, it is creative fire.

Neil Gunn

(Let us) think of whisky as part of Scotland's contribution to humanity, as claret is a great part of the munificence of France. Now the varieties of claret are innumerable, from the thin but honest simplicity of a tenpenny Médoc to the rich yet subtle enchantment of the first growths of the three great Châteaux, in which perfume and flavour and bloom, divisible yet undivided, are as three aspects of perfection in Perfection. This multiplicity of delight, conveyed in the single word claret, is known or acknowledged by all. But to the majority of people whisky is merely whisky, an amber spirit unfairly diluted by obtuse authority, in a bottle whose shape is often more variable than its contents. How wrong is this judgment! And how shameful that there should be grounds for it! For it cannot be denied that under recent legislation, and as a result of commercial arrangements to survive it, there is today an undistinguished monotony in many brands. Yet if distillers were fairly treated, and encouraged to take a pleasure and pride in their art, they could produce whisky as variable in flavour and character as claret.

. . . France, I say again, has given claret to the world, and the world is the better for it. Scotland has it in its power to give the world such whisky as few can dream of; and the world would again be better. Léoville, Margaux, and Latour might be matched with Islay, Glenfiddich and Glengrant. Haut Brion, singing aloud, might hear in reply the *voix d'or* of Highland Park. And the brown streams of Glenlivet would need not envy the sun-warmed slopes of Bordeaux. With such whisky to help it, the world would grow kindlier and more wise, aware of beauty and comforted with friends.

Eric Linklater: *The Lion and the Unicorn* (1935)

Whisky Liqueurs

Of these we have two, one at least two hundred years old, the other of recent birth.

Drambuie is made of Highland malt whisky, heather honey,

and special herbs. According to one legend, the drink was devised for Prince Charles Edward when he was living at the French
Court, and the secret formula for this, his 'personal liqueur', was
presented by the grateful Prince to Mackinnon of Strathaird, a
Skye family, in recognition of services rendered in the dark days
between Culloden and the escape to France. This seems to the
present writer very unlikely. It is incredible that the French, of
all nations, should have abandoned so superb a liqueur if they had
ever invented or even encountered it, and there is not the faintest
tradition of its ever having been known there or elsewhere on
the Continent. Moreover, it was not to Drambuie, nor even to
whisky, but to brandy that the unfortunate Prince turned to
drown his sorrows.

The other and much more probable story is that the drink was
prepared by the Mackinnons in Prince Charlie's honour, or at
least that he was regaled with it during his stay on the island. The
Mackinnons were not the only Highland family to possess a
special liqueur or drink of this type; but whether because of its
superior merits or because of its romantic and indubitable association with Prince Charlie, it soon became namely throughout the
Hebrides. For long the liqueur was made in very small quantities,
and only a few bottles were dispatched from Skye to the mainland
as gifts to friends. Not until 1892 was the name Drambuie[1] regis-
tered as a trade mark. In 1906, a member of the Strathaird family,
Malcolm or Calum Mackinnon, migrated, at the age of seventeen,
to Edinburgh, where he went to work in an old-established
Whisky House; and presently he was making use of the secret
recipe to manufacture Drambuie in a cellar, in small commercial
quantities. By the time the first World War broke out its fame
had spread furth of Scotland; and in less than half a century after
its emergence from the mists of Skye it achieved a signal triumph,
when it obtained the premier award at the International Exhibition of Tourism and Culinary Arts held at Berne in 1954. Thus
Drambuie has been formally recognized as one of the world's
greatest liqueurs.

Drambuie is in colour a sherry brown, showing flecks of gold
in the sun—like sunbeams imprisoned in a peat-bog.

The new whisky liqueur is Glayva, which has already earned
considerable popularity.

1. *An dram buidheach*, the drink that satisfies.

3: *Wine*

FRENCH wines were freely imported to Scotland in early times, and attained a wide popularity in the days of the early Stuart kings, when prolonged English aggression had thrown Scotland into the arms of France. Wine has, indeed, been described as the blood-stream of the Auld Alliance.

In the Acts of the Scottish Parliament there appears 'An Assize of Wine according to the Constitution of King David' (1124-53), which indicates that there was already a considerable consumption in the twelfth century, and the documents we possess relating to our medieval trade make it clear that wine was for long one of our principal imports. The need for something in the nature of a licensing court was met by the appointment of 'the Chalmerlan's Ayr', an official who was required to 'challenge' wine taverners on four distinct points: selling wine without its having been tasted and approved; selling it in measures that had not been duly tested; selling it without having the price fixed by the tasters; and lastly, mixing 'corrupt' wine with wholesome stuff.

French wines were drunk at the court of Alexander III, and in the reign of James I the popular demand reached such proportions that in 1431 an Act was passed requiring that half the price of the salmon exported to France should be paid in Gascon wine. The wines of Bordeaux and the Charente district were extremely popular, and a trade in Rhine wine is indicated in an enactment of 1436. Evidence of a taste for some of the choicer brands is found in the Exchequer Rolls and Household Books that have come down to us. Mary of Gueldres, for example, continued after her marriage to James II to favour the wines of Burgundy to which she had been accustomed, Beaune being her favourite vintage.

Besides French and Rhenish wines, Leith imported many Mediterranean wines for the connoisseurs of the capital; Malmsey, which was brought by Italian traders from Candia and Cyprus and supplied to the chief ports of Western Europe; Muscatel, which came straight from Italy; Alicante and other Spanish wines; and Bastard, a peninsular wine mixed with honey.

In his *Dirige to the King at Stirling*, Dunbar invites James IV to return to the festive halls of Holyrood:

To drink with us the new fresche wyne
That grew upon the rever of Ryne,
Ffresche fragrant clarettis out of France,
Of Angers and of Orliance.

Again, in the 'Ballad of Sir Patrick Spens' (reign of James VI) we read:

The King sat in Dunfermline toun,
Drinking the blude-red wine;

and in the same reign—in 1618, to be precise—Taylor, the London Water-Poet, joined a large hunting-party of Scottish nobles, gentlemen and retainers in Braemar and took part in an *al fresco* feast of salmon, venison, and all manner of feathered game, with 'good ale, sacke, white and cleret, tent [Alicante] with most potent aquavitae [whisky] for a company of about fourteen hundred'.

The excellence, abundance and cheapness of the wines with which they were regaled in Scotland are commented on by successive travellers. The bulk of these wines were shipped direct from Bordeaux and the Charente to Leith, Edinburgh's thriving little seaport. Year in, year out, the merchant ships sailed up the Firth of Forth—sometimes running smoothly over placid waters, sometimes moving warily through a heavy haar, sometimes battering their way against high winds, through heavy seas—and dropped anchor in the sheltered Water of Leith, where the casks were put ashore and carried to the vaults.

Whilst most of the wines were distributed in Scotland, a certain proportion went to the North of England and some even to London, where, after the introduction of bottling, many connoisseurs insisted on Leith-bottled wines because of their quality. The prime favourite was claret.

At one time Scotland was reputed to drink more claret than any other country, and Edinburgh to have a more discriminating taste in that wine than any other city outside France.

The name claret properly applies to the red wines of Bordeaux, which M. André Simon describes as 'the most natural and wholesome of all wines', adding: 'There is no wine other than claret to possess so great a variety of styles and types, such perfection of poise and harmony between all that a wine should give: colour, bouquet, flavour and savour.' Claret, in the words of a Scots connoisseur is 'a kingly wine'.

Wines were, of course, shipped to other Scottish ports and

many remote and quite primitive inns had excellent cellars. Throughout the centuries, however, Leith remained the principal wine port. The vaults used in earliest times still receive their annual consignment of wines. They now form part of the building known as The Vaults—the premises of a famous wine firm— and, incidentally, the oldest building still in daily commercial use in Scotland: for there is a reference to these same vaults in a charter granted by the Abbey of Holyrood in 1138, in the reign of David I, and they may well be much older. On a higher floor there is a fine seventeenth-century room where the merchants and connoisseurs of Edinburgh used to meet and bid for the wines, which were auctioned by the President of the Vintner's Guild; whilst higher still are the extremely up-to-date modern offices. In the vaults themselves, however, the age-old methods are largely preserved, owing to their intrinsic merits. Under the concave roofs which, like those of all good wine vaults in Europe, grow a white fungus, the clarets, burgundies, ports and sherries carried in from the docks are nursed back from sea-sickness—for wines are easily upset by changes of temperature and the motion of the sea—and are then left for some months to mature in a temperature that never varies perceptibly summer or winter. On their removal from the vaults, they go for fining; and when bright, clear and ready for bottling, they are bottled carefully by hand, candlelight being still used to illuminate the wine and test its clarity. The bottles are then corked and stored in huge stone bins, and finally labelled before dispatch. (This firm, like all good firms, also imports wines bottled at the châteaux of their origin.)

In the old days, when claret was virtually the national drink, the handling of wine for popular consumption was somewhat rough and ready. When a cargo of claret from Bordeaux arrived at Leith, the citizens of Edinburgh were notified by the appearance in the streets of a hogshead on a horse-drawn cart and the sound of a horn blown by its attendant. 'Anyone who wanted a sample, or a drink under the pretence of a sample,' says Lord Cockburn in his *Memorials*, 'had only to go to the cart with a jug, which, without much nicety about its size, was filled for a sixpence.' Casks were also trundled round on barrows and the claret sold straight from them in stoups.

'A well-known physician of that olden time,' the story goes, 'who one Sunday evening sent his servant for a jug of red wine fresh from the barrel, was much annoyed at his supply being confiscated by the "seizers"—men who perambulated the streets on that day to see that no person was engaged in "worldly work", and who were empowered to pounce upon evil-doers, and take from them all they were in possession of in the shape of food or drink. The doctor, determined to have his revenge, gave his servant on the next occasion a powder to place in the jug if the "seizers" troubled her. As usual, they were on the watch, and duly, as in duty bound, confiscated the ruddy liquor—and as duly drank it, which was no part of their duty. But they never again confiscated, or at all events never again drank, that physician's claret.'[1]

The practice of bottling was introduced in the eighteenth century, but Sir Andrew Bruce Tulloch relates that as late as the eighteen-thirties his father saw claret sold in draught in the streets of Perth.

The Highland chiefs were as partial to claret as were the lairds and lawyers of the Lowlands. In his *Letters from the North of Scotland*, Captain Burt, who accompanied General Wade to Scotland in 1724, writes that he found there abundance of this wholesome and agreeable drink, as well as brandy of fine quality; but, he adds, 'the glory of the country was Usky [whisky]'. Claret was no less popular in the Hebrides, but in 1616 the Privy Council passed an 'Act agens the drinking of Wynes in the Yllis', and another Act six years later, prohibiting merchants and skippers from sending or carrying wines to the Isles 'except so meikle as is allowed to the chieftains and gentlemen of the Islis', so that the islanders were restricted to water and the more potent beverage of their own distilling.

In Burns's time the best claret cost eighteen shillings a dozen, and inferior but still sound vintages considerably less.

In the taverns situated in the dark wynds of eighteenth-century Edinburgh, claret circulated freely, as is testified by Robert Fergusson, the poet of that place and period:

> The grace is said; it's nae owre lang;
>   The claret reams in bells.
> Quo' Deacon, 'Let the toast round gang:
>   Come, here's our noble sel's,
>   Weel met the day.'

1. James Bertram: *Memories of Men, Books and Events.*

And Sir Alexander Boswell, the father of our Bozzy, records:

> O'er draughts of wine the beau would moan his love,
> O'er draughts of wine the cit his bargain drove,
> O'er draughts of wine the writer penned the will,
> And legal wisdom counselled o'er a gill.

Judges took their bottles of claret into court, and it was the favourite drink of the remarkable fraternity that made eighteenth century Edinburgh the intellectual capital of these islands.

In 1780 the happy days of duty-free claret came to an end. Port, not claret, was the Englishman's favourite wine—a choice dictated less by his palate than by his country's foreign policy—and as the senior partner (or so he deemed himself) in the Union, it seemed to him right and proper that the Scotsman's drink should be taxed in preference to his own. The imposition of the tax on claret grievously offended Scots bred in the old tradition, and inspired John Home (author of the tragedy of *Douglas*), who detested port, to write the well-known epigram, which Sir Walter Scott delighted in repeating:

> Firm and erect the Caledonian stood;
> Old was his mutton, and his claret good;
> 'Let him drink port!' the English statesman cried—
> He drank the poison, and his spirit died.

'About a century ago (1793), Lord Duffus,' we are told, 'imported fifty hogsheads of claret to Barrogill Castle [now known as the Castle of Mey], he being guardian to the Earl of Caithness. Forty-eight hogsheads his Lordship hid in a peat stack, two he put in his own house; he then wrote an information against himself to the revenue officer, and when he came showed him the two, said they were scarcely worth saving, and hoped he would share the last drop with him.'[1]

The ultimate effect of the prohibitive duties on French wines was to banish claret from the dinner-tables of all but the well-to-do classes and substitute the highly alcoholized beverage the abuse of which was to become an evil and a reproach to the nation.

Champagne began to appear on Scottish tables only after the peace of 1815, when the 'Auld Allies' were able to resume their interrupted intercourse. Sir Walter Scott was one of the first to popularize this wine in Scotland. It circulated freely at his dinner-

1. R. Kempf: *Convivial Caledonia* (1893).

parties, and to many of his guests was an agreeable novelty. 'John Ballantyne,' writes a memorialist of that time, 'on his visits to the Continent, was accustomed to bring over considerable quantities of the brands he knew so well how to select, of the wine which the Ettrick Shepherd called "yon kind"; its destination, of course, being the cellars of his patron at Castle Street [Scott's Edinburgh town-house] and Abbotsford, where the bins were at all times stocked with good liquor.'

'It is a fact, which some philosophers may think worth setting down,' says Lockhart, 'that Scott's organization, as to more than one of his senses, was the reverse of exquisite. . . . He could never tell Madeira from Sherry. . . . Port he considered as physic. . . . In truth, he liked no wines except sparkling champagne and claret; but even as to this last he was no connoisseur; and sincerely preferred a tumbler of whisky-toddy to the most precious "liquid ruby" that ever flowed in the cup of a prince.'

It is recorded that in 1879 a London barrister wrote to a friend living in the Isle of Skye asking if the place was sufficiently civilized to be visited by his wife and daughter. 'Judge for yourself,' was the reply; 'the wine-card of the hotel where I am now staying offers you a choice of seven brands of champagne.'

In early Victorian times, when wine was more rarely seen in middle-class houses than formerly, much was done to popularize its use by Mr Charles Tait, brother of the proprietor of *Tait's Edinburgh Magazine*.

'At his sales,' writes James Bertram, 'which took place at his rooms in Hanover Street, the wines disposed of were always of high quality. At first the sales were confined to the disposal of gentlemen's cellars, in which had been accumulated fine old ports and sherries, Madeiras and clarets, not forgetting, of course, the "wine of the country"—whisky. In time, however, the scope of these sales was extended, hocks, Champagnes, Moselle and Burgundies being obtained from outside; and the wine list at Edinburgh dinners, it was observed, extended accordingly. . . . There were a number of cellars of celebrity in Edinburgh. Lord Jeffrey, it was said, could produce over thirty kinds to his guests at Craigcrook; and a Lord Justice Clerk of some forty years ago was as famous for his ports as for his law.'

In the annals of the Cleikum Club—a club of gastronomes— we read of one of the famous dinners provided by Meg Dods—

a contemporary of Sir Walter Scott—at the old Border inn from which the Club took its name:

'Cranberry tart and a copious libation of rich plain cream concluded one of the most satisfactory dinners Dr Redgill had ever made in his life, and the racy flavour of Meg's old claret completed the conquest of his affections.' After much smacking of green seals and red seals, much cracking of nuts and of jokes, 'to conclude the entertainment, the Nabob produced a single bottle of choice Burgundy, Mont Rachet; and a special bumper was dedicated to the newcomer.'

This, Mr Morton Shand once told the present writer, appears to be the first mention of this superb white Burgundy in these islands.

Edinburgh long remained a stronghold of claret-drinkers, and the finer vintages were the almost exclusive dessert wine in the houses of the Scottish nobility, gentry, and well-to-do burgesses. Claret and olives, indeed, appear to have been the Scottish equivalent of the Englishman's port and walnuts. The claret trade of Leith is said to have been at its best from 1848 to 1878, when wines of the great vintages—'54, '58, '61, '64, '69 and '70—were eagerly sought after. The first Lord Kinross, Lord President, told George Saintsbury, who was for twenty years Professor of English Literature at the University of Edinburgh and was as distinguished a connoisseur of wine as of books, that in his early days at the Scottish bar—that is, in the 'sixties—it was customary for knots of four frequenters of Parliament House, when a vintage promised well, to lay down so many hogsheads of the best reputed first or second growths, dividing the produce in bottles among themselves.

'I remember now with gusto', writes Sir James Crichton-Browne, 'that glorious wines were offered at dinner-parties in Edinburgh in the 'sixties—Margaux, Lafite, Léoville, Longueville and Montrose.'

From about 1878 the taste for claret declined steadily—so much so that Professor Saintsbury found it practically useless, he tells us, to open a magnum. The decline is attributed by Sir James Crichton-Browne partly to the late dinner-hour, which gives no time to dwell on the delicate differences in bouquet in various vintages, and partly to cigarette-smoking, which blunts the palate and renders it incapable of fine distinctions.

Traces of the old predilection for claret lingered long in some of the remoter districts. An Argyll magistrate, in a letter to *The Times* about the end of the last century, said that he had been recently in a Lochfyneside hotel and had been told by the proprietor that the herring-fleet fishermen consumed about a hogshead of his light claret every week. They would not touch whisky, being 'temperance' men, but on returning from the fishing they enjoyed their claret, which they drank warm, with sugar, and which they considered to be a 'temperance' drink.

There are still many discriminating wine-drinkers in Scotland, and their numbers have been increasing since 1949, when the Chancellor of the Exchequer made them a gesture by reducing the duty on wine imported in the cask. Since then, the trade between France and Scotland has grown steadily. One hears little wine jargon north of the Tweed, but there are many people who can discuss wine with sense and judgment. Drinking is, happily, much more moderate than formerly and is likely to remain so; and the restoration of a light, sound, relatively non-acid claret to the tables of people of moderate means is generally welcomed.

Among men of law tradition dies hard. At the annual meeting of the Stair Society (for the study of Scots Law) held in Edinburgh in 1953, a suggestion that the Society should hold a sherry party was opposed, says a newspaper account, by Lord President Cooper on the grounds that sherry and the history of Scots Law did not go together. There is but one wine for whose supremacy there will never be contending counsel at the Scottish Bar, and that wine is claret.

D

CONVIVIAL LIFE

1: *The National Tradition*

IT is in conformity with the theory of 'the Caledonian antisyzygy'
—the combination of opposites which the Scot shows at every
turn[1]—that we should be widely credited as a nation with two
apparently incompatible characteristics: an exaggerated careful-
ness with money, and a lavish indulgence in hospitality and conviviality. A remark of Estienne Perlin, a French ecclesiastic who
visited Scotland in 1552, throws light on the apparent paradox.
'Nothing', he says, 'is scarce here but money.' What people had
they shared freely, and for the passing stranger there were always
an open door, a seat by the fire, and a share of whatever food and
drink the house could afford; but, save with the favoured few,
there was little handling of hard cash. Even the lairds were frequently obliged to pay their tradesmen, as they themselves were
paid by their tenants, 'in kind', and after the Union of Parliaments
many of the Scottish members who had lived comfortably
enough in Edinburgh found themselves in sore straits after paying
the cost of their journeys to and from London and the expenses
of residence in a city where money melted like snow. Throughout the country barter was the rule, and in the remoter districts
it remained the rule up to our own time. The value of money is,
of course, relative, and the dismay of the rustic Scot of a bygone

1. 'The angry dichotomy prevails in scission upon scission, creating intense
conflict not only between groups, but between individual persons, and within
individual souls. Scotsmen are metaphysical and emotional, they are sceptical
and mystical, they are romantic and ironic, they are cruel and tender, and full
of mirth and despair.'—Rachel Annand Taylor: *Dunbar.*

age who found that he had hardly set foot in London when 'bang went saxpence' is comparable with the dismay of the post-war Englishman of modest means who finds that he has hardly set foot in Gleneagles or Braemar when bang goes a Treasury note.

But it is with the other side of this particular 'antisyzygy' that we are here concerned. Numerous travellers, early and late, have recorded their impressions of Scotland, and it is noteworthy that our most vociferous critics and kindliest commentators are unanimous on one point—that we possess the virtue of hospitality in an unusual degree. Among the ancient Scots, it was deemed infamous in a man to have the door of his house shut, lest, as the bards expressed it, 'the stranger should come and behold his contracted soul'. Again, lest he should have under his roof an enemy, to whom the laws of hospitality applied as strictly as to a friend, he was prohibited by immemorial custom from asking his guest his name and occupation until a year and a day had elapsed—an extraordinary effort, comments Hugh Miller, for a people so naturally inquisitive.

The sanctity of the old laws of hospitality is illustrated by an incident recorded in the official History of Clan Lamont. Sometime between 1565 and 1579 James, the young laird of Lamont, with some 'lads of the belt' (retainers) in attendance, was travelling north from Cowal towards Inverlochy, in Lochaber, and on the way fell in with a hunting-party under young Ewan Macgregor of Glenstrae (a glen running north from Loch Awe). They supped together at a small change-house at the mouth of Glencoe (probably the forerunner of the present King's House). After the horns had passed round frequently, a heated quarrel arose. Lamont and Macgregor drew dirks, and Macgregor received a fatal thrust. Appalled at his deed, Lamont rushed out into the night and made, as he thought, for home; but striking too far west, he came hotfoot down Glenstrae to Stronmelochan, the home of his victim's father. Now in extremity, he pommelled on the oak. The chief himself appeared, and although the fugitive disclosed that he was wanted by the Macgregors for blood, swore on the naked steel that the youth who claimed his protection should be safe. Confronted shortly with the corpse of his beloved son, deaved with the imprecations of his clansfolk, and harrowed by the cries and lamentations of his wife and daughters, the grief-stricken father refused to break his oath, and next day, accompanied by twelve armed men, he escorted his ill-omened guest as far as the western shore of Loch Fyne and procured a boat to row him across.

'You are safe now,' said the chief at parting. 'No longer can I, or will I protect you. Keep out of the way of my clan, and may God forgive and bless you.'

The two little thought to meet again; but meet they did. It happened that after the famous herschip upon the Colquhouns at Glen Fruin the Clan Gregor was proscribed, Stronmelochan reduced to ashes, and the old chief declared an outlaw. James eagerly seized the opportunity to repay a debt of honour and gave garth at Toward to the hunted man to whom he owed his life.

Corroboration of the story is to be found in the Argyll Papers, 1591-1779 (now lodged in the Register House in Edinburgh) which record Argyll's undertaking to discharge Lamont and some others 'of all paynis for the resset [receipt or harbouring] of the Clan Gregor'.

On the subject of hospitality, our visitors have much to say.

Pedro de Ayala (1498), ambassador from Ferdinand and Isabella of Spain to the court of James IV, reports that 'they [the Scots] like foreigners so much that they dispute with one another who shall have and treat a foreigner in his house'.

In 1618 John Taylor, the Thames Water-Poet, printed an account of his 'Pennyless Pilgrimage' throughout Scotland, where he depended entirely on private hospitality. He accompanied the Earl of Mar and a distinguished company on a shooting expedition into the Eastern Highlands, where they put up in temporary lodges called *lonchards*, erected a huge *al fresco* kitchen on the side of a bank, and feasted sumptuously on the produce of the chase. Everywhere he went his needs, including money, were generously supplied by gentlemen who seem to have been amply recompensed by the society of so unusual and entertaining a guest. 'So much of a virtue comparatively rare in England,' comments Chambers, 'and so much plenty in a country which his people were accustomed to think of as the birthplace of famine, seems to have greatly astonished him.'

William Lithgow (1623) writes: 'Now as for the Nobility and Gentry of the Kingdome . . . for a general and compleat worthiness, I have never found their matches amongst the best people of forrane Nations: being also good housekeepers, affable to strangers, and full of Hospitality.'

A distinguished American visitor, Benjamin Franklin, who visited Scotland in 1759 and 1771, declared that 'on the whole, I must say, I think the time we spent there was six weeks of the densest happiness I have ever met in any part of my life; and the agreeable and instructive society there in such plenty has left so pleasing an impression on my memory, that, did not strong connexions draw me elsewhere I believe Scotland would be the country I should choose to spend the remainder of my days in.'

Several English visitors of the late eighteenth century have also recorded their impressions. First Pennant, who writes of the Highlanders: 'As for the common people, they were chiefly characterized by good manners, pride, inquisitiveness, and a genius for hospitality and religion.' He adds: 'The Scots preserve with a narrow income a dignity too often lost among their brethren south of the Tweed.'

Then Captain Topham, who spent the year 1774-5 among us: 'The virtue which is peculiarly characteristic of the Scotch nation is Hospitality. In this they excel every country in Europe: both the men and the women equally share it, and indeed vie with each other in showing politeness and humanity to strangers. When you are once acquainted with a family you are made part of it, and they are not pleased unless you think so yourself.' And he goes on, 'Though England and Scotland are very minute in comparison with many of the countries on the European continent, yet you cannot conceive a greater dissimilarity of manners. I speak of the common people only, for the polished and polite are everywhere nearly the same in many respects.

'... In a wild, uncultivated country, in a miserable hovel, destitute of every convenience of life ... you meet with souls generous, contented and happy, ever ready to the call of humanity religious and charitable. In a short tour that I lately made in the Highlands, I mixed with them, conversed on a variety of subjects, lived with their families, and passed with them many a happy hour.

'... I daresay you will be astonished to find so many virtues in a family in the Highlands, where the inhabitants are thought by us to be in a state of barbarism. But such, I assure you, they all are. . . . Even in Edinburgh the same spirit runs through the common people, who are infinitely more civilized, humanized and hospitable than any I have ever met with.'

In 1776 Dr Samuel Johnson, of whom more anon, was amazed at the scale and magnificence of the hospitality he and Boswell enjoyed—'veal in Edinburgh, roast kid in Inverness, admirable venison and generous wine in the Castle of Dunvegan. . . . Everywhere', he writes, 'we were received like princes in their progress.'

An Irishman of the same period, Sir Richard Sullivan, writes: 'Much as we had heard of Scots hospitality, we did not conceive that it could ever have been carried to the extreme in which we found it. Our first intent was merely to stay a night with our friend: instead of which, the neighbouring gentlemen leaguing themselves together, agreeably detained us a considerable number of days. No sooner had we visited one than another threw in his claim; and thus loading us with a profusion of unmerited, though most gratifying kindness, they baffled our firmest resolves, and compelled us to enjoy as much satisfaction as an enlightened well-bred liberal society could afford.

'But disinterestedness is not exclusively confined to the better sort; the poor even share it in this country, and according to their humble means, are as anxious to show their hospitality and friendship as those of the amplest extent of fortune. Many Highlanders would be offended at the offer of a reward; accept of their services, appear satisfied, and they are usuriously repaid for everything they can do for you; nay, what is more surprising, this extends itself to many of the lowest servants; one of whom, from Lord Breadalbane, having been pressed to accept some acknowledgement for the trouble he had been at to oblige us, flew out of the house with all imaginable trepidation, resolutely declining the offer, and seeming hurt that he should be supposed capable of accepting a pecuniary gratification.'

All these passages are in praise of Scotland, but there is plenty of dispraise too—much of it legitimate, a fair amount mere Scotophobia. The smells and dirt and squalor characteristic of all cities until fairly modern times were greatly intensified in Edinburgh by the congestion of the population in the tall 'lands' of the Old Town, and travellers very naturally expressed their disgust. So, for that matter, did some of Edinburgh's own

citizens—William Dunbar, for instance, one of the galaxy of
poets that illumined the court of James IV:

> May nane pass throw your principall gaittis
> For stink of haddockis and of scaittis,
> For cryis of carlingis and debaittis,
> For fensum flyttingis of defame,
>   Think ye nocht schame,
>   Befoir strangeris of all estaittis
> That sic dishonour hurt your name!

Gaittis, streets; *scaittis*, skates; *carlingis*, old women; *fensum*, offensive; *flyttingis*,
quarrels in words; *estaittis*, degrees; *sic*, such.

Our social life, too, had its critics. Goldsmith, who spent a
year (1752-3) in Edinburgh as a medical student, waxes sarcastic
over a dance he attended. The ladies 'sat dismally' at one side of
the dancing-hall and their 'pensive partners' at the other, with 'no
more intercourse between them than between two countries at
war'. The lady directress having interrupted the hostilities, the
minuet is danced 'with a formality that approaches to despon-
dence', after which they all stand up to country dances. 'So they
dance much and say nothing, and this concludes the assembly.'

It may well be that these dances were conducted with an excessive formality that would appear ridiculous to a lively young
Irishman, especially if he were better acquainted with an Irish
fair than with a .Dublin ballroom, but apparently he did not
realize that neither the slow and stately minuet nor the Scottish
country dances with their intricate pattern lend themselves to
chatter and merriment—although one hardly imagines the latter
danced without smiling faces—nor that in sheer liveliness not
even the Irish jig excels the Scots reel.

'The Scotch ladies', says Captain Topham, 'will sit totally un-
moved at the most sprightly airs of an English country dance,'
but the moment a reel strikes up, 'up they start, animated with
new life, and you would imagine they had received an electrical
shock or been bit by a tarantula.' And he makes an interesting
point: 'The young people of England only consider dancing as
an agreeable means of bringing them together; and was not
gallantry to be of the party, I am afraid we should most of us
think it a very stupid sort of a meeting. But the Scotch . . . may
truly be said to dance for the sake of dancing.'[1]

1. 'The Scots are a nation whose lightness is all in their feet.'—Catherine
Carswell: *Open the Door.*

Sydney Smith, too, poked fun at the same trait as Goldsmith observed—over-solemnity.

'They are so imbued with metaphysics that they even make love metaphysically. I overheard a young lady of my acquaintance at a dance in Edinburgh exclaim, in a sudden pause in the music, "What you say, my Lord, is very true of love in the *aibstract*, but"—here the fiddlers began fiddling furiously, and the rest was lost.'

What a pity the fiddlers did not pause a little longer! All the same, it is surprising that so shrewd an observer did not realize that the noble (or learned) lord and the young lady were not *making* love, but merely *talking* love, which is a very different thing. If a well-bred young woman is rash enough to discuss love with a gentleman who is not her lover, is she not wise to keep the discussion on a metaphysical basis? And is it not conceivable that that same young lady, alone with her lover, would let metaphysics go hang and be more than ready to discuss the subject empirically?

Xenophobia is one of the commonest—and most childish—of human failings. In every country there are plenty of otherwise sensible and kindly folk who are wont to declare that they 'can't stand' the inhabitants of this, that or the other country. Naturally, with nations, as with individuals, we all find some less sympathetic than others; but that is an instinctive reaction and very different from xenophobia, which is founded and nourished on ignorance and prejudice. Every nation produces some thoroughly objectionable types, and heaven knows Scotland has her share of them; but the mistake of the xenophobe is to persist in regarding the exception as the norm. It is hardly surprising that after centuries of feud there was a good deal of mutual dislike between the Scots and the English. (Sir Walter Scott, incidentally, did more than anyone else to dissipate it, and to create, through his novels, mutual understanding and respect.)

'I have been trying all my life to like Scotchmen', declared Charles Lamb, 'and am obliged to desist from the experiment in despair. The tediousness of these people is certainly provoking. I wonder if they ever tire one another.'

Lamb, it appeared, had met a Scot who was an unmitigated bore, and that particular bore had remained for him the prototype of all Scots.

The sycophant, as John Buchan points out, is rare in Scotland, but the Scottish sycophant is a peculiarly unpleasant variety of the species. Hazlitt had the misfortune to encounter one of these gentry, and thereafter the Scots were for Hazlitt a nation of sycophants.

The most noted of Scotophobes was Dr Samuel Johnson. Even after his visit to Scotland, whence he returned, as Boswell tells us, with his prejudices greatly lessened, he still took delight in disparaging and abusing his biographer's compatriots—though his Scotophobia sometimes appears less a conviction than a convention. Occasionally it is really amusing. 'Once, in Skye, Dr Johnson', we are told, 'got into one of his fits of railing at the Scots. He owned that they had been a very learned nation for a hundred years, from 1550 to about 1650; but that they afforded the only instance of a people among whom the arts of civil life did not advance in proportion with learning; that they had hardly any trade, any money, or any elegance, before the Union. *Boswell*: "We had wine before the Union." *Johnson*: "No sir; you had some weak stuff, the refuse of France, which would not make you drunk." *Boswell*: "I assure you, sir, there was a great deal of drunkenness." *Johnson*: "No sir; there were people who died of dropsies, which they contracted in trying to get drunk." '

'Pray, Sir,' Boswell asked him once, 'can you trace the cause of your antipathy to the Scotch?' *Johnson*: 'I cannot, Sir.'

'The truth is,' says his biographer, 'like the ancient Greeks and Romans he allowed himself to look upon all other nations but his own as barbarians.... If he was particularly prejudiced against the Scots, it was because he thought their success in England rather exceeded the due proportion of their real merit; and because he could not but see in them that nationality which I believe no liberal-minded Scotsman will deny. He was indeed, if I may be allowed the phrase, at bottom much of a John Bull, much of a blunt true-born Englishman. There was a stratum of common clay under the rock of marble.... When I humour any of them [the English] in an outrageous contempt of Scotland, I fairly own I treat them as children. And thus I have, at some moments, found myself obliged to treat even Dr Johnson.'

The secret of hospitality lies, of course, far deeper than in the provision of material comforts. An old Gaelic rune, translated by Kenneth MacLeod, runs:

I saw a stranger yestreen;
I put food in the eating-place,
Drink in the drinking-place,
Music in the listening-place;
And in the sacred name of the Triune
He blessed myself and my house,
My cattle and my dear ones.
And the lark said in her song
Often, often, often
Goes the Christ in the stranger's guise,
Often, often, often,
Goes the Christ in the stranger's guise.

Above all, it is the *blessing* that matters—the mutual goodwill, the desire to welcome and be welcomed, the genuine, as distinct from the politely assumed, interest of host and guest in each other. If this be lacking, even with the softest bed and the finest food and drink in the world, you have only a travesty of hospitality.

'Highland hospitality', remarks a later traveller, 'was never boasted of, yet never failing.' Indeed, the people he met had never heard of hospitality—happily, for 'when once the term has crept in, the virtue is apt to creep out'. Their civility is a true *politesse de coeur*, or what he describes as 'that civility which arises from kindness or good nature: a desire to assist you, or to remove your inconveniences, not that *politesse qui est l'art de se passer des virtus qu'elle imite.*'

But, alas, commercial values are being gradually superimposed on the old human values, and, to quote the same author, it is now not hard to find evidence of 'the spirit of commerce, the artificial graft, vegetating on the radical generosity of the species'.

Still, neither the commercialized civilization of modern times nor the austerity of the War and post-War years has been able to extinguish the old delight in entertaining the stranger in our midst.

'Edinburgh's love of hospitality', writes Moray McLaren, 'is like a banked, glowing fire, not easily put out. It does not display itself easily to the newcomer with the flash of flames or the crackle of burning, but it does give out a slow, deep, steady heat. One has to look for it, to advance to it and be warmed by it. It is not the easy, open-handed hospitality that in America makes one feel so delightfully free of a whole town the day one enters it. It is a hospitality which one has to do something about. One has to go to meet it as well as to be met by it.' He approves Mr George Scott-Moncrieff's comparison of Edinburgh to a theatre where a play is always going on, in contrast with the cinema-like atmosphere of most other large towns. 'In a cinema you go in and sit down and passively accept the wave of entertainment that passes impersonally over you; without your having to do anything about it, it comes at you. In a theatre there is not only a certain formality that must be obeyed, but there must also be a give-and-take between the real actors and the real playgoers. It is so with Edinburgh hospitality, which is the real, conventionalized, sometimes over-formal, but human hospitality of the theatre and not the mechanical and automatic hospitality of the cinema. It is a direct legacy from the hospitality of an older age.'

Hospitality and conviviality are not, of course, the same thing, but in Scotland they are inextricably mingled. The Scots have always been a highly convivial folk, and every social occasion used to centre round a tappit-hen, brimming with claret, a reeking punch-bowl, a grey-beard of malt whisky, or a bowie reaming with home-brewn ale.

In rural communities copious libations of the national beverages—ale and whisky—attended each and all from the cradle to the grave. Drink was provided for the howdie (midwife) and the kimmers (neighbour wives) who attended the lying-in, to celebrate the canny-moment (the moment of birth); and it appeared again at the kirstenin'. It contributed to the merriment of the Highland *reiteach*, or betrothal feast, and at every rustic wedding the 'bride's cog' (a loving-cup), filled with 'braithel ale' (bridal ale—an especially strong brew), was freely circulated. It was in evidence at the 'foondin' o the hoose' (the laying of the foundation stone); at the 'hoose-heatin' '; at the fisherman's foy, the farewell party when the boats were drawn up at the end of the season; at the Martinmas foy of the farm hands, who moved, more often than not, to a new farm on the term-day; and notably at the kirn (harvest home), or clyack, as it is called in the north-east, when the meal-and-ale (an immemorial harvest drink) was carried round by the farmer himself, in token of the friendly bond between master and men. But for hilarious conviviality, the greatest occasion of all was the funeral, when the spirit of the departed seemed to linger hospitably among 'the sib and the fremd' (the relatives and those who were not kin) who had assembled to bid him farewell, and urge them on to fresh libations.

'For God's sake, give them a hearty drink!' were the last words of a dying laird to his son; and it is told of the faithful retainer of another that when the funeral guests were about to depart after a moderate refreshment he barred the exit and declared solemnly, 'It was the express will o the deid that I should fill ye fou, and I maun fulfil the will o the deid.'

It is hardly surprising that English officers who had witnessed such occasions pronounced a Scots funeral to be merrier than an English wedding!

The obsequies of a Highland laird or chief were a truly sumptuous affair. The Highland gentleman in Smollett's *Humphry Clinker* considered it a grave disparagement on his family that not above a hundred gallons of whisky were consumed at his grandmother's funeral; and this was typical of the times. At the funeral of a chief, the *daoin'uasal* (gentry of the clan), clansfolk, retainers, neighbours and friends within a hundred miles were present, and the entertainment of the guests went on for several days, wine and whisky being emptied in hogsheads. A cortège, miles long, would at last set out for the churchyard with flaring torches, the chanting of coronachs (laments), and the wailing of the pipes. But this unique blend of mourning and merrymaking had sometimes unforeseen results. So lavish was the hospitality dispensed by Forbes of Culloden at his mother's funeral that the mourners arrived at the grave only to find that the corpse had been left behind!

A similar tale is told of an ancient maiden lady in Strathspey. An extremely exhilarated funeral party reached the kirkyard after a long journey broken by a prolonged halt at a roadside inn.

'But whaur's Miss Ketty?' asked the gravedigger. Miss Ketty, it transpired, had been left at the place of refreshment on this, her last journey.

The only occasion that rivalled a funeral as a Bacchanalian orgy was Hogmanay, when a communal welcome was, and still is, given to the New Year. In the cities and burghs, the traditional gathering-place is the Mercat Cross, though in Edinburgh the crowd has slid a few yards down the hill to the Tron Kirk, lured, no doubt, by the four-faced clock in the tower. Whilst awaiting 'the chappin' o Twal', folk pass their hip-bottles round freely. Formerly, steaming kettles of Het Pint—a sort of Hogmanay wassail-bowl—were carried through the streets an hour or two before midnight, and a cupful pressed on all and sundry. When midnight has struck, the bells have ceased to peal, greetings have been exchanged and the last strains of *Auld Lang Syne* have died away, the crowd disperses and the young folk set off on their first-footing expeditions.

First-footing, in the loose sense of the term, means visiting in the early hours of New Year morning; but the first-foot, strictly speaking, means the first person, other than a member of the household, who crosses the threshold after midnight. His appearance is held to indicate the character of the luck that will attend the household throughout the coming year, and it is a matter of concern that he (or she) should be sonsie and well-favoured. The first-footers all carry handsel, which may be anything from an orange to a bottle of whisky.

The first-foot, on crossing the threshold, immediately greets the household: 'A gude New Year to ane and a', and mony may ye see!' or simply, 'A Happy New Year'. He pours out a glass from the bottle he carries and proffers it to the head of the house, who must drink it to the dregs, for luck. The host then pours out a glass of his own whisky for each of his visitors. The glass handed to the first-foot proper must also be drunk to the dregs. Toddy, punch or het pint are sometimes substituted for whisky. In the Highlands, and particularly in the Highland regiments, the popular Hogmanay drink is Atholl Brose.

The first-footers visit only those families to whom they desire to show goodwill, and the attention is always welcomed. The greater the number of first-footers, the more honoured the household. But a dram or two at each of half-a-dozen houses is a fairly severe test for a youth habitually sober during the rest of the year, and one may sympathize with the predicament of the Glasgow undergraduate who, trying to make his way home in the wee sma' oors of Ne'er Day, encountered a lamp-post, made several futile attempts to get past it, and was heard to mutter, 'Losht, losht! Losht in an impenetrable foresht!'

In Edinburgh, the zenith of conviviality was reached in the

eighteenth century, an age of hard drinking. People drank un-ashamedly, and apparently without ill effects to their constitution.

'It's no the love o the drink that gars a body get the waur o't,' remarked an old Scots worthy; 'it's the conveeviality o the thing.'

When a gentleman entertained his friends, he invariably pressed the bottle as far as it could be made to go; indeed, a host worthy of the name was offended with a guest who had not to be carried to bed.

During dinner every glass had to be dedicated to the health of some one or other, and everyone present, following his host, drank to every other guest, individually. The more bashful guests were permitted 'merely to look the benediction'; but to do this well, we are told, required some grace, and 'consequently it was best done by the polite ruffled and frilled gentlemen of the olden time'. But that did not end the drinking; for before the ladies retired, there generally began what were called 'rounds of toasts', when each gentleman named an absent lady, and each lady an absent gentleman. The toasts were usually accompanied with 'sentiments'—short epigrammatic sentences expressing moral feelings and virtues, which were considered refined and elegant productions. In Lord Cockburn's time (1779-1854) they were out of fashion and rather scoffed at; but though at their worst they had a touch of the ridiculous, and were often a sad trial to the timid and the awkward, at their best and in the right hands, they added a touch of dignity and grace to private society; and they are certainly worth preserving as period pieces.

A curious custom known as 'saving the ladies' had a consider-able vogue in the eighteenth century.

'When after any fashionable assembly the male guests had con-ducted their fair partners to their homes, they returned to the supper-room. Then one of the number would drink to the health of the lady he professed to admire, and in doing so would empty his glass. Another gentleman would name another lady, also drinking a bumper in her honour. The former would reply by swallowing a second glass to his lady, followed by the other, each combatant persisting till one of the two fell upon the floor. Other couples followed in like fashion. These drinking competitions were regarded with interest by gentlewomen, who next morning inquired as to the prowess of their champions.'[1]

1. Lord Cockburn: *Memorials*.

'There was a sort of infatuation', says Dean Ramsay, 'in the supposed dignity and manliness attached to powers of deep potation, and the fatal effects of drinking were spoken of in a manner both reckless and unfeeling. Thus, I have been assured that a well-known laird of the old school expressed himself with great indignation at the charge brought against hard drinking that it had actually killed people. "Na, na, I never knew onybody killed wi' drinking, but I hae kenn'd some that dee'd in the training." '

In Ramsay's time, drunkenness had largely passed away in the higher circles, but the evil had in some quarters taken deeper root. This was also true of England; but in Scotland, says Ramsay, 'the system of pressing, or compelling guests to drink seemed more inveterate'. The Scots on the other hand, though their tables were abundant, were more abstemious eaters.

'It seems difficult', comments Chambers, 'to reconcile all these things with the staid and somewhat square-toed character which our country has obtained among her neighbours. The fact seems to be that a kind of Laodicean principle is observable in Scotland, and we oscillate between a rigour of manners on the one hand, and a laxity on the other, which alternately acquire an apparent paramouncy. In the early part of the last [eighteenth] century, rigour was in the ascendant; but not to the prevention of a respectable minority of the free-and-easy, who kept alive the flame of conviviality with no small degree of success. In the latter half of the century—a dissolute era all over civilized Europe—the minority became the majority, and the characteristic sobriety of the nation's manners was only traceable in certain portions of society.'

All over the Highlands, a glass of whisky served as ready-money payment for any small service. Habitual tippling was rare, but strangers were often astonished at the number of glasses of undiluted whisky a Highlander could dispose of without appearing any the worse.

In 1860, on a tramp through the mountains from Kinlochawe to Ullapool, Dr Archibald Geikie, the geologist, took with him an old shepherd to act as guide over thirty miles of rough, trackless ground. The refreshments they carried included a bottle of whisky. Dr Geikie, who was not used to it, hardly touched it all day, and he was all the more astonished when, on reaching the ferry opposite Ullapool, Simon pitched the empty bottle into the loch, he himself remaining as cool and collected as when they had set out.[1]

The liberality of a man's disposition was often judged by his manner in dispensing whisky. Two Highlanders were on one occasion discussing a gentleman of their acquaintance.

'What ails ye at him, Duncan?' asked one of them.

'Och, I wass up at his house last week, and he wass pouring me out a glass of whisky, and of course I said, "Stop!"—and man, wad ye believe it, he stoppit!'

Of a different calibre was the newly arrived minister who had received a call from one of his elders.

'What think ye o the meenister, Tammas?'

'A grand chap, yon! He opened a fresh bottle o whisky as sune as I sat doun, and flang the cork intae the fire!'

Elizabeth Grant gives us a picture of life at Rothiemurchus in the early nineteenth century. Her father, the seventh laird, was the 'chief and father' of that part of the country, and his house was filled with relatives and retainers, 'including a piper who refused all work unconnected with whisky, for fear of spoiling the delicacy of his touch'.

Describing a visit to Inverness and Forres, 'the hospitality', she writes, 'was tremendous. The doors were never locked and visitors poured in during the summer and autumn. No one then passed a friend's house in the Highlands, nor was it ever thought necessary to send invitations on the one part, or to give information on the other. No barefoot boy with a message from the gamekeeper or forester went empty away; whisky, oatcake and cheese were given to all comers.' The Laird's lady, handing the horn cup to a woodman's wife, was startled to see her, after taking a good pull, pass it on to the wee thing toddling beside her. 'My goodness, child,' said Lady Grant, 'doesn't it bite you?' 'Aye, but I like the bite,' replied the creature.[2]

'The last act of manorial hospitality', Scott reminds us, 'was enacted upon the lawn. On each, in front of the mansion, was a platform of masonry—the loupin'-on stone. Here gentlemen mounted their horses, and were supplied with the deoch-an-doruis or stirrup-cup. Drunk from a quaich (a timber bowl with two ears) it was otherwise known as a bonalay.'[3]

---

1. *Scottish Reminiscences.*   2. *Memoirs of a Highland Lady.*   3. *The Pirate.*

E

2: *Tavern Life*

THE eighteenth century was the age of tavern clubs, and, until well into the nineteenth, tavern dissipation prevailed in Edinburgh to an incredible extent among all ranks and classes. Many highly esteemed citizens, including some of the ablest judges, were noted for their convivial habits. M. Simond, who in 1811 published a *Tour of Scotland*, mentions his surprise when, on entering Parliament House one morning, he found 'in the dignified capacity of a judge and displaying all the gravity suitable to the character', the very man with whom he had spent the previous night in a fierce debauch. This was Lord Newton.

Unfortunately not all his contemporaries enjoyed his Lordship's constitution. Many men of robust intellect, and some of apparently robust physique, fell by the way, overcome, as Mr Moray McLaren puts it, by the 'combination of liquor and logic, of conviviality and creed'.

Most of the taverns were situated in the thoroughfare leading from the Castle to the Watergate, and in its adjacent wynds and closes. They suited all tastes and purses, and round the clock—or, in the old phrase, 'from the gill-bells to the drum'—the taps were overflowing. The bells of St Giles, which on Sundays summoned the citizens to worship, summoned them on week-days to the good-fellowship of the tavern or the home. Half an hour before noon came the chiming of the gill-bells—so called from the general custom of stopping work for a midday gill or whetting-dram; the kail-bell announced the approach of two o'clock, the fashionable hour for dinner;[1] and the tinkle-sweetie, at eight o'clock, set the shopkeepers and apprentices at liberty, thus earning its popular name. At ten o'clock the drum of the Town Guard went round to warn sober folks to call for their 'lawin' ' or reckoning.

> Some to porter, some to punch
> Retire, while noisy ten-hours drum
> Gars a' the trades gang danderin' hame.
> Now mony a club, jocose and free,
> Gi'e a' to merriment and glee;
> Wi' sang and glass they fley the power
> O' care, that wad harass the hour.[2]

1. Kail, a common name for broth in Scotland, was used metonymically for the whole dinner.   2. Robert Fergusson. *Fley*, scare away.

The 'meridian',[1] as the mid-morning dram was commonly called, was as popular with business men in its day as is their mid-morning coffee in our own time. A favourite regale was 'a cauld cock and feathers'—that is, a gill of brandy and a bunch of raisins —over which it was customary to fee counsel in St John's coffee-house, the favourite resort of the writers and clerks belonging to Parliament House. The merchants who congregated at the Mercat Cross to discuss business frequented kindly Mrs Rutherford's tavern in Craig's Close, and on the stroke of noon would cross the street to have their meridian of whisky or beer, with perhaps a saucer of mussels.

Further afield, in the Potter Row, was Mrs Flockhart, better known as Luckie[2] Fykie, who is believed to have been the original of Mrs Flockhart of *Waverley*. Every morning she put her little shop in the neatest order, and set out on the bunker-seat in the window three bottles, containing severally brandy, whisky and rum, with a tray of her famous 'parlies'[3] (a species of gingerbread), in readiness for the lawyers and bankers of George Square who came daily for their 'meridian'.

'Her customers', says Chambers, 'were very numerous and respectable, including Mr Dundas, afterwards Lord Melville; Lord Stonefield; Lord Braxfield; Sheriff Cockburn; Mr Scott, father of Sir Walter; Mr Donald Smith, Banker; and Dr Cullen. The use and wont of these gentlemen, on entering the shop and finding Mrs Flockhart engaged with customers, was to salute her with, 'Hoo do you do, mem?' and a *coup de châpeau*, and then walk *ben* to the room. . . . They seldom sat down, but after partaking of what bottle they chose, walked quickly off.'

In the evenings the taverns were busier than ever. Owing partly to the lack of public amusements, and partly to the restricted accommodation in private houses, all classes of the community were in the habit of frequenting them after the day's work was over, for relaxation and discussion. There were many convivial coteries centring on some recognized wit or worthy, and many

1. Glasgow used to have its Meridian Club. The appellation, writes Dr Strang, the historian of the Glasgow Clubs, 'will appear as appropriate as it is descriptive when it is recollected that some of the brotherhood were ever busy in their vocation of taking spiritual comfort ere the sun had attained to its "high meridian".'   2. *Luckie*, goodwife, goody.
3. Properly Parliament-cakes, so called from their having been popular with the members of the old Scottish Parliament.

a congenial gathering would be arranged on the spur of the moment, the host summoning his guests by the 'caddies', or town messengers, to meet him at his favourite howff.

The Luckies

The Luckies who presided over many of the city's taverns were the descendents of the brewster-wives of an earlier age. They were a highly-assorted crew. Some, like Mrs Flockhart, had a quiet dignity; some, like Lucky Wood, were kind and motherly; some were slapdash and slatternly; not a few, such as Lucky Thom, whose tavern off the Cowgate was popular with aristocratic young rakes, and Lucky Spence (of whom more anon) were deep in the underworld.

The Luckies owed much to their poet-patrons. Allan Ramsay, who has left us many pictures of the couthie, clarty, bawdy life of the clubs and taverns in the early eighteenth century, wrote elegies on three of them. One of these was Lucky Wood, an ale-house keeper in the Canongate, who had so long provided him and his cronies with 'gude belly-baum'.

> She gaed as fait as a new prin,
> And kept her housie snod and bien;
> Her peuther glanc'd upon your een,
> 　　　Like siller plate;
> She was a donsie wife and clean,
> 　　　Without debate.
>
> 　　·　　　·　　　·　　　·
>
> She ga'e us aft hale legs o lamb,
> And didna hain her mutton-ham;
> Then aye at Yule whene'er we cam',
> 　　　A braw goose-pye;
> An' wasna that gude belly-baum?
> 　　　Nane dare deny.

And the elegy closes thus:

> Beneath this sod
> Lies Lucky Wood,
> Wham a' men might put faith in;
> 　　Wha wasna sweer
> 　　While she winn'd here,
> To cramm our wames for naethin!

Fait, trim; *prin*, pin; *snod*, neat, trim; *bien*, comfortable; *donsie*, affectedly neat; *hain*, spare; *belly-baum*, belly-timber, provender; *sweer*, unwilling; *winn'd*, dwelt.

Then there was Maggie Johnstoun, whose little farm-tavern lay just beyond the Bruntsfield Links. Maggie's home-brewed ale was famous. 'Certainly it was small beer, very pale and clear, but nevertheless potent, and many a guess was made as to the secret process of her "pawky knack of brewing ale a'maist like wine!" '

> Some said it was the pith o broom
> That she stow'd in her maskin'-loom,
> Which in our heids raised sic a foom,
>   Or some wild seed
> Which aft the chapin stoup did toom,
>   But filled our heid.
>
> When we were wearied at the gowff,
> Then Maggie Johnstoun's was our howff;
> Noo a' our gamesters may sit dowff
>   Wi' hearts like lead,
> Death wi' his rung rax'd her a yowff,
>   And sae she dee'd.

Maskin'-loom, mash-tub; *chapin*, quart; *toom*, empty; *gowff*, golf; *howff*, tavern; *dowff*, gloomy; *rax*, reach out; *yowff*, a smart blow.

Another poem of Ramsay's, *Lucky Spence's Last Advice*, purports to be the dying testament and admonitions of a notorious bawd.

Mistress Spence took considerable pride in her profession, had ladylike manners and conducted her establishment with decorum, summoning her lasses with a 'siller ca' ' (silver whistle). On her death-bed, so far from showing any signs of remorse about her way of life, the old procuress instructs her pupils with her latest breath in the arts of their vocation, and dies with a glass of gin in her hand.

> Lass, gi'e us in anither gill,
> A mutchkin, jo, let's tak our fill,
> Let death syne registrate his bill;
>   When I want sense,
> I'll slip awa wi' better will,
>   Quo' Lucky Spence.

Mutchkin, pint.

Ramsay's poem has been compared with Villon's *Heaulmière aux Filles de Joie*, but in fact the two differ considerably in character. 'The coarse-grained, sardonic brutality of Ramsay's poem,' comments Mr Harvey Wood, 'is as characteristic of the age as of the city in which it was written.'

Just as Allan Ramsay has preserved for us the spirit of the convivial life of Edinburgh in the early eighteenth century, so Robert Fergusson that of the latter half. There were taverns where the most impecunious poet could be sure of an evening's entertainment. One such was Lucky Middlemass's, in the Cowgate, where 'with sixpence he'll purchase a crown's worth of bliss', and the poet has very properly immortalized this, his favourite Lucky.

> When big as burns the gutters rin,
> Gin ye hae catch'd a droukit skin,
> To Lucky Middlemiss's loup in,
>   And sit fu' snug
> O'er oysters and a dram o' gin,
>   Or haddock lug.

droukit, drenched; *lug*, ear, so *haddock lug*, part of the head (a titbit).

At Jock's Lodge, then a little way out of the city, was Pudding Lizzie's Tavern, which specialized in 'Popish Whisky'—rum sold under that name to evade the tax. This worthy is commemorated by one of her customers, a young poet named Richard Gall, who died at the age of twenty-five.

> Did ony relish cauler water?
> Na, faith, it wasna in our natur!
> We boot to hae a wee drap cratur,
>   Gude Papish Whisky.

cauler, fresh.

Lizzie was famous, too, for her mealie puddings, which she carried in to the company seated round her ingle,

> A pipin' like a roastit hen,
>   Braw healthy eatin'!
> Wi' timmer pins at ilka en'
>   To haud the meat in.

timmer, wooden; *ilka*, each.

But the most outstanding name in the Scots tradition of convivial literature is Burns himself. *Willie Brew'd a Peck o Maut*, which is perhaps the greatest of all drinking-songs, was written in an Edinburgh tavern, and the scene of *The Jolly Beggars* was, of course, Poosie Nansie's at Mauchline. This was a tavern of the lowest description, where vagrants and beggars, the 'randie gangrel bodies' of the poem, were able to obtain bed and board and a comforting draught of their 'dear Kilbagie', which, at a penny a gill was the cheapest (and nastiest) whisky to be had.

'The natural reaction against the harsh and ignorant bigotry of Presbytery rule', writes Mr Harvey Wood, 'was an affectation of wine and women, and this was encouraged in Burns by his study of Ramsay and Fergusson, and coincided with an ardent, genial and gregarious temper. It was this defiant impulse of reaction that impelled Burns, while pillorying the parish Pharisees, to erect for worship "muse-inspiring aquavitie" and sing the praises of "browster-wives and whisky stills". But however foolish the affectations that motivated them, we cannot regret or reject "Scotch Drink", "Tam o Shanter", and "The Jolly Beggars", any more than we can wholly regret the drug-inspired dream to which we owe "Kubla Khan".'[1]

It is true that there was plenty of harsh and ignorant bigotry under Presbytery rule, just as there was plenty of domestic tyranny in Victorian times; but it would be as wrong to assume that all ministers of the kirk resembled the Rev. William Auld of Mauchline, whom Burns found so objectionable a character, as to assume that all Victorian fathers resembled Mr Barrett of Wimpole Street. In both categories there were numerous men who possessed, beneath the conventional attitude of their time, natural intelligence, good sense, and humour, and who retained the respect and affection of their families and friends.

Bigotry and integrity, however, often go together. This same Mr Auld had his merits. He worked strenuously, for instance, for the abolition of the popular but cruel sport of cock-fighting in his parish.

The last of the long line of Luckies of the old school to achieve more than local fame was Tibbie Shiels, whose little inn still stands on St Mary's Loch. 'A cosy bield, this o Tibbie's,' quoth the Ettrick Shepherd, 'just like a wee bit wren's nest', and Christopher North made it the scene of one of his *Noctes*. Besides North and Hogg, Tibbie's clients included Sir Walter Scott, de Quincey, Lord Aytoun, Allan Cunningham and Robert Chambers, and in later years, Robert Louis Stevenson. Tibbie is described as 'a sagacious woman, gifted with a large amount of common sense and a fund of dry, quiet humour, and at the same time deeply religious and a strict Sabbatarian'.

1. From an article in *Scotland*, ed. by Henry W. Meikle.

The Taverns

One of the most popular of the old Edinburgh taverns was Johnny Dowie's in the steep and narrow Libberton's Wynd, by West St Giles. It had a descending scale of small rooms, accommodating from fourteen to six people, the smallest being known as 'the coffin'.

Dowie, a dignified figure in an out-moded costume of cocked hat, knee breeches and shoe buckles, greeted his clients with mingled geniality and politeness. The tavern was renowned for its ale—the well-known 'Edinburgh Ale'—which was brewed at Croft-an-Righ by Archibald Younger.

> O Dowie's Ale! Thou art the thing
> That gars us crack, that gars us sing.

'Nothing could equal the benignity of his [Johnny's] smile,' says Chambers, 'when he brought in a bottle of ale to a company of well-known and friendly customers; and it was a perfect treat to see his formality in drawing the cork, his precision in filling the glasses, his regularity in drinking the healths of all present in the first glass (which he always did, at each successive bottle), and then his douce civility in withdrawing.'

Dawny Douglas's Tavern in Anchor's Close housed the Crochallan Fencibles, with whom Burns associated during his Edinburgh visits.

> As I cam by Crochallan,
> I cannily keekit ben—
> Rattlin', roarin' Willie[1]
> Was sittin' at yon board en'.

Here ceremonial dinners were held and more than one convivial club had its meetings.

'The guests', writes Chambers again, 'before getting to any of the rooms, had to traverse the kitchen—a dark, fiery pandemonium, through which numerous ineffable ministers of flame were constantly flying, like devils in a sketch of the Valley of the Shadow of Death, in *The Pilgrim's Progress*. Close by the door of the kitchen sat Mrs Douglas, a woman of immense bulk, dressed out in the most splendid style. . . . She never rose from her seat upon the entry of the guests, either because she was unable from fatness, or that from sitting, she might preserve the greater dignity.

1. William Smellie.

She only bowed to them as they passed, and there were numerous waiters and slip-shod damsels, ready to obey her directions. . . . The genius and tongue of his wife had evidently been too much for [Dawny], for she kept him in the most perfect subjection and he acted only as a sort of head waiter under her.'

Among Dawny's clients were Adam Smith, Adam Ferguson, Dr Blair, Dr Beattie, Henry Mackenzie, and the law lords Hailes and Monboddo.

Less couthie, perhaps, but certainly more spacious and elegant was Fortune's Tavern, formerly the mansionhouse of the Earl of Eglintoune, where gentlemen of fashion met to toast the Flowers of Edinburgh, as the belles of the city were known. The Royal Commissioner to the General Assembly held his levées at Fortune's until, in 1833, he took up residence in Holyrood; and it was here, in 1784, that fifty gentlemen met and formed the Highland Society of Scotland. Though a rendezvous of the *élite*, the clientèle of the tavern was by no means confined to what our American friends call 'socialites', but included poets, scholars and philosophers, as well as more ordinary citizens; for the Scots, although they had considerable respect for 'good family', never took class distinctions too seriously.

The Cross Keys Tavern, which was situated in what is now called the Old Assembly Close, was in the early eighteenth century the great rendezvous of music-lovers. Hither ladies and gentlemen resorted in the afternoons to hear the compositions brought back from their travels on the Continent by nobles and gentlemen performed by amateur and professional musicians. The Laird of Newhall would play on his viol-da-gamba, Lord Colville on the harpsichord, and Sir Gilbert Elliot (later Lord Minto) on the German flute; whilst an enthusiastic group of amateurs would perform the overtures of Handel and the concertos and sonatas of Corelli.

The tavern was also frequented by the opponents of the Union of Parliaments. Feelings ran high, and it must have required a quantity of good claret to assuage them. 'Here, it is most likely,' surmises Marie Stuart, 'would be the tavern in which Fletcher (of Saltoun) sat nursing his wrath after high words with the Duke of Roxburgh in the Parliament House.'

The Star and Garter Inn, popularly known as Cleriheugh's Tavern, was frequented by the Provost and Magistrates of the

City, and much civic business was transacted here. Hither, too, came Dr Webster, the claret-loving minister of the Tolbooth and a man of great practical genius, to discuss with Lord Provost Drummond the plans for the New Town. Cleriheugh's has been immortalized by Scott in *Guy Mannering*, where Councillor Pleydell describes one of his sederunts in the tavern: 'There we sat birling till I had a fair tappit-hen under my belt.'

James Mann's tavern in Craig's Close was the home of the Cape Club, one of the most distinguished coteries in the city. The 'Knights of the Cape' included members so diverse in talents and character as Henry Raeburn, our greatest portrait-painter, David Herd, the song-collector, Stephen Kemble, manager of the Theatre Royal, and Deacon Brodie, a respectable burgess by day and house-breaker by night, who was to inspire Robert Louis Stevenson's *Dr Jekyll and Mr Hyde*.

Chief among the Stablers' Inns was the White Horse, which had theatrical associations, and was a haven for runaway couples, who were able to fee an unofficial parson at a shilling; and among other guests were Cromwell, Burns and Wordsworth. To Boyd's Inn James Boswell came hotfoot to welcome Dr Samuel Johnson on his arrival in Scotland in the autumn of 1776.

Jenny Ha's (Janet Hall's) opposite Queensberry House, was the resort of the Jacobites and Episcopalian clergy, who were wont to toast 'The King owre the Water!' in claret from the butt. One of its most popular clients was Jamie Balfour, long remembered as a great singer, a great drinker, and a great golfer, who would regale his companions with 'Owre the Water to Charlie', 'The King shall enjoy his Own Again', and other Jacobite songs.

'There used to be a portrait of him', writes Chambers, 'in the Leith golf-house representing him in the act of commencing the favourite song of "When I hae a saxpence under my thoomb", with the suitable attitude and a merriness of countenance justifying the traditionary account of the man. . . . The powers of Balfour as a singer of Scotch songs of all kinds, tender and humorous, are declared to have been marvellous; and he had a happy gift of suiting them to occasions. Being a great peacemaker, he would often accomplish his purpose by introducing some ditty pat to the purpose, and thus dissolving all rancour in a hearty laugh.

'Jamie's potations here were principally what was called "cappie ale"—that is, ale in little wooden bowls—with wee thochts o brandy in it. But indeed no one could be less exclusive than he as to liquors. When he heard a bottle drawn in any house, and observed the cork to give an unusually smart report, he would call out: "Lassie, gi'e me a glass o *that*": as knowing that whatever it was, it must be good of its kind.'[1]

Jenny Ha's was frequented, too, by Gay on his visit to Edinburgh in 1729, whenever he could escape from his lovely but eccentric and possessive patroness, the Duchess of Queensberry. It is noteworthy that he set some of the lyrics in *The Beggars' Opera* and other works to lively Scottish airs.

In the latter part of the eighteenth century oyster-parties were all the rage, and ladies as well as gentlemen resorted to the oyster-cellars where they were held. Of these none was more popular than Lucky Middlemass's. At that time the famous osyter-beds of the Forth supplied the city's needs, and these were not small.

'They tell me,' says the Ettrick Shepherd in the *Noctes Ambrosianae*, 'that Embro devours a hunder thoosand every day.'

Visitors to the city were delighted with the cheap and abundant supplies.[2] The Firth of Forth natives were usually served on the deep shell and eaten without condiments in their own juice.

'In winter,' says Chambers, 'when the evening had set in, a party of the most fashionable people in town, collected by appointment, would adjourn in carriages to one of those abysses of darkness and comfort, called, in Edinburgh, laigh (low) shops, where they proceeded to regale themselves with raw oysters and porter arranged in huge dishes upon a coarse table in a dingy room lighted by tallow candles.... The rudeness of the feast ... seems to have given a zest to its enjoyment.

'One of the chief features of an oyster-cellar entertainment was that full scope was given to the conversational powers of the company. Both ladies and gentlemen indulged, without restraint, in sallies the merriest and the wittiest; and a thousand remarks and jokes, which elsewhere would have been suppressed as improper, were here sanctified by the oddity of the scene, and appreciated by the most dignified and refined.... It is not [in 1824] more than thirty years since the late Lord Melville, the Duchess of Gordon, and some other persons of distinction, who happened to

1. *Traditions of Edinburgh.*
2. 'In 1837 the price was 10d. for a board (36-66) with bread and butter ad lib.' —James Bertram.

meet in town after many years of absence, made up an oyster-party, by way of a frolic, and devoted one winter evening to the revival of this almost forgotten entertainment of their youth.'

A similar tavern life prevailed in Glasgow. In the forenoons business was transacted and lawyers were consulted, the bill being paid by the client, and in the evenings clubs met and assemblies were held in the taverns. The liquor in common use was, however, not claret, but sherry, which was presented in mutchkin stoups. The quantity swallowed, says Dr Strang, the historian of the clubs, was almost incredible.

Edinburgh had no monopoly of notable men. The University of Glasgow, founded under a Papal Bull in 1450, was considerably older than the 'Tounis College' of Edinburgh, which was founded by James VI in 1582. Adam Smith occupied the Chair of Moral Philosophy for some years—James Boswell was one of his students —although he was always 'running through' to Edinburgh before he finally moved there for good. Among his colleagues were Robert Simson, the mathematician, Dr Cullen, one of the greatest physicians of his time, Joseph Black, the discoverer of latent heat, and Dr Moore, a man of literary tastes, the friend of Smollett, and father of Sir John Moore of Corunna fame. The brothers Foulis, with their admirable book and printing shop were other notable citizens, and, not least, there was James Watt, who arrived from Greenock in 1754. In the taverns where such men foregathered there must have been plenty of good talk; whilst others—for an age of religious tyranny had passed and the genial qualities of the sober, honest citizens of Glasgow blossomed anew—resounded with laughter and lively songs.[1]

During the latter half of the eighteenth century, the Saracen's Head was the resort of the élite of Glasgow and the favourite hostelry of wealthy and aristocratic travellers. Here the magistrates held their celebrated dinners, the waiters resplendent in embroidered coats, red plush breeches, white stockings and powdered hair. A prominent feature on such occasions was the famous punch-bowl of blue and white china, decorated with the tree, the

1. 'Glasgow is a city I never visit without a more intense awareness of the warmth of human nature than any city gives me, though God knows it is a city over which not even its own Lord Provost can afford to rhapsodize.'— Compton Mackenzie: *The North Wind of Love*.

bell and the fish of the city's coat of arms, together with a rollicking procession of revellers. The bowl held no less than five gallons of liquor. A sporting Duke of Hamilton, who was a frequenter of the cockpit in the Gallowgait, 'used to foregather', we are told, 'with his cock-fighting cronies at the Saracen's Head and celebrate his gains, or drown his losses, in reaming rummers of Jamaica punch'.[1] It was here, too, that Boswell brought Dr Johnson on the completion of their tour of the Hebrides, and hither came several of the professors of the University to pay their respects to the distinguished travellers.

'Aberdeen,' says the author of *Convivial Caledonia*, is 'a city renowned for mirth and music.' At the time of the founding of the University (1495), when the duty was negligible, Gascony wine was sold at sixpence a pint. In the sixteenth century, the Town House 'could boast of an excellent stock of ancient and choice wines, and was distinguished for the hospitality of its civic feasts'. For generations University professors and notables of the town and 'twal mile roun'' met in howffs. The spirit of good fellowship so characteristic of Aberdeen, which has always striven to live up to its motto *Bon Accord*, found expression in a custom already spoken of as ancient in 1622—that of waiting upon distinguished visitors to the burgh and presenting them with a libation of wine called 'a cup of Bon-Accord'—in other words 'a richt gude-willy waught'.

A version of the song, 'Up in the Mornin' Early' recounts the drinking feats of a number of boon companions, all Aberdeenshire gentlemen of the late eighteenth century.

> Frae nicht till morn our squires they sat,
>> And drank the juice o the barley.
> Some they spent but ae half-croun,
>> And some sax crouns sae rarely.
>
> .   .   .   .
>
> 'Let's a' gang hame,' said Lord Aboyne,[2]
>> 'Na, bide awhile,' quo' Towie;
> 'O, ne'er a fit,' said Lochnagar,
>> 'As lang's there's beer i' the bowie.'

1. C. Stewart Black: *Glasgow's Story.*
2. Lord Aboyne, afterwards the fourth Duke of Gordon (1743-1827), was the husband of the famous Duchess Jean, the friend and patroness of Burns, and was the author of the well-known convivial song, 'The Reel o Bogie'. It was he who induced the Westminster Government to cease their persecution of distilling in the Highlands and permit the establishment of the large distilleries.

O there they sat the lee-lang nicht,
    Nor stirred ere the sun shone clearly,
Then made an end as they began
    And gae'd hame i' the mornin' early.

Good food and good wine were quite as much appreciated in
Aberdeen as in Edinburgh. We read that in pre-Victorian days,
'Affleck's tavern, in the Exchequer Row, enjoys among the
choice spirits of the town an unrivalled reputation for poignancy
of cookery and excellence of potations; and the curious in gastro-
nomy flock hither to explore the deeper mysteries of the science.'[1]

A famous Aberdeen restaurant still going strong is commemorated by Eric Linklater in *White-maa's Saga*:

'Sandy's was a chop-house with a tradition. . . . The creative
spirit of the original proprietor had survived his body and passed
into his son's son. Father, son and grandson were Alexander
Broun, mortal men. But Sandy Broun's their living and their
monument did not die. Its grill-fire was like a vestal hearth that
never went cold, and a livelier than vestal atmosphere was warmed
by it. The restaurant was a high room, black and gilded about
the ceiling. The smoke of the richest, reddest steak in Scotland
had darkened its mouldings and ghostly vineyard perfumes
haunted every corner, for Alexander Broun, the First and Second,
had been men with a nose and a palate who bought up the rem-
nants of famous cellars and did business with the great wine-
shippers. . . . It might be of little material moment that the riches
of France, the Peninsula and the Rhineland lay under foot when
whisky was most often on the table, but yet there was a satisfaction in the knowledge. The wine list was a liberal education, a
commentary on history and a handbook to the aesthetics of
drinking.'

Country Inns

It was precisely because there was so much free and open
hospitality that the development of the inn in the Highlands was
so long retarded. Inns were few and the majority of them were
cheerless and unattractive, whilst at their worst they were miser-
ably poor and dirty.

1. Joseph Robertson: *The Book of Bon-Accord.*

At Moffat, in 1705, Joseph Taylor 'met with good wine, and some mutton pretty well drest; but looking into our beds, found there was no lying in them, so we kept on our cloaths all night and enjoyed ourselves by a good fire, making often protestations never to come into that country again.'

His experience was far from unique. Some travellers, however, fared better. As early as 1635, Sir William Brereton found to his surprise that in most places he could rely on 'great entertainment, good lodging, a respectable host, and an honest reckoning'; whilst John Wesley, who made frequent visits to Scotland from 1751 onwards, writes, 'We were most surprised at the entertainment we met with in every place, so far different from common report. We had all things good, cheap, in great abundance, and remarkably well dressed.'

On their way from Aberdeen to Skye Dr Johnson and Boswell had a varied experience of inns. At Elgin, Dr Johnson could not eat the dinner set before him; but, he says, 'this was the first time, and, except one, the last, that I found any reason to complain of a Scottish table.'

At an inn in Glenmoriston, the landlord attended them with great civility. They found on his shelves a small but good library which included a volume of *The Spectator*. Boswell adds, 'his pride seemed much piqued that we were surprised at his having books'. His daughter, who made tea for them, had received a good education in Inverness, and 'her conversation,' says Dr Johnson, 'like her appearance, was pleasing. We knew that the girls of the Highlands are all gentlewomen and treated her with great respect, which she received as customary and due, and was neither elated by it nor confused, but repaid my civilities without embarrassment, and told me how much I honoured her country by coming to survey it.'

The inn at Glenelg where the travellers were obliged to spend a night was bare and miserable, and they slept on beds of hay; but here they had what Dr Johnson calls 'a very eminent proof of Highland hospitality. Along some miles of the way, in the evening, a gentleman's servant had kept us company on foot with very little notice on our part. He left us near Glenelg, and we thought on him no more till he came to us again, in about two hours, with a present of rum and sugar. The man had mentioned his company, and the gentleman, whose name, I think, was Gordon, well knowing the penury of the place, had this attention to two men whose names perhaps he had not heard, by whom his kindness was not likely to be ever repaid, and who could be recommended to him only by their necessities.'

From Glenelg they crossed to Skye.

'It need not, I suppose, be mentioned,' writes Dr Johnson, 'that in countries so little frequented as the islands there are no houses where travellers are entertained for money. He that wanders about these wilds either procures recommendations to those whose habitations lie near his way, or when night and weariness overcome him, takes the chance of general hospitality. If he finds only a cottage, he can expect little more than shelter, for the cottagers have little more for themselves. But if his good fortune brings him to the residence of a gentleman, he will be glad of a storm to prolong his stay.'

Returning to the mainland after their tour of the Hebrides, 'We got at night to Inverary,' says Boswell, 'where we found an excellent inn. . . . We supped well; and after supper, Dr Johnson whom I had not seen taste any fermented liquor during all our travels, called for a gill of whisky. "Come (said he), let me know what it is that makes a Scotchman happy!" He drank it all but a drop which I begged leave to pour into my glass, that I might say we had drunk whisky together.

' . . . He owned tonight that he got as good a room and bed as at an English inn.'

Faujas de Saint-Fond, who followed close in Dr Johnson and Boswell's wake, has a good word to say of the inn at Dalmally, in Argyll.

'We were astonished at its elegance in so desert a place. The threshold of the door, as well as the stairs, were scoured and strewn with fine shining sand, the dining-room was covered with a carpet; the beds were clean and good, and the landlord was a worthy man.

' . . . Our supper consisted of two dishes of fine game, the one of heathcock, the other of woodcock, a creamy fresh butter, cheese of the country, a pot of preserved *vaccinium* (blaeberries), a wild fruit which grows on the mountains, and port wine—all served up together. It was truly a luxurious repast for the country.'

The Wordsworths, having no Boswell to arrange private hospitality for them, and no one to recommend addresses, took pot luck as they travelled, and had occasion to lament the backward state of the inns. They had two unpleasant encounters, one with that *rara avis*, a surly inn-keeper, who refused to put them up, although they were convinced he had beds to spare, and, further on, 'a heartless and uncivil woman', overgrown with fat, who ruthlessly turned the weary travellers adrift. But these experiences were exceptional. A lovable thing about Dorothy is that she never minded how primitive her lodging was provided it had the glow of kindliness, and happily that was seldom lacking. She and William had one thoroughly bad meal—'a shoulder of mutton so hard that it was impossible to chew the little flesh that may be scraped off the bones, and some sorry soup made of barley and water, for it had no other taste'—and one exceptionally good one—'fresh salmon, a fowl, gooseberries and cream, and potatoes'—for which, together with good beds, breakfast, liquor, and stabling for their horse, they were agreeably surprised to be charged only seven shillings and sixpence.

'The best taverns in the days of my youth', writes James Bertram, 'were undoubtedly the Rainbow and the Café Royal.' Both were inexpensive. At the Café Royal, 'hunting and racing men were wont to meet and hold high revel over devilled bones and claret, a wine . . . which was always good at this house. Many of the wealthier merchants held their snug little dinners in the Rainbow . . . one of its chief attractions being the dishes prepared by Kirsty Bell, who was famous for her "devils". Its cheese, lovingly kept and cared for, and dosed judicially with ale or port, was a speciality. So was the hock, which took rank with the best bins of port at the Café. Banquets and great political or literary dinners were usually held at the Royal Hotel, in Princes Street, or in one of Barry's Rooms in Queen Street. It was in Barry's that Dickens was first fêted in Edinburgh.'

Tripe suppers were very popular, those esteemed the best being served at the Guildford Tavern in Register Street. 'It was served as it came to be named, "à la de Quincey", viz. smothered in a thick white sauce, richly stocked with thin slices of well-boiled onions. All sorts of people supped on tripe at the Guildford, and "the English Opium-Eater", very frequently, when he was "lost" might have been found there. "Prime Edinburgh Ale" was the usual accompaniment.'

F

Near, 'Paterson's' was a humbler house famous for its potted head. A plateful of this with mashed potatoes and a bottle of Prestonpans table beer was considered 'cheap and filling' for sevenpence.

Edinburgh was long famous for its pie-shops. And so, according to James Bertram, was Glasgow.

'The eating of many pies and the drinking of much ale and porter in public-houses and pie-shops was the habit in the minor literary men in Glasgow in the 'forties. Several of these "howffs" were situated in queer corners, known only to their frequenters.'

England is infinitely richer than Scotland in ancient and picturesque inns; nevertheless we have a few interesting old howffs, especially in and around Edinburgh. One of the oldest is the Sheep's Heid, at Duddingston, which dates to the fourteenth century. Among its reputed patrons were Mary Queen of Scots, James VI, and Prince Charlie; and it was James, according to tradition, who presented the inn with the embellished ram's head and horns from which it derives its name.

Many of the older Edinburgh citizens used to walk out to Duddingston for a plateful of powsowdie, or sheep's head broth. In winter Duddingston Loch was crowded with curlers and skaters, and the tavern had an immense custom in the traditional curler's fare, salt beef and greens. Dr Robert Chambers and Sheriff Henry Glassford Bell were among its regular customers.

The old Golf Tavern on Bruntsfield Links stands cheek by jowl with the still older tavern built in 1717. There is a tradition that the original inn dates from 1456, but there is no charter evidence for that date. The Beehive Inn, in the Grassmarket, originally a coaching inn, dates from 1500. It is now completely modernized. The seventeenth-century Old Ship's Inn, on the quayside at Leith, has a stained-glass window that commemorates the landing there of George IV in 1822.

Two seventeenth-century inns are associated with Robert Louis Stevenson—the Cramond, four miles from the city, whose innsign depicts a scene characteristic of the days when the Roman galleys harboured nearby at the mouth of the Almond, and which treasures a table with his initials carved upon it, and the Hawes Inn at South Queensferry, close by the Forth Bridge, where, in Room 13, he began to write *Kidnapped*. This inn has also honourable mention in Scott's *Antiquary*. The modern Café Royal, in West Register Street, incorporates the celebrated Ambrose's Tavern (kept by one Ambrose) the scene of the *Noctes Ambrosianae* in which Christopher North, the Ettrick Shepherd, and other notabilities of the age of Scott, took part.

The Peacock Inn at Newhaven has always been celebrated for its fish teas and suppers. It was here that Charles Reade stayed when collecting material for his novel of fisher-life, *Christie Johnstone*.

Dickens, John Blackwood, Macready, Sheriff Alison, Charles Kean, Thackeray, Douglas Jerrold, the brothers Chambers, Lord Robertson, Russel of *The Scotsman*, Henry Irving, and many other celebrities, 'were wont to delight in a fish dinner at Newhaven', says James Bertram, 'despite the outside dirt and discomfort of the little town and its ancient and fish-like smell.

'The Newhaven fish-wives—who has not been in love with "Christie Johnstone"?—have always excited the admiration of visitors, especially the artists. George IV—who was surely a connoisseur—when taken down incog. to the village by Sir Walter, declared he had never seen a handsomer set of women. The verdict pronounced by Dickens on his first visit was—"This is immense! The service is not so fine as it is at Greenwich, but the fish! and the cooking!" Peter Fraser the bookseller, who was the host of the day, had arranged for the two girls who usually waited at Mrs Clark's table to dress themselves for the occasion in the picturesque costume of the fish-wives, so as the more to gratify the author of *Pickwick*.'

Few counties possess more attractive hostelries than Perthshire, and The Salutation Hotel in Perth claims to be the oldest established hotel in Scotland. It was used in evidence against a suspected Jacobite that, wearing a white cockade in his bonnet, he was seen shaking hands with Prince Charlie in a room which is still pointed out to visitors. Many other inns have history and romance to offer in addition to hospitality.

It must be frankly owned that as regards the position of the public house in the social life of the community today, Scotland has much to learn from England. It is true that London and other English cities have their quota of cheerless public houses and garish gin-palaces, but the old village pubs scattered all over the country have character and charm, and many of the modern

public houses have been imaginatively designed by skilled archi-
tects. In Scotland, on the other hand, the old-time tavern, which,
however small and unpretentious, was a couthie, friendly place
where all classes rubbed shoulders, has been replaced by some of
the most drab and dismal houses of public entertainment that
these islands contain. True, an occasional picturesque little howff
survives, but that is exceptional. However well-managed they
may be, our public houses are still looked on askance by many
worthy citizens, and any respectable woman who is venturous
enough to enter one is liable to set censorious tongues wagging.
The reason for the odium attached to them is, of course, their long
association with the drunkenness and squalor of the old industrial
life. Happily the rising generation is not haunted by such memories, and the beautifying and humanizing of the Scottish public
house may be looked for in the not too distant future. Indeed,
the process has begun.

In a letter to Moray McLaren, James Bridie makes some interesting comments on the ways of the patrons of the public house
north and south of the Tweed.

'The Englishman's drinking habits are different from those of
his neighbours though they approach perhaps most nearly to
those of the Germans in that he likes to stupefy himself with large
quantities of weak beer. He does not appear to use alcohol as an
instrument for the rapid release of his intellectual faculties as do
the Irish and the Scots. He is no doubt wise in this.

' . . . Correct me if I am wrong, but I think rural pub conversation is better in Scotland than in England. The slow rumble of
"'Ar be the missus, Jarge?" and the "'Oo's" and the "'Ar's" of
the English pub are not stimulating but soporific and they are
probably meant to be. In Scotland, the customers try to be funny
and are quite often successful and it is not uncommon to hear
philosophy raising its bulging head. This is in spite of the fact
that the pubs are usually dirty dispensaries and the customers are
by no means the pick of the population. In very many rural
districts in Scotland a social stigma hangs over the pub and really
serious drinking is done at home by respectable people.'[1]

When the stigma disappears, when we learn not to equate
temperance with total abstinence, it will be possible for 'nice'
women to resort to the public house (whether for cocktails or

1. *A Small Stir.*

lemonade) with their husbands and sweethearts, as they so sensibly do in England, and indeed as the witty and well-bred women of Edinburgh resorted to their oyster-taverns in the eighteenth century.

3: *Private Hospitality*

'WHEN dinners are given here,' writes Captain Topham from Edinburgh, 'they are dinners of form. The entertainment of pleasure is their suppers, which resemble the *petits soupers* of France. . . . These little parties generally consist of about seven or eight persons, which prevents the conversation from becoming particular, and which it must be in larger companies. During the supper, which continues for some time, the Scotch ladies drink more wine than an English woman could well bear; but the climate requires it, and probably in some measure it may enliven their natural vivacity. . . . After supper is removed, and they are tired of conversing, they vary the scene by singing, in which many of the Scots excel. There is a plaintive simplicity in the generality of their songs which, from the mouth of a pretty Scotch girl, is inconceivably attractive.'

Again, 'the Scotch gentlemen, in their families, at their tables, or in company . . . always seem pleased with you, and converse on subjects with which you are most acquainted, so that their guest leaves well pleased with himself, and consequently with them. They entertain their visitors with the highest degree of courtesy, without compliment or formality, and rather choose to listen to the sentiments of others, than to give their own opinion in a general company.'

When not at church, where, to quote Mr Michael Joyce, 'they looked as sorrowful as if they were going to bury not only their sins, but themselves,' Mr Topham's hosts overflowed with good humour and gaiety. 'They are extremely fond of jovial company,' he tells us; 'and if they did not too often sacrifice to Bacchus the joys of a vacant hour, they would be the most entertaining people in Europe; but the goodness of their wine and the severity of their climate are indeed some excuse for them.'

Another observer noted that 'people visit each other in Edinburgh with all the appearance of cordial familiarity, who, if they lived in London, would imagine their differences of rank to form an impassable barrier against such intercourse'. As a consequence, 'upon the whole [Edinburgh] society is less elegant than might otherwise have been expected in the capital of such a country as Scotland.'

From the middle of the eighteenth century to the end of the second decade of the nineteenth, Edinburgh possessed a remarkable aristocracy of native talent, which included David Hume, Adam Smith, Raeburn, Dugald Stewart, Walter Scott and other names that achieved international fame. Many pen-pictures of these men are to be found in the various Memorials of the time.

In 1769 David Hume, philosopher and bon-vivant, and the idol of intellectual Paris, returned to Edinburgh, which had already begun to draw the eyes of the civilized world to Scotland. Lord Cockburn describes him as 'a man of great knowledge, of a social and benevolent temper, and truly the best-natured man in the world'.

'I have been settled here for two Months,' Hume wrote to a friend, 'and am here Body and Soul, without casting the least Thought of Regreat to London, or even to Paris. . . . I live still, and must for a twelve-month, in my old House in James's Court, which is very chearful, and even elegant, but too small to display my great talent for Cookery, the Science to which I intend to addict the remaining Years of my Life. I have just now lying on the Table before me a Receipt for making *Soupe à la Reine*, copy'd with my own hand. For Beef and Cabbage (a charming Dish), and old Mutton and old Claret, no body excels me. I also make Sheep Head Broth in a manner that Mr Keith speaks of it for eight days after, and the Duc de Niverois would bind himself Apprentice to my Lass to learn it.'

Hume's elegant dinners and select suppers became a feature of Edinburgh's social life. He provided the best wines, and, better still, 'he furnished the entertainment with the most instructive and pleasing conversation, for he assembled whoever were among the most knowing and agreeable among either the laity or the clergy. . . . For innocent mirth and agreeable raillery I never knew his match,' writes a contemporary.

Hume lived on terms of affectionate intimacy with the leading

Moderates in Edinburgh; indeed his friendship with the younger clergymen is said to have enraged the zealots on the opposite side (the Evangelicals), who failed to realize that he could not if he would, and would not if he could, shake their principles.

Henry Mackenzie (The Man of Feeling) relates a characteristic anecdote of Hume:

'When Provost Stewart, who was a distinguished wine-merchant at that time [1746—the year of Culloden] and Provost of Edinburgh, was called to account for an alleged breach of duty in delivering the City to the rebels, Hume wrote a volunteer pamphlet in his defence showing most convincingly that the City could not have been defended, and that standing a siege would have been attended with the most disastrous consequences; the Provost on finding out his anonymous advocate, made him a present of a batch of uncommonly good Burgundy. "The gift", said David, in his good-humoured way, "ruined me. I was obliged to give so many dinners in honour of the wine." '

Henry Mackenzie, a shrewd and able lawyer who enchanted his own generation with the most lachrymose of novels, is one of those men whose talents are greatly overrated by their contemporaries; but his many real gifts and qualities, and above all his generous spirit, deservedly won him a high place in the intellectual society of Edinburgh. Another much overrated writer was Dr Blair, Professor of Rhetoric and Belles Lettres, whose sermons are, in fact, the worst sort of eighteenth-century prose; yet he enjoyed the close friendship of Hume.

Lord Elibank, the most cultivated and literary of peers, resembled Hume in his talent for collecting agreeable companions about him, and had a house in town for several winters chiefly to enjoy their society. Another notable host was Lord Monboddo, an able judge but an intellectual eccentric, who aroused Dr Johnson's derision by maintaining that men were born with tails, and that a savage state of life was preferable to a civilized one. 'Classical learning, good conversation, excellent suppers, and ingenious though unsound metaphysics were', we are told, 'the peculiarities of Monboddo.' His suppers were, indeed, reputed 'the most Attic of their day'. This 'shrivelled, learned oddity' was, surprisingly, the father of Burns's 'heavenly Miss Burnett', for whom, on her early death, he wrote an elegy.

Lord Monboddo entertained Dr Johnson and Boswell at his

country house on their way to Aberdeen. 'I knew Lord Monboddo and Dr Johnson did not love each other,' wrote Boswell before their visit, 'yet I was unwilling not to visit his lordship; and was also curious to see them together.' After the visit, he wrote: 'My lord was extremely hospitable, and I saw both Dr Johnson and him liking each other better every hour.'[1]

When Adam Smith, forsaking his Glasgow chair, settled in Edinburgh in 1778, 'his unpretentious Sunday suppers soon became famous as the resort of intellect and talent.... He had none of Hume's almost childlike gaiety of conversation, but, when perfectly at ease in the society of those he loved, his features were sometimes brightened by a smile of inexpressible benignity.'

The clergy had an assured place in Edinburgh society.

'In my younger days', writes Henry Mackenzie, 'there were very eminent men among them. One met [them] at dinners among literary men, and indeed in all good companies.' They included, besides William Robertson, John Home, Dr Hugh Blair, Adam Fergusson, Dr Henry, Dr Erskine, Sir Harry Moncrieff and Dr Alexander ('Jupiter') Carlyle.

One of the most outstanding personalities of this period was William Robertson, Principal of the University, who was equally distinguished as churchman and historian. He achieved European fame, his historical works being acclaimed by Voltaire and Catherine II of Russia as well as by Burke, Gibbon and Chesterfield in England.

'High as was the character of the eminent men of letters who were then the glory of Edinburgh, there was not one of them who surpassed Robertson in amiability of temper and sweetness of disposition. All who knew him testify to his integrity and uprightness, his temperance and discretion, his possession, in short, of all the "virtues".'[2]

1. 'Sir Adolphus Oughton, then our Deputy Commander in Chief (at Edinburgh), who was not only an excellent officer, but one of the most universal scholars I ever knew, had learned the Erse (Gaelic) language, and expressed his belief in the authenticity of Ossian's poetry. Dr Johnson took the opposite side of that perplexed question; and I was afraid the dispute would have run high between them. But Sir Adolphus, who had a very sweet temper, changed the discourse, grew playful, laughed at Lord Monboddo's notion of men having tails, and called him a Judge *a posteriori*, which amused Dr Johnson; and hostilities were prevented.'—James Boswell: *Journal of a Tour to the Hebrides*.
2. J. H. Millar: *A Literary History of Scotland*.

It was Robertson who, with Robert Adam as designer, raised funds and started work on the present University buildings, which remain his monument.

The only fault his friends had to find with him were his love of dissertation and consequent propensity to lead the talk—a habit which, as such habits do, increased with the years.

In his *Autobiography*, Dr Alexander ('Jupiter') Carlyle tells us that 'there were two men whose coming into a convivial company pleased more than anybody I knew. The one was Dr George Kay, a minister of Edinburgh, who, to a charming vivacity when he was in good spirits, added the talent of ballad-singing better than anybody I ever knew; the other was John Home.'

John Home, who scandalized the less tolerant clergy of his day by the production of his tragedy, *Douglas*, was one of David Hume's closest friends. Though far from being a great dramatist, he had many gifts, and was spoken of as one of the most lovable men of his century.

When Home visited his friend, he always enjoyed Hume's excellent claret, but could not be induced to share his host's taste for port. In revenge, David inserted this clause in a codicil to his will:

'I leave to my friend, Mr John Home of Kilduff, ten dozen of my old claret at his choice; and one single bottle of that other liquor called port. I also leave to him six dozen of port, provided that he attests under his hand signed John Hume, that he has himself alone finished that bottle at two sittings. By this concession he will terminate the only two differences that ever rose between us concerning temporal matters.'[1]

Another example of David Hume's humour—though it has nothing to do with wine:

'He wanted a book out of the Advocates' Library, of which the learned antiquarian Goodall, author of the first Vindication of Queen Mary, was then acting Librarian. He was sitting in his elbow-chair so fast asleep that neither David nor a friend who accompanied him could wake Goodall by any of the usual means. At last David said, "I think I have a method of waking him" and bawled into his ear, "Queen Mary was a strumpet and a murtherer" —"It's a damn lie," said Goodall, starting out of his sleep, and David obtained the book he sought.'[2]

1. J. T. Y. Greig: *David Hume*.   2. Henry Mackenzie.

All the clergy of that fine old crusted school were, we are told, bon-vivants according to their lights and means. Among them was Dr Alexander Carlyle, who, though the associate of all the eminent men of his time, appears never to have achieved any special distinction of his own. 'His hold over his comrades was derived from the charm of his private manners, which were graceful and kind. And he was one of the noblest looking old gentlemen I have ever beheld. . . . That he could carry his liquor with gentlemanly aplomb is proved by a servant lassie's remark, "there he ga'ed, dacent man, as steady as a wall after his ain share o five bottles o port".'

Another popular minister was Sir Harry Moncrieff. This 'most admirable and somewhat old-fashioned gentleman' used to walk from his house in the east end of Queen Street to his church, with his bands, his little cocked hat, his tall cane and his cardinal air, and home in the same style. On Sunday evenings, after family worship, to which he welcomed the friends of any of his sons; 'the whole party sat down to the roasted hens, the goblets of wine and the powerful talk. Here was a mode of alluring young men into the paths of pious pleasantness. Those days are now past, but the figure, and the voice, the thoughts, and the kind and cheerful manliness of Sir Harry, as disclosed at those Sunday evenings, will be remembered with gratitude by some of the best intellects in Scotland.'[1]

But the most outstanding figure of them all was Dr Alexander Webster, popularly known as Dr Magnum Bonum—a nickname earned by his capacity to put away liquor, which, however, he always carried discreetly. Although he belonged to the rigid Calvinistic party of the Church, 'he shone', we are told, 'in social life; and the pleasantry and gaiety of his conversation, his command of amusing anecdotes, and the sprightliness of his wit, always good-natured and inoffensive, rendered him the most delightful companion to persons of every age and rank.[2] In the choice of his company, he always showed a preference for those who notoriously differed from him in theological matters or

1. Lord Cockburn: *Memorials.*
2. 'At supper we had Dr Alexander Webster, who, though not learned, had such a knowledge of mankind, such a fund of information and entertainment, so clear a head and such accommodating manners, that Dr Johnson found him a very agreeable companion.'—James Boswell.

party attachments. At the same time he was extremely popular with his congregation, at all times a friend of the poor, and constantly accessible. He was reputed to be the most beloved and popular preacher of his time, one admirer declaring that "it was easier to get a seat in the Kingdom of Heaven than in the Tolbooth Kirk".'

It is related that on his way home one night from a long supper at a tavern, somewhat elated by the good claret and the merriness of the company, he was chaffed by one of his companions:

'Dr Webster, what would your kirk session say if they saw you now?'

'Tut, man,' he replied with a chuckle, 'they wadna believe their een!'

On another occasion, a friend promised to regale him with a forty-year-old claret which, when produced, proved to be only a pint bottle.

'Dear me,' said the disappointed guest, 'it's unco wee for its age.'

Although his indulgences were frequent, 'he lived and died respected and almost venerated'.[1]

It was into this society that Robert Burns was introduced when, at the age of twenty-eight, his new-found fame brought him to Edinburgh. He spent his evenings with his brother Masons, with the Crochallan Fencibles, and with the Knights of the Cape. 'In circles such as these,' we are told, 'his gaiety, his wit, and what he himself called his violent propensity to bawdry, had soon become a legend.' His 'rollicking zest for life' affected all listeners. In more serious vein, 'the grasp and range of his conversation', writes Principal Robertson, 'were such that his hearers could almost forget that he had been bred to the soil. His manner, countrified but never clownish, had a firmness and simplicity that carried him triumphantly thro' the most novel and flattering situations. Above all, there was a compelling vitality—the stamp of genius—in all he said and did, which charmed both men and women, frivolous and learned.'

1. A man of many parts and interests, Dr Webster was the founder of the Widows' Fund of the Church of Scotland, and his mathematical knowledge is said to have been utilized in planning the New Town of Edinburgh. His tolerance, however, did not extend to the theatre and it was he who led the opposition to Home's *Douglas*.

Among the frivolous, or at least unlearned, were the waitresses and hostlers at country inns who, on hearing of his arrival, would get out of bed and come crowding to hear him talk. Also that Burns had no Boswell!

The Scotswoman

Writing of Scotland in 1498, Pedro de Ayala says, 'The women are courteous in the extreme. I mention this because they are really honest, though very bold. They are absolutely mistress of their houses and even of their husbands in all things concerning the administration of their property, income as well as expenditure. They are very graceful and handsome women. They dress much better than here [England] and especially as regards the head-dress, which is, I think, the handsomest in the world.'

The women of eighteenth-century Scotland appear to have been true to type. They are described as of independent mind, with free and affable manners.

'There was a singular race of old Scots ladies,' writes Lord Cockburn, 'a delightful set—strong-headed, warm-hearted and high-spirited,' and he proceeds to give us several lively sketches.

Captain Topham found his Edinburgh hostesses 'peculiarly attentive in their own houses', and adds, 'they discharge the duties of their families with much ease, economy and politeness. At their tables they share with their husbands the greatest assiduity to entertain, and show more desire to make everything free from ceremony than in any nation with which I have yet been conversant.'

The younger women receive many bouquets from southern visitors, even from those who are supercilious about many aspects of Scottish life. They are described as pleasing in face and figure, and their fresh complexions, free from artifice, their carriage, and their firm tread were all admired. In addition, they are credited with a 'winning frankness, a charming simplicity of manners, and sprightly talk'.

One of the 'Flowers of Edinburgh' of this period was immortalized by an anonymous admirer. Though known to posterity as Bonnie Mallie Lee, she was in fact Mallie or Mary Sleigh, the S having been dropped in the passage of time, probably through an unconscious desire for euphony.

As Mallie Lee cam doun the street her capuchin did flee;
She cast a look ahint her back to see her negligee;
She had twa lappets at her heid, that flauntit gallantlie,
And ribbon knots at back and briest o bonnie Mallie Lee.
    And we're a' gane east and west, we're a' gane agee,
    We're a' gane east and west, a-courtin' Mallie Lee.

A' doun alang the Canongate were beaux o ilk degree,
And mony a ane turned round about the comely sicht to see;
At ilka bab her ping-pong gi'ed, ilk lad thocht, 'That's to me,'
But feint a ane was in the thocht o bonnie Mallie Lee.
    And we're a' gane east and west, we're a' gane agee,
    We're a' gane east and west, a-courtin' Mallie Lee.

The dame gae'd through the Palace ha', and wha sae braw as she?
A Prince spiered leave to dance wi' her, and Earlies twa or three;
But Hielan' Brodie fleered them a' wi' proud and glancin' e'e:
He's won for aye the heart and hand o bonnie Mallie Lee.[1]
    And we're a' gane east and west, we're a' gane agee,
    We're a' gane east and west, a-courtin' Mallie Lee.

Character in the middle and higher ranks of society is described as singularly honourable. It is true that strangers were often disconcerted by a lack of delicacy in the speech of well-born women; but they soon learned that though the tongue was free, conduct was strict. Intrigue was virtually unknown—'the men have no talent for it', says Topham—and there were few scandals of married life. (This does not mean that the city lacked its low life.)

In the eighteenth century, while Englishwomen were writing pamphlets, Scotswomen were writing songs, and at many of the reunions or at card-parties of quality were women who had written songs all society was singing. Among them were Lady Anne Lindsay, 'a bright, blushing girl' who frequently heard her own song, 'Auld Robin Gray', sung to the harp; Miss Jean Elliot, author of the exquisite 'Flo'ers o the Forest'; and Miss Oliphant of Gask (later Baroness Nairne), author of 'Caller Herrin' ', 'The Laird o Cockpen', 'The Rowan Tree', 'The Land o the Leal', and many well-loved Jacobite songs, including one still universally sung to speed the parting guest, 'Will Ye No Come Back Again?' All these ladies strove to maintain anonymity.

Of our early women writers, two, Mrs Elizabeth Hamilton,

1. 'Alexander Brodie of Brodie, Lord Lyon King of Arms 1725-54. b. 17 March 1697, m. 3 Sept. 1724 Mary Sleigh (b. 3 Oct. 1704).'—Burke's *Landed Gentry*.

author of *The Cottagers of Kilburnie*, and Mrs Grant of Laggan, widow of a Highland minister, who wrote *Letters from the Mountains*, were 'remarkable', says Lord Cockburn, 'for their literary conversational gatherings;' and he adds, 'their evening parties had the greater merit from the smallness of their houses and their means.' Good company and good talk could be had, too, in the rooms of dowager ladies such as Lady Balcarres, who with 'small genteel incomes' and one maid-servant gave 'slender entertainments' in a fourth flat.

Balls were held under the patronage of ladies of high degree, such as my Lady Panmure and the beautiful Susanna, Countess of Eglintoune, who with her seven lovely daughters were borne off in their sedan chairs after the ball to their lodging in Jack's Land, escorted by gentlemen with drawn swords. Another notable hostess was Lady Colville, 'to whom', writes Boswell, 'I am proud to introduce any stranger of eminence, that he may see what dignity and grace is to be found in Scotland'. But the most outstanding hostess of them all was Jean, Duchess of Gordon, a leader of fashion in London as well as in Edinburgh. As a high-spirited lassie she had ridden a pig down the High Street. Her reckless wit and her genius for mimicry would, it is said, have made her a host of enemies but for the charm of her broad, warm-hearted gaiety. She was the friend of Pitt and Dundas, 'the uncrowned King of Scotland', but when she met Burns—and it was chiefly through her support that he became the lion of the season —she declared that his conversation carried her off her feet as no other man's had ever done.

When Dr Johnson was staying at Auchinleck, Sir Alexander Boswell's Ayrshire home, James Boswell insisted on taking him to see Lady Eglintoune, then advanced in years.

'In the course of our conversation', he writes, 'it came out that Lady Eglintoune was married the year before Dr Johnson was born; upon which she graciously said to him that she might have been his mother; and that she now adopted him. . . . My friend was much pleased with this day's entertainment.'

He was no less pleased with the sequel. When they returned to Edinburgh, at a party at Sir Alexander Dick's, 'from that absence of mind to which every man is at times subject', continues Boswell, 'I told, in a blundering manner, Lady Eglintoune's complimentary adoption of Dr Johnson as her son, for I unfortunately stated that her ladyship had adopted him as her son in consequence of her having been married the year *after* he was born. Dr Johnson instantly corrected me. "Sir, don't you perceive that you are defaming the countess? For supposing me to be her son, and that she was not married till the year after my birth, I must have been her *natural* son." A young lady of quality who was present very handsomely said, "Might not the son have justified the fault?" My friend was much flattered by this compliment, which he never forgot. When in more than ordinary spirits, and talking of his journey in Scotland, he has called to me, "Boswell, what was it that the young lady of quality said to me at Sir Alexander Dick's?" Nobody will doubt that I was happy in repeating it.'

Dr Johnson had, in fact, a conspicuous success with the women of Scotland, from Boswell's infant daughter, who looked up at the heavy pock-marked, twitching face and made happy, cooing noises, to her father's great delight—'I'll give her five hundred additional pounds for this when she marries', he swore—to the octogenarian Lady Eglintoune. There was the maid of the inn at Inverness; there was Flora Macdonald, now Mrs Macdonald of Kingsburgh, in Skye, who told him the story of her adventures with Prince Charlie and insisted on his sleeping on the same bed that the fugitive prince had occupied; and there was the Duke of Argyll's stepdaughter at Inverary, where, Boswell tells us, 'Dr Johnson talked a great deal, and was so entertaining that Lady Betty Hamilton, after dinner, went and placed her chair close to his, leaned upon the back of it, and listened eagerly. It would have made a fine picture to have drawn the Sage and her at this time in their several attitudes. He did not know, all the while, how much he was honoured.'

All through his tour of the west, Dr Johnson was struck by the natural good manners in all classes, if classes be the word. At Corriechatachin, in Skye, 'we were treated with very liberal hospitality', he writes, 'among a more numerous and elegant company than it could have been supposed easy to collect.' Miss MacLeod of Ullinish, daughter of the Sheriff-Substitute of the island, 'though she was never out of Skye, was a very well-bred woman', and it is probably true of others there that they had never seen the mainland; for Skye is a little world in itself. Raasay, too, delighted him. 'Such a seat of hospitality, amidst the winds and waters, fills the imagination with a delightful contrariety of images. Without is the rough ocean and the rocky land, the beating billows and the howling storm; within is plenty and elegance, beauty and gaiety, the song and the dance.' And at the Castle of Dunvegan, the seat of MacLeod of MacLeod, 'I had tasted lotus, and was in danger of forgetting that I was ever to depart, till Mr Boswell sagely reproached me with my sluggishness and softness.'

As for the food: 'A dinner in the Western Isles,' says Dr Johnson, 'differs little from a dinner in England, except that in place of tarts there are always different preparations of milk.' (These include curds and cream, hattit kit, o'on [Gaelic *omhan*] or frothed whey, and crowdie.) The wine was excellent. There was also plenty of good talk, especially among the ministers, of whom 'I saw not one', he writes, 'whom I had reason to think either deficient in learning or irregular in life: but found several with whom I could not converse without wishing, as my respect increased, that they had not been Presbyterians.' Nor was music lacking. At the Manse of Sleat, 'Miss McPherson', says Boswell, 'pleased Dr Johnson much by singing Erse (Gaelic) songs and playing on the guitar. He afterwards sent her a present of his *Rasselas*. In his bedchamber was a press stored with books, Greek, Latin, French and English, most of which had belonged to the father of our host, the learned Dr McPherson.' Indeed, 'I was never in any house of the islands,' says Dr Johnson, 'where I did not find books in more languages than one.' This is explained by the fact that it was long customary for the sons of Highland chieftains and the more promising youth of the clans to finish their education on the Continent and spend a year or two in the French or Spanish service, thus acquiring an urbanity and a knowledge of languages and life which, on their return, enriched their native inheritance.

Another young lady who charmed the travellers with her music was Miss Maclean of Torloisk in Mull, who played Italian music on the harpsichord and sang Gaelic songs. Faujas de Saint-Fond, who visited Torloisk a little later, was equally impressed.

'Miss Maclean,' he writes, 'an only daughter, pretty, with a graceful figure, interesting from her talents, her acquirements, and her modesty, played extremely well upon the harpsichord, and was in every respect the charm of that society. She had attentively studied the language, poetry and music of the Hebrideans.'

Sir Walter's Edinburgh

In due course Sir Walter Scott succeeded to the eminence that had formerly belonged to David Hume, Adam Smith and Henry Mackenzie; and he, in turn, gave way to his son-in-law, John Gibson Lockhart, Christopher North and the Edinburgh Reviewers. Scott was himself a prince of hosts, and the lavish hospitality he dispensed at Abbotsford is known to all the world. Peer, poet, peasant, all were made welcome, for personality was valued above birth, wealth or high office.

In 1815 Jeffrey set up house at Craigcrook, on the side of Corstorphine Hill, and here all his subsequent summers were passed. Of the tart, sarcastic manner which had hindered his progress at the Bar there was no vestige when he sat at the head of his own table, and the Craigcrook Saturdays during the summer session became an extremely popular feature of the social and intellectual life of the city. 'Nothing can efface the days they have passed there from the memory of his friends,' wrote one of them; 'No unofficial house in Scotland has had a greater influence on literary or political opinion.'

A frequent visitor to Craigcrook was Elizabeth Grant of Rothiemurchus. 'It was not a big-wig set at all', she writes. 'My father, Lord Gillies, and such-like dignatories would have been quite out of place in this rather riotous crew. . . . Individually, almost all of our party were agreeable, cleverly amusing. Collectively, there was far too much boisterous fun for my taste. I preferred being with Mrs Jeffrey, that naturally charming woman, not then by any means sufficiently appreciated by those so much her inferiors. She and I spent our time gardening—she was a perfect florist—playing with little Charlotte, to whom all my old nursery tales and songs were new, preparing for the company, and chattering to each other.

' . . . The dinners were delightful, so little form, so much fun, real wit sometimes, and always cheerfulness; the windows open to the garden, the sight and the scent of the flowers heightening the flavour of the repasts unequalled for excellence; wines, all our set were famous for having of the best and in startling variety —it was a mania . . . Mrs Jeffrey's home-fed fowl and home-made bread, and fine cream and sweet butter, and juicy vegetables, all so good, served so well, the hot things *hot*, the fruits, cream and butter so cold, gave such a feeling of comfort everyone got good-humoured, even cranky William Clerk. They were bright days, those happy summer days at Craigcrook.'

Many men were attracted to Edinburgh by the fame of Dugald Stewart, who occupied the Chair of Moral Philosophy. His lectures were attended by Sydney Smith, Francis Horner, Henry Erskine, Lord Webb, Lord Jeffrey, Lord Brougham, Sir Archibald Alison, Lord Palmerston, Lord John Russell, and many others who achieved distinction in various spheres. Stewart was not an original thinker, but rather an exponent of his own teacher Thomas Reid's philosophy; and what he attempted to impart was not so much a profound knowledge of his professed subject, as moral sensibility and a discriminating taste—in short, a liberal, well-balanced outlook on life. This he achieved through his remarkable gift of didactic oratory, his personal attractions and grace of manner, and, not least, his high personal character.

'No intelligent pupil of his ceased to respect philosophy,' writes Lord Cockburn. 'To me, his lectures were like the opening of the heavens. I felt that I had a soul. His noble views, unfolded in glorious sentences, elevated me into a higher world. . . . They changed my whole nature.'

Stewart's gifted and aristocratic wife added to the pleasure of hospitality in his home.

One of the most popular guests during his five years' stay in Edinburgh (1798-1803) was Sydney Smith, who combined extravagant wit and shrewd commonsense. It has been said that Anglo-Scottish friendship thrives on banter, and Smith was always ready to raise a laugh at our expense. 'It requires a surgical operation', he averred, 'to get a joke well into a Scotch understanding.' That is certainly true of some kinds of English joke, but it might be retorted that the Scot sometimes finds it equally difficult to get what *he* considers a good joke into an English understanding. What appeals most to him is terseness and pithiness. Here is a characteristic Scottish joke. Illustrated, it is told in four words, and by omitting the name of the man addressed can be reduced to three. The scene is a village street. A sober villager meets a toper of his acquaintance who is zigzagging down 'the croun o the causey' (the middle of the highway). The following dialogue ensues:

The sober one: 'Gaun hame, Sandy?'
The unsteady one: 'Whiles.'

Of course it loses in English, as jokes are apt to do in translation. 'Going home, Sandy?'—'Occasionally.'

The truth is that humour is just about the most distinctively national thing in the world, and the humour of one nation is the last thing to be understood by members of another.

Still, for all his chaff Smith had as warm a regard for his hosts as they for him. In serious mood, he asserts, for example, that 'they [the Scots] are perhaps in some points of view the most remarkable nation in the world; and no country can afford an example of so much order, morality, economy and knowledge among the lower classes of society.' After that, we can forgive him a lot!

Besides Francis Jeffrey and Francis Horner, a notable member of Sydney Smith's circle was James Gregory, Professor of the Practice of Medicine, who is described as 'a man of great stature and commanding presence, an accomplished scholar, a notable talker, and a lecturer of the highest ability'. Gregory had two special claims to fame: he was a cousin of Rob Roy,[1] and he invented or perpetrated that compound known to generations of children—and, incidentally, still going strong—Gregory's Mixture.

In spite of the fact that he was the fifth of his family to hold a University Chair, his Macgregor blood remained untamed.

'The Professor was immensely popular with his students, to whom he always lectured in a cocked hat. When walking down the streets of Edinburgh it was his habit to carry a stout cane at the trail or over his shoulder, as if prepared for action, and in one of his too frequent professional controversies he actually applied it to the shoulders of an eminent obstetrician. For this piece of self-indulgence he was fined a hundred pounds, a sum he could well afford since he had built up the most lucrative consulting practice in Scotland; indeed he was heard to say when judgment was delivered that he would be glad to pay the fine twice over for the chance of repeating the assault.'[2]

These were some of the men who sat round the table at the

1. After the clan was proscribed in 1603, several Macgregors changed their names to Gregory, Grigor, Grieg and other forms. The Norwegian composer, Grieg, belongs by descent to Clan Gregor. In the Introduction to *Rob Roy*, Scott relates how the outlaw offered to take his young cousin to the Highlands and make a man of him.   2. Michael Joyce: *Edinburgh: The Golden Age*.

celebrated Saturday-night suppers given by Jeffrey and his brethren of the Bench, when a party of a dozen or fifteen—these were 'gentlemen only' occasions—would spend the evening in 'more or less refined revelry'. 'Foremost in all topics—wit, merriment, literature, politics', we are told, 'was the voice of Henry Cockburn.'

Lord Cockburn, an able though perhaps a less distinguished lawyer than some of his contemporaries, is gratefully remembered for his delightful books, *Memorials of Our Own Times* and *Circuit Journeys*. He is described as 'the model of a high-bred Scottish Gentleman of the last distinctive school which his country possessed.... His face was handsome and intellectual. His manner and address was, among his friends and intimates, singularly winning and attractive.' To see Cockburn as he really was he should have been encountered among that congenial circle of whom Sydney Smith says: 'Never shall I forget the happy days spent there, amidst odious smells, barbarous sounds, bad suppers, excellent hearts and the most enlightened and cultivated understandings.'

Smith, who, incidentally, had a French mother, turned up his nose at our plain, wholesome Scottish fare; but then he had never been subjected to a prolonged diet of frozen ewe mutton and unpalatable synthetic foods.

'Any writer of 1950,' writes Mr Moray McLaren, 'looking back upon the Edinburgh of two hundred years earlier, feels more envious than squeamish when he reads of the collations of fresh fowls, game from the moors, eggs and cheese from the farm, and, above all else, a large variety of white and shell fish from the Firth of Forth. This abundance of food, especially the fish, was put upon the table very simply, and without those spices and sauces which may please the palate, but which may also conceal a lack of freshness as well as irritating the digestion if taken in large quantities.... All this for the most part was preceded by, washed down with, and followed by good cheap claret and ale or sherry.'[1]

The 'savoury and inexpensive' supper dishes popular in Edinburgh in the early nineteenth century include, according to James Bertram (who, as 'Jenny Wren', wrote a cookery book commended by George Saintsbury), 'broiled "finnans", eggs and bacon, devilled kidneys, curried rabbits, oysters in a hundred

1. *The Capital of Scotland.*

"ways", partan pies, baked crabs, minced collops, lobsters, an-
chovy toasts, and Welsh rabbits'. Bottled ale, Prestonpans table-
beer, followed by whisky-toddy, he adds, were the usual accom-
paniments, and richer people provided wines.

What characterizes the men of the Golden Age is their *mens
sana in corpore sano*. We may attribute their *mens sana* at least in
part to the philosophers and divines they 'sat under'. As regards
their physical well-being, can it be questioned that it owes much
to the simple, wholesome fare of the period? And what part does
claret play? Possibly the revival of our derelict oyster beds and of
claret drinking would help to revive the *perfervidum ingenium
Scotorum* of which we stand in such need today.

Christopher North of the *Noctes Ambrosianae* was the alter ego
of John Wilson, the unerudite but eloquent and immensely popular Professor of Moral Philosophy at the University of Edinburgh.

'It is in the *Noctes Ambrosianae* that Wilson lives,' writes Dr
John Oliver. 'In them, as Christopher North, he presides over a
group of lively characters who eat and drink and talk and disport
themselves in the most riotous and extravagant way. Tickler,
O'Doherty, the Ettrick Shepherd and the rest: they must have
been as familiar and as engaging to the readers of *Blackwood's* as
the characters of ITMA recently were to their much wider
public.'[1]

Wilson sowed his literary wild oats in *Blackwood's Magazine*,
where he attracted the scandalized attention of the public, but
lived to earn the affection and admiration of that same public.
His magnificent figure and leonine appearance earned him the
name, 'The Lion of the North'. North's splendour has long since
faded, but his memory retains the faint perfume of Edinburgh's
great age, of which he was the last survivor.

A feature of social life in Edinburgh in the second quarter of
the century was Mr C. B. Tait's auction-room dinners. These
were often got up at an hour or two's notice in honour of some
passing celebrity.

'Many desired to be present on such occasions,' writes James
Bertram; 'but the company was usually restricted to "interesting
people"—painters, preachers, professors, poets, lawyers, literary
men, comedians, and a sprinkling of epicures.'

1. Centenary article in *The Scotsman*, April 3, 1954.

Mr Bertram's services were frequently called upon by Mr Tait's factotum, who acted as butler on such occasions.

'My first duty was to run through the city in a hackney-coach and collect the guests. . . . Then I would hasten over to Hewart's perhaps to expedite them with the oyster-soup or the mulligatawny. A man who kept a cook-shop near the auction-room always supplied the fowls and ham—the latter usually baked in paste. Other portions of the dinner required to be collected from various places. A special feature of these impromptu dinners was the curry, of which there were usually two or three kinds, prepared by an unattached East Indian expert. . . . He was called "the Baboo", and was a protégé of Mr Falconer, of Falcon Hall, a retired East Indian Civil Servant. His curried oysters, crab-claws, and ox-cheek, were famous in those days.

'At these dinners the wines and liquors formed a chief attraction —whatever was accounted rich or rare, from "Imperial Tokay" to humble Edinburgh ale, was placed at the service of the guests. One invariable feature of the feast was cheese in great variety; some native, some foreign—never less, I think, than half a dozen kinds.'[1]

James Bertram also alludes to Mr James Ballantyne's 'Waverley-Novel banquets' and the 'Candlemaker-Row festivals' held in honour of the Ettrick Shepherd. The Royal Company of Archers, the Honourable Company of Golfers, the Yeomanry Mess, the Merchant Company and other corporations all entertained liberally; and 'what perhaps is peculiar to Edinburgh is that Banks and Insurance Offices feasted their friends, some of the Banks supplying their table on such occasions from their own great cellars of fine old wines'.

Tea

The convivial life of the women of Scotland may be spelt in one word—tea. Throughout the eighteenth and nineteenth centuries there has been a continuous flow of tea-table hospitality, and it still goes cheerfully on.

It was Mary of Modena, the lovely and gracious wife of James VII and II, who formally introduced tea to Scotland—though

1. *Some Memories of Books, Authors and Events.*

doubtless she had unknown forerunners. That was in 1681, when her husband, then Duke of York, was holding court at Holyrood as Lord High Commissioner to the General Assembly of the Church of Scotland. In 1705, green tea at 16s. a pound and Bohea at 30s. were advertised and sold by one George Scott, a goldsmith in the Luckenbooths. The denunciations of both doctors and clergy only gave a fillip to the sales, and by 1750 the conquest of the women of Scotland was complete. The ale and claret that were formerly the sole drinks served at the 'four-hours' were now reserved for gentlemen, until, in the process of time, they, too, capitulated.

There may be two opinions as to whether Scotswomen can cook, but there can be no two opinions as to whether they can bake, and the cult of afternoon tea gave them unlimited scope. The ideal setting is a cosy interior on a grey winter day. The tea equipage on a low table beside a glowing fire—the delicate china on the finely embroidered tea-cloth, the polished silver reflecting the dancing flames, the hot buttered toast, freshly baked scones, and tempting home-made cakes—for many of us these have made the tea hour the pleasantest hour of the day.

And the farm-house tea! How one used to tuck in after a long tramp over the hill! There is no tea like it, plain or high, with its variety of scones and light teabread, its velvet-textured sponge sandwiches, spread with strawberries (or other berries) and cream or fresh lemon curd; its thick crisp shortbread, rich almond-covered Dundee cake and what not besides; its pyramids of yellow butter-balls, its crystal dishes of jams and jellies, red, green and yellow; and the big brown teapot, as couthie and comforting as any tappit-hen—the very symbol of feminine conviviality!

It is surprising to think that, unlike the coffee-house, the tea-room dates only from the close of the nineteenth century. Its birthplace was Glasgow. The original tearoom, according to well-established tradition, was the back parlour of an unpretentious shop near the corner of Argyll Street and the Broomielaw. Here the shopkeeper's wife, a kindly body, used to refresh her husband's country customers with a cup of tea—at first, for love, but eventually, on their insistence, and as the numbers who desired tea increased, at a penny a cup. But it was the Cranstons—Stuart Cranston, and his gifted sister Catherine who established in Glasgow the modern tearoom. Catherine had the imagination to employ that brilliant, though as yet hardly recognized architect, Charles Rennie Macintosh, and his wife, Margaret Macdonald, a decorator of great originality; and the beauty of her tearooms, the dainty fare, and the modest charges gave a tremendous incentive to tea-table conviviality in the city. The idea caught on, and in a few years the tearoom, like our national game, golf, our national drink, whisky, and our national song, 'Auld Lang Syne', swept the world.

Later Times

About the end of the eighteenth century, the exuberant life of the crowded 'lands' of the Old Town burst its bounds and overflowed into the spacious elegant squares and circuses of the New. It was a complete civic revolution. No longer did all ranks of society jostle good-naturedly together in the wynds and closes. Broadly speaking, the Nor' Loch now separated the upper classes from the commonality, and a class consciousness alien to the old life, at least in kind, began to show itself. The snug little suppers of an earlier age gave place to formal dinners; the assemblies were more imposing but less lively; and in spite of its superficial impressiveness, the new Edinburgh refinement had a deadening influence on creative activities.

'The society of Edinburgh', writes Lord Cockburn, 'continued in a state of high animation till 1815, or perhaps till 1820. Its brilliancy was owing to a variety of peculiar circumstances which only operated during this period. The principal of these were— the survivance of several of the eminent men of the preceding age, and of the curious old habits which the modern flood had not yet obliterated; the rise of a powerful community of young men of ability; the exclusion of the British from the Continent, which made this place, both for education and for residence, a favourite resort of strangers; the war, which maintained a constant excitement of military preparation, and of military idleness; the blaze of that popular literature which made this the second city in the empire for learning and science; and the extent and the ease with which literature and society embellished each other, without rivalry, and without pedantry. The first abstraction from this

composition was by the deaths of our interesting old. Then
London drew away several of our best young. There was a gap
in the production of fresh excellence. Peace in 1815 opened the
long-closed floodgates, and gave to the Continent most of the
strangers we used to get. A new race of peace-formed native
youths came on the stage, with but little literature, and a comfort-
less intensity of political zeal, so that by about the year 1820 the
old thing was much worn out, and there was no new thing of the
same piece, to continue or replace it. Much undoubtedly remained to make Edinburgh still, to those who knew how to use
it, a city of Goshen, and to set us above all other British cities
except one, and in some things even above that one. But the
exact old thing was not.'

For all its splendour, the Golden Age does not lack its critics,
particularly in the renascent Scotland of our own time.

'It is the age,' writes Mr Ian Finlay, 'in which Scotland has been
least conscious of her nationhood, most abject in her relations with
England, least subject to her emotions, most oblivious of the
sterner issues. It was in fact an age of rarified intellectual life upon
which no Scot can look back with unmixed pride.

'A vital fervour had gone out of Scottish thought, leaving it a
prey to that tendency to speculation for its own sake which has
dogged it since the days of John Major—a tendency which dogs
it still. . . . It was nearly the end of the century before she [Scot-
land] found another champion of her independence—Robert
Burns. Burns led no movement. His was the voice of the labori-
ously enriched earth asserting again the liberty of which it had so
long been impoverished. By his eloquence he re-established
consciousness of the ancient Border of Tweed and Cheviot. In
no sense is his achievement a revival of the old enmity against
England: it is a challenge to his own people to retain their
identity and character and to assert themselves before their qualities become merged and lost. His patriotism is the reverse of
jingoism. He preaches the brotherhood of man; but has the
wisdom to recognize that such brotherhood can best be attained
by men whose roots are deep in the earth they have sprung
from. That is why his appeal is so universal today, even in Russia
and China and other countries outside the stream of Western
European thought, and why his importance to Scotland is so

much greater than the importance of all the intellectuals of the Golden Age put together.'[1]

As the nineteenth century advanced, the character of the city gradually changed; the tempo slowed down; the colours faded. Apart from Robert Louis Stevenson, Edinburgh produced a certain amount of critical writing and of medical and scientific research; but its glory declined into what Moray McLaren calls 'a pompous and torpid conservatism'. True, the city remained the centre of those indigenous institutions which the Treaty of Union had permitted Scotland to retain—her law-courts, her unique system of education, and her Kirk. True, there continued to be men of distinction in the University, in the Pulpit, and at the Bar. But lively young minds gravitate naturally to the Capital. where 'life' is, where history is being made. To London Scotland had lost first her Court, then her Parliament, and now, in increasing numbers, she was losing her aristocracy and her intelligentzia. An English education was the correct thing. As a corollary, confirmation in the Church of England was the correct thing, and more and more the landed families abandoned the 'laird's pew' in the parish kirk for a seat in the episcopal chapel. Nothing wrong with that, except that it fostered the growing cleavage between the laird and his folk. An educated English accent became a social asset. Nothing wrong with that—indeed, an educated English accent is something all, or nearly all Scots admire—but unfortunately the majority of those who acquire it acquire at the same time an English accent of the mind, which, though becoming in an Englishman, is less becoming in a Scot. (I speak of the conventional accent of the mind, not of that of the minority of free-minded folk to be found in every country.)

'If you un-Scotch us,' said Sir Walter Scott, 'you will find us damned mischievous Englishmen.'

'If you un-Scotch yourselves,' he might have added, 'you will find yourselves damned dull Englishmen.'

In Skye, where, we learn from Boswell, 'my fellow-traveller and I were now full of the old Highland spirit,' Dr Johnson said, 'Sir, the Highland chiefs should not be allowed to go further south than Aberdeen. A strong-minded man like Sir James Macdonald

1. *Scotland.*

may be improved by an English education, but in general they
will be tamed into insignificance.'

The truth is, a man may be a good Londoner and a good Scot,
but he cannot be a good Englishman and a good Scot; just as an
Englishman may be a good Parisian and a good Englishman, but
not a good Frenchman and a good Englishman.

Of course one doesn't deliberately set about being a Scot, or an
Englishman, or any other national. That would simply lead to
eccentricity. If one is content to be oneself, one's nationality will
make itself felt unobtrusively, like the scent of a flower. Just as a
flower draws its sustenance both from the soil from which it has
sprung and from the sun and air in which it unfolds, so the human
being in relation to the civilization and traditions of his own
country and those of the wider world that gradually opens up
to him.

There is undoubtedly much that the Scot can advantageously
learn from the Englishman, and vice versa, but the indiscriminate
adoption of alien traditions and customs is both foolish and disastrous for any people. In Scotland, our deepest roots lie in the
Celtic tradition. As our present Lord Lyon[1] has pointed out, the
basic social divisions in Scotland are not, as in England, horizontal
into classes, but vertical into clans and families, the humblest
member of the clan having a sense of kinship with his chief.

'The paradox of loyalty to one's fellows with loyalty to a lord',
writes Dr Arthur Geddes, 'of stoutly equalitarian thinking bound
up with fervid admiration for an aristocracy is nowhere more
marked than among the Gael'; and he adds, that the people
'sought to reconcile these conflicting loyalties by claiming common ancestry for chief and people, as the children (clann) of a
hero of history or myth.'[2]

The fact that Scotland, though many times occupied, was never
conquered by the sword, and that her people thus escaped sub-
ordination to an alien ruling caste, has profoundly influenced the
national psychology. It is to this that we owe what G. K. Chester-
ton calls 'the really valuable historic property of the Scots, their
independence, their fighting spirit, and their instinctive philo-
sophic consideration of men as men'.

'Scotland has always been the most democratic of feudal
societies,' writes Florence MacCunn, 'till now, when, in country

1. Sir Thomas Innes of Learney.   2. *The Isle of Lewis and Harris.*

places, at least, she is the most feudal of democracies. . . . The servants of all his friends were distinct personalities to Scott, to be warmly welcomed and inquired after.' And she quotes his relations with the faithful Tom Purdie: 'Laird and servant both being Scots, they had their wrangles over trees and pathways. When Scott's orders became final, Tom would save his dignity by turning up in the evening to inform his master that "on thinking the matter over he had decided to follow his advice".'[1]

Tom Purdie could be trusted, as Scott told Washington Irvine, with untold gold, but not with unmeasured whisky.

Elizabeth Grant of Rothiemurchus, describing the rural festivities of her youth, tells us that 'we were accustomed to dance with all the company as if they had been our equals; it was always done. There was no fear of undue assumption on the one side, or low familiarity on the other; a vein of good breeding ran through all ranks influencing the manners and rendering the intercourse of all most particularly agreeable.

' . . . Both Lord Huntly and my father were promoters of this sort of mixed meeting. . . . They themselves were the life and soul of such gatherings, courteous to all, gay in manner, and very gallant to the fair. . . . Besides the renewal of intercourse between the ranks, leading to a continuance of kind feeling, a sort of stimulus was given to the spirits of those whom Belleville called *the bodies*. . . . Husbands were proud of producing handsome wives nicely dressed; mothers looked forward to bringing with them pretty daughters to be introduced to grander friends. The dress and the manners of the higher portion of the company had a sensible effect on the lower. Mrs John Macnab's first cap was greatly moderated on her second appearance, and Janet Mitchell's boisterous dancing fined down into a not unbecoming sprightliness of movement.

'All this is over now. The few grandees shut themselves up rigorously in their proud exclusiveness. Those who could have perpetuated a better tone are gone, their places know them no more. Our former wise occasional reunions are matters of history; each section appears now to keep apart, unnoticed by the class above, and in turn not noticing the class below.'

That was in the East Highlands. The same process of decay,

1. *Sir Walter Scott's Friends.*

or progress, according to one's point of view, was noticeable in the West. In Dr Norman Macleod's *Reminiscences of a Highland Parish* (Argyll), Finlay the Piper describes the lively Hogmanay festivities, in which the whole community took part, at the house of the laird. '(We) passed the night amid music and enjoyment, and parted not until the breaking of the dawn guided us to our homes.

'Many good results', he goes on, 'followed from this friendly mingling of gentles and commons. Our superiors were at that time acquainted with our language and our ways. . . . There were kindness, friendship and fosterage between us; and while they were apples on the topmost bough, we were all fruit of the same tree. . . . (But now) our superiors dwell not among us, and cannot converse with us. All this has passed as a dream, or the breaking of a bubble on the top of a wave.'

This is what 'civilization' has done for the Highlands, or the 'roving clans and savage barbarians', as Dr Johnson designates our not very remote ancestors. In point of fact, the people who assume Highland history to be a tale of feuds and forays and nothing else err as absurdly as would the men of Mars if, looking down on the Earth, they assumed its history to be a tale of battles and ruthless struggling for wealth and power, and nothing else. Happily, there is much else.

'What kind of mental fabric could that have been,' asks Lytton Strachey, 'which had for its warp the habits of filth and savagery of sixteenth-century London and for its woof an impassioned familiarity with the splendour of *Tamburlaine* and the exquisiteness of *Venus and Adonis*?' And what kind of mental fabric could that have been, we may ask, which had for its warp the filth and savagery of the warring clansmen and for its woof an impassioned familiarity with an oral literature, if such it may be called, of singular beauty and power, in which were enshrined the history and aspirations of the Gael? Around the leaping fire in the hall of the chief, these ragged clansmen, the meanest of them as tenacious of his honour as any medieval knight, heard the songs and the harping and the heroic tales that were his racial heritage. Thus it came about that 'this people, shut off from civilizing influences by impassable mountains and trackless wastes, without schools or churches, and without any genuine form of ordered government, had nevertheless more of the polish of mind and elevation of sentiment which constitutes true civilization than the same class in the south.'[1]

Poor in material things, the people of the remoter Highlands and Islands have retained something that our modern materialistic civilization lacks and is sorely in need of—something that led a sober lawyer to say to the present writer on his return from a first visit to one of the Outer Isles: 'These are the most civilized people I ever met.' Is it fancy to see in such an island a microcosm of the world civilization of the future? Dr Geddes, in the Survey of Lewis and Harris already mentioned, urges the need to revive there 'the traditional community spirit, the essential feature of Hebridean civilization'; and he devotes many pages to the redis-covery of 'the basic communalism of the Gaelic way of life, as expressed in the family, the farm team, the boat crew, and the democratically organized township'. In its social aspect, this communalism flowers into the *ceilidh*.

What exactly is a *céilidh*? It is an institution peculiar to the Highlands and Islands, and one that only an old and mellow civilization could produce. It might be defined as an informal gathering of friendly neighbours for music and talk; but such gatherings are not confined to Gaeldom. The peculiar quality of the *céilidh* is that it reflects what Douglas Young describes as

> That old lonely lovely way of living
> In Highland places. . . .
> The yearly rhythm of things, the social graces,
> Peatfire and music, candlelight and kindness.

This is convivial life in its perfection.

The old way of life is passing, but its spirit can and must be preserved.

Edinburgh Today

Meanwhile what of Edinburgh? In the years preceding the first World War, Scottish national consciousness had reached its lowest ebb, and during the late nineteenth and early twentieth century those Scots who were allergic to anglicizing influences were sadly irked by the 'imperturbable conservatism and frigid

1. Duncan MacGillivray: Art, 'Development of Education' in *Home Life of the Highlands, 1400-1746.*

self-assurance' that characterized the social life of the Capital. These were particularly evident in the clubs that had been established in the New Town.

'Some of these clubs,' writes Moray McLaren, 'particularly the more socially elevated, have been influenced by London imitation and have been over-weighted by nineteenth-century pomposity, a pomposity made only the more ridiculous by the theatrical beauty of their situation and outlook in Princes Street—their great windows facing and seeming to dream upon the ancient and grander glories of the Castle, the Rock, and the Old Town. Others have admirably maintained themselves in the Scottish and Edinburgh tradition that gave them birth.'

The shock of two world wars roused Scotland from her long sleep, from her supine acceptance of provincial status and standards. The heart of the people has always been sound, but the surprising and gratifying and hopeful thing is the return of the prodigals. Many of our aristocratic families who formerly accepted the convention that Scotland shuts down in September are settling down happily (if often, to begin with, needs must) on their own soil; and that is all to the good, for every country needs an aristocracy, provided it is a genuine one. (Unfortunately there is always a proportion of chaff among the wheat.) A generation ago, every ambitious writer and most ambitious artists made for London as a matter of course. Whilst it is natural that a certain number should migrate, it is unnatural and disastrous that there should be a wholesale migration. That has ceased. More and more our intellectuals and artists are taking London and Paris in their stride, and making their homes in Scotland.

'It is a community of purpose,' says Disraeli, 'that constitutes society. Without that, men may be drawn into contiguity, but they still continue virtually isolated.'[1]

Happily for Scotland, the liveliest minds and soundest hearts in all walks of life are being drawn together by a community of purpose—the preservation and development of their country. Once upon a time it was our pride to be good Scots and good Europeans, and it looks as if the wheel had at last turned full circle. Edinburgh's International Festival has made Scotland Europe-conscious and world-conscious, and it has made Europe and the world Scotland-conscious. The old delight in entertaining the

1. *Sybil.*

stranger in our midst persists (even with those who, in these degenerate days, are obliged to make a charge for bed and breakfast), and the social, intellectual and artistic life of the community is thereby quickened. There are wonderful gatherings during the three weeks of the year when some of the greatest musicians, artists and writers in the world are to be met in Edinburgh; but even after the city has settled down to her normal life, there are many supper-parties and informal evenings that would have delighted the men of the Golden Age. It may be that there is less intellectual brilliance, but we have one incalculable advantage over our Georgian predecessors—a community of purpose.

4: *Convivial Occasions*

Return from the Reiving

MacNeill of Barra returns from a reiving expedition on the high seas to Kisimul Castle, his island fortress, which is built on a rock out in the bay. His bard, or bardess, sings this exultant song to welcome his return. The period is the sixteenth century.

Latha dhomh am Beinn a' Cheathaich,
    Air fal-il-o
    O-i-o-u,
Gu'n deach bata Chloinn Neill seachad.
    O hi-o hu-o, fal-u-o.

B'ait leam do bhata 's i gabhail,
    Air fal-il-o
    Ho rionaso.
Mach o dhuthaich Mhic 'Illeathain.
    O hi-o hu-o, fal-u-o.

Steach gu Ceisemul an athair,
    Air fal-il-o,
    Ho rionaso,
Far an faighteadh cuirm ri gabhail.
    O hi-o hu-o, fal-u-o.

Fion o oidhche gus an latha,
　　Fa-li-o-hu,
　　O-i-o-u,
Is clarsach bhinn 'ga gleusadh marris
　　O-i-o hu-o fal-u-o.

.　　　.　　　.　　　.

High from the Ben-a-Hayich
　　On a day of days,
　　Seaward I gaze,
Watching Kishmul's galley sailing.
　　O hee-oh hoo-oh, fal-oo-oh.

Homeward she bravely battles,
　　'Gainst the hurtling waves,
　　Nor hoop nor yards,
Anchor, cable nor tackle has she,
　　O hee-oh hoo-oh, fal-oo-oh.

Now at last 'gainst wind and tide
　　They've brought her to,
　　Neath Kishmul's walls,
Kishmul Castle our ancient glory.
　　O hee-oh hoo-oh, fal-oo-oh.

Here's red wine and feast for heroes,
　　And harping too—
　　O-ee o-oo
Sweet harping too—o ee-o oo-o
　　O hee-oh hoo-oh, fal-oo-oh.

Gaelic Words Traditional
English version by Marjory Kennedy-Fraser

A Highland Stirrup-Cup

1662.—In January, my Lord Lovat was invited by Sir Hugh
Calder to witness his espousals and contract at Tarnaway [Darna-
way Castle], and, though the storm was great, would not decline
the call. . . . We [Lord Lovat and his train] came to Tarnaway to
dinner, where we got a generous welcome. . . . The Earl waited
upon Lovat to his bedchamber, telling him this was the King's

H

apartment and bed, where he was to lodge while he stayed at Tarnaway. Next morrow, the Lady Henrietta Stuart was solemnly espoused to Sir Hugh Calder of Calder, but I deem that she loved my Lord Lovat better, and had he not been married already, this had been a meeter marriage by far. The loves and contract ribbons being distributed in state, we had a most solemn feast—a wedding rather than a contract dinner. . . . After a surfeit of sincere friendship and feasting, my Lord Lovat the fourth day takes leave of that noble family of Moray; and at parting the final compliment was my Lord Lovat, taking horse, rides up the scale-stairs of Tarnaway, and in the great hall drinks the King's health, with sound of trumpet and pistol-shot. The meanest drunk bowls of wine, with snowballs cast in for sugar. And after many a loath farewell, sounded goodnight and joy be with you!

From *The Wardlaw Manuscript*

Christmas in the Baronial Hall

Heap on more wood!—the wind is chill,
But let it whistle as it will,
We'll keep our Christmas merry still.

.   .   .   .

The damsel donn'd her kirtle green;
The hall was dressed with holly green;
Forth to the wood did merry-men go
To gather in the mistletoe.
Then open'd wide the Baron's hall
To vassal, tenant, serf and all.

.   .   .   .

The fire, with well-dried logs supplied,
Went roaring up the chimney wide;
The huge hall-table's oaken face,
Scrubb'd till it shone the day to grace,
Bore then upon its massive board
No mark to part the squire and lord.
Then was brought in the lusty brawn
By old, blue-coated serving-men.
Then the grim boar's head frown'd on high,
Crested with bays and rosemary.

.   .   .   .

The wassel round, in good brown bowls,
Garnished with ribbons, blithely trowls.
There the huge sirloin reek'd; hard by
Plum porridge stood, and Christmas pie;
Nor fail'd old Scotland to produce
At such high tide, her savoury goose.
Then came the merry maskers in,
And carols roar'd, with blithesome din.

. . .

'Twas Christmas broach'd the mightiest ale,
'Twas Christmas told the merriest tale;
A Christmas gambol oft could cheer
The poor man's heart through half the year.

Sir Walter Scott: *Marmion*, Introduction to Canto VI, written at Mertoun Hall, Tweedside.

Noctes Ambrosianae

I

A Scottish nobleman of the olden time was in the habit of indulging pretty freely at the hospitable tables of his friends. He took the precaution to have always with him a trustworthy retainer who never failed to avoid all temptation to excess, in order to make sure of taking his master safely home. On one occasion Donald was induced to join in the festivities in the servants' hall, and feeling himself quite overcome, managed to stagger upstairs and whisper to his master, who was in full swing of enjoyment at the table, 'My lord, ye'll hae to tak care o yersel the nicht, for it's a' owre wi' me!'   R. Kempf: *Convivial Caledonia*

II

There had been a carousing-party at Castle Grant, many years ago, and as the evening advanced towards morning two Highlanders were in attendance to carry the guests upstairs. . . . One or two [of the guests], however, whether from their abstinence or their superior strength of head, were walking upstairs and declined the proferred assistance. The attendants were astonished and indignantly exclaimed, 'Ach, it's sair changed times at Castle Grant, when gentlemens can gang to bed on their ain feet!'

Dean Ramsay: *Reminiscences of Scottish Life and Character*

III

Henry Mackenzie was once at a festival at Kilravock Castle, towards the close of which the exhausted topers first sank down upon their chairs and eventually disappeared below the table. Those who were too far gone lay still from necessity; while those who, like the Man of Feeling, were glad of a pretence for escaping, fell into a doze from policy. While Mackenzie was in this state he was alarmed by feeling a hand working about his throat, and called out. A voice answered, 'Dinna be feared, sir, it's me!' 'And who are you?' 'A'm the lad that lowses the cravats.'

Lord Cockburn: *Journal*

IV

Scottish galraviches, as these drinking-bouts were called, are well known to all acquainted with the 'annals of the bottle', and the one in which Garscadden took his last draught has been often told. The scene occurred in the wee clachan of Law, where a considerable number of Kilpatrick lairds had congregated for the ostensible purpose of talking over some parish business. And well they talked and better they drank, when one of them, about the dawn of the morning, fixing his eye on Garscadden, remarked that he was looking 'unco gash' (ghastly). Upon which Kilmardinny coolly replied, 'Deil mean him, since he has been wi' his Maker these twa hours. I saw him step awa, but I didna like to disturb good company!'   Dr John Strang: *Glasgow and Her Clubs*

A Perpetual Dinner-Party

At Cambo (in Fife), a branch of the noble house of Erskine maintained a perpetual dinner-party, from which guests might retire, subsequently to return. When Colonel Monypenny of Pitmally was about to proceed to India to take command of his regiment, he called at Cambo to express an adieu. Mr Erskine was at dinner; but the Colonel, who was invited to join the party, speedily retired. On his return from India, four years afterwards, the Colonel again waited on Mr Erskine, who was still dining. Unconscious of his friend's long absence, he asked the Colonel to take his chair and pass round the bottle.

If there exists a record of a longer dinner than the above, it would be a pleasure to read it.

Edward Emerson: *Beverages Past and Present*

Compulsory Hospitality

The lairds of Newtyle, in Forfarshire (Angus), used to keep cannon pointed to the road near by their old castle, so as to *compel* the wayfarers to come in and be regaled.

It is also worth the telling that the lairds of Hangingshaw, in Selkirkshire, kept a large goblet, known far and wide as 'The Hangingshaw Ladle', which they administered full of reaming ale to every person, of whatever degree, whether willing or unwilling, who entered the house.

A circumstance still more in point is related regarding a former proprietor of Crichton Castle, in Edinburghshire (Midlothian). A stout baron, with a goodly retinue, having presumed to pass this person's gates, without the usual homage of stopping to take refreshment, the Laird of Crichton mounted horse, with all his merry men, and overtaking the recreant traveller, brought him back and threw him, with all his attendants, into the massymore of the castle. Afterwards, taking fear to himself for the result of such a strange exploit, he liberated the baron, and, planting him at table, endeavoured to restore him to good humour by formally waiting upon him personally.

A. Hislop: *Book of Scottish Anecdote*

An Oyster-Party

A few evenings ago I had the pleasure of being asked to one of these entertainments by a lady. At that time I was not acquainted with this scene of 'high life below stairs'.... The door opened, and I had the pleasure of being ushered in not to one lady, as I expected, but to a large and brilliant company of both sexes, most of whom I had the honour of being acquainted with. The large table, round which they were seated, was covered with dishes full of oysters and pots of porter. For a long time I could not suppose that this was the only entertainment we were to have, and I sat waiting in expectation of a repast that was never to make its appearance. The table was cleared, and glasses introduced. The ladies were now asked whether they would choose brandy or rum punch? I thought this question an odd one, but I was soon informed by the gentleman who sat next to me, that no wine was sold here, but that punch was quite 'the thing'; and a large bowl was immediately introduced. The conversation hitherto had been insipid, and at intervals; it now became general and lively. The women, who, to do them justice, are much more entertaining than their neighbours in England, discovered a great deal of vivacity and fondness for repartee. A thousand things were hazarded, and met with applause; to which the oddity of the scene gave propriety, and which could have been produced in no other place. The general ease with which they conducted themselves, the innocent freedom of their manners, and their unaffected good-nature, all conspired to make us forget that we were regaling in a cellar, and was a convincing proof that, let local customs operate as they may, a truly polite woman is everywhere the same.

Captain Edward Topham: *Letters from Edinburgh, 1774-5*

Dr Johnson and Boswell on Raasay

The approach to Raasay (from Skye) was very pleasing.... Our boatmen sung with great spirit. As we came near the shore, the singing of our rowers was succeeded by that of reapers, who were busy at work, and who seemed to shout as much as to sing, while they worked with a bounding activity.... (On landing) I perceived a large company coming out from the house. We met them as we walked up. There were Raasay himself; his brother Dr Macleod; his nephew the Laird of MacKinnon; the Laird of Macleod; Colonel Macleod of Talisker, an officer in the Dutch service; ... Mr Macleod of Muiravenside, best known by the name of Sandie Macleod, who was long in exile on account of the part which he took in 1745; and several other persons. We were welcomed upon the green, and conducted into the house, where we were introduced to Lady Raasay, who was surrounded by a numerous family.

... It was past six when we arrived. Some excellent brandy was served round immediately, according to the custom of the Highlands, where a dram is generally taken every day. They call it a *scalch*. On a side-board was placed for us, who had come off the sea, a substantial dinner and a variety of wines. Then we had coffee and tea. I observed in the room several elegantly bound books and other marks of improved life. Soon after a fiddler appeared, and a little ball began. Raasay himself danced with as much spirit as any man, and Malcolm bounded like a roe. Sandy Macleod, who has at times an excessive flow of spirits, and had it now . . . made much jovial noise. Dr Johnson was so delighted with this scene, that he said, 'I know not how we shall get away.' It entertained me to see him sitting by, while we danced, sometimes in deep meditation—sometimes smiling complacently . . . and sometimes talking a little, amid the noise of the ball, to Mr (the Rev.) Donald MacQueen. . . . He was pleased with Mr MacQueen, and said to me, 'This is a critical man, sir. There must be great vigour of mind to make him cultivate learning so much in the isle of Skye, where he might do without it.' . . . Soon after we came in, a black cock and grey hen, which had been shot, were shewn, with their feathers on, to Dr Johnson, who had never seen that species of bird before. We had a company of thirty at supper, and all was good humour and gaiety, without intemperance.

James Boswell: *Journal of a Tour to the Hebrides* (1773)

Boswell has one over the eight

At Corriechatachin, in Skye: It was about eleven when we arrived. We were most hospitably received by the master and mistress, who were just going to bed, but, with unaffected ready kindness, made a good fire, and at twelve o'clock at night had supper on the table.

. . . Dr Johnson went to bed soon. When one bowl of punch was finished, I rose, and was near the door, on my way upstairs to bed; but Corrichatachin said, it was the first time Col[1] had been in his house, and he should have his bowl;—and would I not join in drinking it? The heartiness of my honest landlord, and the desire of doing social honour to our very obliging conductor, induced me to sit down again. Col's bowl was finished; and by that time we were well warmed. A third bowl was soon made, and that, too, was finished. We were cordial and merry to a high degree; but of what passed I have no recollection, with any accuracy. I remember calling Corrichatachin by the familiar name of Corri, which his friends do. A fourth bowl was made,

1. 'Young Col', son and heir of Maclean of Col.

by which time Col, and young McKinnon, Corrichatachin's son, slipped away to bed. I continued a little with *Corri* and *Knockow*; but at last I left them. It was near five in the morning when I got to bed.

I awaked at noon, with a severe headache. I was much vexed that I should have been guilty of such a riot, and afraid of a reproof from Dr Johnson. I thought it very inconsistent with that conduct which I ought to maintain, while the companion of the Rambler. About one he came into my room, and accosted me, 'What, drunk yet?'—His tone of voice was not that of severe upbraiding; so that I was relieved a little.—'Sir' (said I) they kept me up.' He answered, 'No, you kept them up, you drunken dog.' This he said with good-humoured English pleasantry. Soon afterwards Corrichatachin, Col and other friends assembled round my bed. Corri had a brandy bottle and glass with him, and insisted I should take a dram. . . . I took my host's advice and drank some brandy, which I found an effectual cure for my headache. When I rose, I went into Dr Johnson's room, and taking up Mrs McKinnon's Prayer-book, I opened it at the twentieth Sunday after Trinity, in the epistle for which I read, 'And be not drunk with wine, wherein there is excess.' Some would have taken this as a divine interposition.   Ibid.

Dinner with a Mull laird

Faujas de Saint-Fond, a well-known mineralogist and the King of France's Commissioner for Wines, visited Scotland in the seventeen-eighties (the exact date is uncertain). He was bent on seeing Staffa, and was the guest of Maclean of Torloisk—in a small laird's house, simply appointed—in the Isle of Mull.

At dinner, the lady of the house did the honours, and served everyone. The first toast is given without delay; it is still the mistress who is in charge of the ceremony. She is brought a great cup filled with port (the grace-cup) and drinks first to the company's health and sends the cup to one of her neighbours, and from one to another it goes round the table. . . . The cloth is taken up after dessert, and the table, of polished mahogany, appears in full brilliance. It is soon covered with decanters of English glass, full of port, sherry and madeira, and great pitchers of punch. Then a profusion of small glasses is set out for everyone.

In England the ladies leave the table as soon as the moment arrives for the toasts. Here it is different: they stay for half an hour at any rate, and rightly share the gaiety where, ceremony being set aside, the Scots openheartedness and friendliness can show. It is certain the men gain by it, while the ladies do not lose. The health of each lady is drunk; to the guests each in turn by name, to the *patrie*, to liberty, to the happiness of mankind, to friendship: we foreigners drank more than once to our good friends, the Highlanders, who answered in chorus, 'To your friends of France!' and, more quietly, in sweet madeira, 'To your ladies!' The ladies then go to order tea. . . . (Later) there is music and talk, reading of somewhat ancient newspapers, and, weather permitting, a walk.

Such is the life that one leads in a country where there is no road, and not a tree.

On the difference of manners in England and Scotland in regard to the ladies' leaving the table, Moray McLaren writes in a letter to James Bridie:

The average Scot, unless he has passed through an Anglican education, is much more habituated to female society from early youth than is the Englishman. . . . He does give the impression that as a sex women interest him, play a part in his life. Not so the Englishman. The English dislike of women is not due to low sexual powers nor to a lack of romantic imagination—far from it. He can love as violently and devotedly as any other man under the sun. But he just doesn't like the company of women when he's not loving them. It is the English who have invented all the ingenious devices for escaping from women's company. He invented that luxurious monastery, the man's club. . . . It is the English who first thought of shooing away the women from the dinner table at the end of the meal for over an hour or even through all the rest of the evening. For over two centuries the ceremony of the circulation of the post-prandial port in purely masculine society has been regarded by many Englishmen as the most delightful part of the dinner. There are men still living who can remember a time when the men did not rejoin the ladies until bed or carriage time.[1]

1. *A Small Stir* (1949).

At Inverary Castle

(Faujas de Saint-Fond dines with the Duke of Argyll.)

The table is usually set for twenty-five or thirty covers. When everyone is seated, the chaplain, according to custom, makes a short prayer and blesses the food, which is eaten with pleasure, for the dishes are prepared after the manner of an excellent French cook; everything is served here as in Paris, except some courses in the English [sic] style, for which a certain predilection is preserved. . . . The *entrées*, the rôtis and the entremets are all served as in France and with the same variety and abundance. If the poultry be not so juicy as in Paris, one eats here in compensation hazel-hens, and above all moorfowl, delicious fish, and vegetables, the quality of which maintains the reputation of the Scottish gardeners who grow them.

At the dessert, the scene changes; the cloth, the napkins, and everything vanish. The mahogany table appears in all its lustre; but it is soon covered with brilliant decanters, filled with the best wines; comfits, in fine porcelain or crystal vases; and fruits of different kinds in different baskets. Plates are distributed together with many glasses; and in every object elegance and convenience seem to rival each other. I was surprised, however, to see on the same table, in so cold a climate, and in the middle of the month of September, beautiful peaches, very good grapes, apricots, prunes, figs, cherries and raspberries, though the figs could hardly be called juicy by a person born in the south of France. It is probable, however, that the greater part of these fruits were produced with much care and expense in hot-houses.

Towards the end of the dessert, the ladies withdrew to a room destined for the tea-table. . . . Although the ceremony of toasts lasts for at least three-quarters of an hour, no person is made uncomfortable, and everyone drinks as he pleases. This, however, does not prevent a great number of healths being drunk with pleasure and good grace. Wines are the great luxury of the table in England [sic], where they drink the best and dearest that grow in France and Portugal. If the lively champagne should make its diuretic influence felt, the case is foreseen, and in pretty corners of the room the necessary convenience is to be found. This is applied with so little ceremony, that the person who has occasion to use it, does not even interrupt his talk during the operation. I suppose this is one of the reasons why the English [*sic*] ladies, who are exceedingly modest and reserved, always leave the company before the toasts begin.

At last we proceed to the drawing-room, where tea and coffee abound, and where the ladies do the honours of the table with much grace and ceremony; the tea is always excellent, but ... their coffee is weak and bitter, and has completely lost its aromatic odour.

... After tea, those who wished retired to their rooms; those who preferred conversation or music remained in the drawing-room; others went out to walk. At ten o'clock supper was served, and those attended it who pleased.

Fête Champêtre at Inverness

In the eighteenth century the Magistrates of Inverness appear to have been as zealous wine-bibbers as those of the capital, their favourite wine being also claret. In summer, their convivialities were held *al fresco*. A favourite spot was the wooded island in the Ness, about half a mile up the river, which was the property of the town. On the grand occasions of the judges' visits, a salmon-dinner was served on the island, which at that time was approached by boat. Having doffed their robes and cares of office, their lordships and their hosts stretched themselves under a canopy of oak and birch, through which the sunlight filtered, and 'watched the fishermen as, with shouts and laughter, the nets were drawn down the rapid flashing stream, or the silent depths of some clear pool were dragged.... When the salmon were dispatched, the drinkables were forthcoming, and the whole party got as merry as ever were Robin Hood and his foresters. For one of these occasions there was provided "a hogshead to make punch in". A hogshead! The only wonder is how the river was crossed after the hogshead was empty.'   Angus B. Reach: *Camillus*

Bumper John

I

What a gay and jovial place Culloden (House) must have been in the days of 'Bumper John', the elder brother of Duncan Forbes!

There was always a pipe of claret at the door for all comers, and the house was one unvaried round of social festivals. 'It is the custom of that house,' says Captain Burt, 'at the first visit, or introduction, to take up your freedom by "cracking his nut", as he terms it, that is, a cocoa shell which holds a pint, filled with champagne or such other wine as you shall choose. You may guess from the *introduction* at the contents of the *volume*. Few go away sober at any time, and for the greatest part of his guests, in the conclusion they cannot go at all.'

The portrait of Bumper John, in the family collection, shows a ruddy and lively countenance, but the wine does not seem to have blown him to the size of a gross toper.

Robert Carruthers: Highland Notebook

II

The types of true hospitality in a Scottish farmer's house of old were said to be an anker of whisky always on the spiggot, a boiler with perpetual hot water, and a cask of sugar with a spade in it. Culloden's hospitalities were of a more aristocratic order, and the custom of the house was to prize off the top of each successive cask of claret and place it in the corner of the hall to be emptied in pailfuls. The massive hall table, which bore so many carouses, is still preserved as a venerated relic, and the deep saturation it has received from old libations of claret prevent one from distinguishing the description of wood of which it was constructed. John Hill Burton: *Life of Duncan Forbes*

The Hecht o Hospitality

In the bad old days there prevailed a custom which, like the *jus primae noctis*, is in the Norman rather than the Celtic tradition, and which appears to have been kept up longest among the lairds of Caithness. These hospitable gentlemen were not content to provide for their male guests 'food in the eating-place, drink in the drinking-place and music in the listening-place'—they added 'a Scotch warming-pan'[1] in the sleeping-place. Not so many generations ago, an old minister was being entertained at a country house. The night was cold, and the hostess, having no

1. A Scotch warming-pan i,.e. a wench. The phrase derives from the story of the traveller who asked to have his bed warmed, whereupon the maidservant immediately undressed and lay down on it.

John Ray: English Proverbs (1768).

'pig' (earthenware jar) to spare, asked one of her sonsie servant lasses to go upstairs, lie down in the visitor's bed, and stay there till it got warmed up. It happened that the guest retired a little earlier than was expected, his host, unaware of the arrangement, accompanying him to his room. The lamplight revealed the occupant of the bed. The old man, speedily recovering from his astonishment, turned to his host:

'Ech, sirs, but this is the hecht [height] o hospitality!'

This story, apocryphal or not, enjoyed a long and widespread popularity, and we may still occasionally hear a genial but entirely circumspect host solemnly apologize to a guest for not being able to provide him with 'the hecht o hospitality'.

A Frolic

Mr John Bennet, who became President of the Royal College of Surgeons in 1803, shared in the fashionable frolics of his time.

On one occasion, having lost a bet, he had to pay the forfeit of entertaining his companions to dinner and the theatre. The feast took place at a tavern in Leith, and Mr Bennet plied his guests so well with wine that they were soon in exceeding merry mood. To their delight, their host had provided a string of mourners' coaches to carry them at funereal pace to the theatre, where the onlookers' bewilderment was increased on seeing the jovial party that staggered out with roars of laughter.

Marie Stuart: *Old Edinburgh Taverns*

Dinner at Abbotsford

I

At Abbotsford, Scott always entertained his dinner guests with piping. The windows were open, and on the lawn before the house a tall and stalwart piper in full Highland dress paced up and down. This was John of Skye, who, incidentally, was a capital hedger and ditcher.

When the cloth was drawn, and the never-failing salver of quaichs introduced, John of Skye, upon some well-known signal, entered the room, but *en militaire*, without removing his bonnet, and taking his station behind the landlord, received from his hand the largest of the Celtic bickers brimful of Glenlivet. The man saluted the company in his own dialect, tipped off the contents (probably a quarter of an English pint of raw aquavitae) at a gulp, wheeled about as if the whole ceremony had been a movement on parade, and forthwith recommenced his pibrochs and gatherings.   John Gibson Lockhart: *Life of Scott*

II

On the night of the Abbotsford Hunt, Sir Walter Scott entertained thirty or forty guests or more to dinner. After describing the groaning tables, his biographer continues:

Ale was the favourite beverage during dinner, but there was plenty of port and sherry for those whose stomachs they suited. The quaighs of Glenlivet were filled brimful, and tossed off as if they held water. The wine decanters made a few rounds of the table, but the hints for hot punch and toddy soon became clamorous. Two or three bowls were introduced, and placed under the supervision of experienced manufacturers—one of these being usually the Ettrick Shepherd—and then the business of the evening (song and story) commenced in good earnest.   Id.

Les Neiges d'Antan

In *Peter's Letters to His Kinsfolk*, Lockhart describes a visit to Henry Mackenzie, then an old man. He was seated in a high-backed easy chair, the woodwork 'carved richly in the ancient French taste', with a low cap of black velvet on his head; and the visitor notes the clear transparency of skin, the fresh complexion, the fine features—teeth gone—the innumerable fine wrinkles, and, beneath 'bleached and hoary brows', eyes 'tenderly, brightly blue, full of eloquence and passion'. The only other guest was an old friend and contemporary of Mackenzie's, a distinguished lawyer.

He gave us an excellent bottle of Muscat-de-Rivesaltes during the dinner, and I must say I am inclined very much to approve of the old-fashioned delicacy. We had no lack of Château-la-Rose afterwards, and neither of the old gentlemen seemed to have the slightest objection to its inspiration. . . . They began to give little sketches of the old time. . . . According to the picture they gave, the style of social intercourse in this city, in their younger days, seems, indeed, to have been wonderfully easy and capti-vating. . . . They did not deal in six weeks' invitations and formal dinners; but they formed, at a few hours' notice, little snug supper-parties, which, without costing any comparative expense, afford opportunities a thousand-fold for all manner of friendly communication between the sexes. As for the gentlemen, they never thought of committing any excess, except in the taverns, and at night.

. . . At that time, the only liquor was claret, and this was sent for just as they wanted it—huge pewter jugs, or, as they called them, *stoups* of claret, being just as commonly to be seen travelling the streets of Edinburgh in all directions *then*, as mugs of Mieux and Barclay are in those of London *now*.

Of course I made allowance for the privilege of age, but I have no doubt there was abundance of good wit, and, what is better, good humour among them, no less than of good claret.

Dinner with a Glasgow Merchant

A dinner for sixteen people at the house of a Glasgow merchant in or about 1819 is described in *Peter's Letters to his Kinsfolk*:

'The dinner was excellent. . . . Capital salmon, and trout almost as rich as salmon, from one of the lochs—prime mutton from Argyllshire, very small and sweet, and indeed ten times better than half the venison we see in London—veal not inferior —beef of the very first order—some excellent fowls in curry; everything washed down by delicious old India Madeira which went like *elixir vitae* into the recesses of my stomach. . . . A single bottle of hock, and another of white hermitage went round, but I saw plainly that the greater part of the company took them for perry or cider. After dinner we had two or three bottles of port, which the landlord recommended as being *real stuff*. Abundance of the same Madeira, but to my sorrow no claret, the only wine I ever care for more than half a dozen glasses of.'

During dinner there was too much 'noise and racket of coarse mirth' to please Peter; but after the ladies had withdrawn he

enjoyed a demonstration of 'the noble science of making a bowl'
—a bowl of the famous Glasgow punch (see p. 221).

'The punch being fairly made', continues Peter, 'the real business of the evening commenced, and giving its due weight to the
balsamic influence of the fluid, I must say the behaviour of the
company was such as to remove almost entirely the prejudices I
had conceived in consequence of their first appearance and external
manners. In the course of talk I found that the coarseness which
had most offended me was nothing but a kind of waggish disguise
assumed as the covering of minds keenly alive to the ridiculous
and therefore studious to avoid all appearance of finery—an
article which they are aware always seems absurd when exhibited
by persons of their profession. In short, I was amongst a set of
genuinely shrewd, clever, sarcastic fellows, all of them completely
up to trap—all of them good-natured and friendly in their dis-
positions—and all of them inclined to take their full share in the
laugh against their own peculiarities. Some subjects, besides, of
political interest were introduced and discussed in a tone of great
good sense and moderation. As for wit, I must say there was no
want of it . . . and on the whole I was really much disposed at
the end of the evening . . . to congratulate myself on having made
a good exchange for the self-sufficient young Whig coxcombs of
Edinburgh.'

Dinner at a Country Manse, c. 1819

The dinner took place on the Sunday after the Sacrament. The guests included Peter, the participating ministers and the laird.

I have very seldom eat a dinner which I should have been more
sorry to have missed. I don't mean as to the viands in particular,
although these, too, were not to be sneezed at. Besides *hotch-potch*,
a truly delicious soup quite peculiar to Scotland, but worthy of
being introduced into the very first leaf of the Almanach des
Gourmands, there were Loch Fyne herring, singed sheeps' heads,
and prime old mutton; and, to end with, a whole regiment of
gooseberry pies, with bowls of cream.
. . . After dinner we had a few bottles of excellent port and
sherry, and then two punch-bowls were introduced. . . . The
bowl at the top was presently filled with hot whisky toddy—that

at the bottom with the genuine Glasgow mixture, in compounding which our croupier displayed talents of the very highest order. Bye and bye, we were all in a state of charming merriment, although nothing could be more moderate than the measure of our indulgence. The conversation of the ministers was extremely picturesque and amusing, and opened up to me new glimpses at every turn, into the whole penetralia of their own existence and that of their parishioners. They all seemed to be most worthy persons, but nothing could be more striking than the diversity in their carriage and demeanour. . . . Before they departed, the Croupier called loudly for the stirrup-cup.

Peter's Letters to his Kinsfolk, by J. G. Lockhart and Others (1819)

Unusual Guests

Edinburgh's better-class establishments of a certain type were long reputed to be conducted with dignity and decorum, nor did *mesdames* lack self-respect. Witness the story told of an old country minister of the last century. One dark and stormy night two ladies arrived at the Manse door seeking shelter, their carriage being unable to proceed. One was middle-aged, one young; both were charming. With the aid of the housekeeper, everything was arranged for their comfort, and the old man enjoyed their company as much as they appeared to enjoy his hospitality.

On their departure next day, the elder lady gave him her card, saying how glad she would be to have an opportunity of returning his hospitality when next he was in Edinburgh. A few months later, when attending the General Assembly, he decided to pay a morning call. He received a kind and gracious welcome and was pressed to stay for lunch. At table, he was surprised to see several attractive young ladies, but nothing was said to account for their presence. After lunch and a pleasant chat, he took his leave. As he was walking down the steps to the street, he saw two men he knew, both Edinburgh citizens, coming along. They stopped and gazed at him aghast.

'Good heavens, man!' exclaimed one of them, who knew the old man to be guileless, 'Do you know what sort of house you've been visiting? If you value your reputation, you'll never be seen there again!'

I

Convivial Golfers

Golf matches were also convivial occasions.

The gentlemen golfers of Fife and Lothian were combatant first and convivial after. As Carnegie of Pitarrow (1780-1851) author of *The Golfiad*, tells us, claret and champagne, as well as fashion and betting, were the cups of victory or consolation. They were also the medium of paying for lost wagers or breaches of club rules. Claret was more precious than port. In the record book of the Honourable Company of Golfers it was set down in 1782 that 'Port and Punch shall be the ordinary Drink of the Society, unless upon those days when the Silver Club and Cups are played for. At those meetings Claret or any other Liquor more agreeable will be permitted.' In 1837 Mr Wood, of the Society, was fined two 'tappit hens' . . . for appearing on the links without a red coat. . . . At St Andrews in 1825 'the present Captain, having imposed on himself a Magnum of Claret for failure in public duty, imposed a similar fine on all old Captains present'. The evenings usually ended with 'harmony and melody'.

. . . An old friend of mine who used to go with the Hoylake men for matches with the Lothian clubs told me that there was a dinner every night of the visit, at which a bottle of whisky was set before each man and finished during the evening. But all were early and steady on the tee next morning.

Ivor Brown: *Summer in Scotland*

5: Toasts and Sentiments

Blythe may we a' be,
Ill may we ne'er see,
Here's to the King
And the good companie!

The Majestie o this Realm, being the Land o Cakes!

The Land o Cakes and brither Scots
Frae Maidenkirk to Johnny Groats!

Freedom and Whisky gang thegither—
Tak aff your dram! Robert Burns

Here's our noble sel's, weel met the day!
Robert Fergusson

Here's tae us! Wha's like us? Deil the yin!

The Lasses!

Here's to the heath, the hill and the heather,
The bonnet, the plaid, the kilt and the feather!

Here's to them that lo'es us, or lends us a lift!

Here's a health to the sick,
Stilts to the lame,
Claes to the back,
And brose to the wame!

Here's health, wealth, wit and meal!

May the honest heart ne'er feel distress!

May the winds o adversity ne'er blow open our (your) door!

When we're gaun up the hill o fortune, may we ne'er meet a frien'
comin' doun!

May the mouse ne'er leave your meal-pock wi' a tear in his ee!

May ye aye be happy,
And ne'er drink frae a toom cappie!

May puirtith ne'er throw us in the mire or gowd in the high saddle!
[May we never be cast down by adversity or unduly elated by prosperity.]

The ingle neuk, wi' routh o bannocks and bairns!

May we a' be canty and cosy,
And ilk hae a wife in his bosy!

A cosy but and a canty ben
To couthie women and trusty men!

Yin, one; *lo'es*, loves; *claes*, clothes; *wame*, belly; *toom*, empty; *cappie*, a wooden
bowl; *puirtith*, poverty; *gowd*, gold; *routh*, plenty; *canty*, cheery; *ilk*, everyone; *bosy*, bosom; *but and ben*, the two main rooms (kitchen and parlour or
inner room) in a typical small cottage; *couthy*, agreeable.

Mair frien's, and less need o them!

Mair sense and mair siller!

May ye ne'er want a frien', or a dram to gi'e him!

May the hinges o frien'ship ne'er rust, nor the wings o love lose a feather!

May the pleasures of the evening bear the reflections of the morning!

> Blythe to meet,
> Wae to pairt,
> Blythe to meet aince mair!
> [Toast at parting]

> Gude nicht to ye, and tak your nappie:
> A willie-waught's a gude nicht-cappie.

> To the King owre the watter!
> [Jacobite]

All absent friends, all ships at sea, and the auld pier o Leith!

> Horn, corn, wool and yarn!
> [At an Agricultural Dinner]

> Horny hands and weather-beaten chaffets!
> [Mason's toast—implies desire for work]

> The rending o rocks and the pu'in doun o auld houses!
> [Mason's toast—the erecting of new buildings]

> Lang may Auld Reekie's lums reek rarely!
> [An Edinburgh toast—a tongue-twister]

A fou purse—the gudewife to the booth and the gudeman to the cutting-knife!

[Trade toast of the Corporation of Edinburgh Cordiners (shoemakers). The wives helped their husbands at the weekly fairs]

The stock o broom!

[The centuries-old toast of the Edinburgh Merchant Company. The 'stock o broom' was the symbolic trade-mark and toast, chosen because the broom is 'a modest shrub, but with a great tendency to increase']

The Water-yett! The Treasurer's Auld Wife!

[The Magistrates of the Canongate (Edinburgh) thus expressed their thanks for the profitable dues which had to be paid at the Watergate]

Mair, more; *siller*, silver; *wae*, sorrowful; *aince mair*, once more; *tak your nappie*, drink your ale; *willie-waught*, friendly drink; *chaffets*, cheeks; *fou*, full; *yett*, gate.

The Buirdly Barons o the Borders and the Auld Road to Carlisle!
[Old Border Toast]

The Cassin' o the Wanchancie Covenant! [The repeal of the unlucky Union.]
[Old anti-Union toast]

Slainte mhor! Slainte mhath! [Your good health!]

Tir nam beann, nan gleann, nan gaisgeach! [To the land of the bens, the glens and the heroes!]

> Then let us toast John Barleycorn—
> Each man a glass in hand—
> And may his great posterity
> Ne'er fail in auld Scotland!
> Robert Burns

Buirdly, stalwart; *cassin'*, breaking; *wanchancie*, unlucky.

The Grace Cup

The grace cup is the cup or health drunk at the end of the feast. Its origin is attributed to Margaret Atheling, wife of Malcolm Canmore (1057-93). 'It was the law of her table that none should drink after dinner who did not wait the giving of thanks.'
Edward Emerson: *Beverages Past and Present*

The Signal Toast

During dinner liquor was used sparingly. So long, indeed, as the ladies remained in the dining-room, excess was eschewed. But there was a *signal toast*, on the proposing of which the ladies withdrew. Eighty years ago [from 1884], the signal toast in Glasgow was 'The Trade of Glasgow and the Outward Bound!'
Charles Rogers: *Social Life in Scotland*

Toasting with Highland Honours

At a ceremonial dinner, when it is desired to show special honour to a guest or absent friend, his health is drunk with Highland honours. The proposer of the toast, who must, of course, wear the kilt and be a fluent Gaelic speaker, rises to his feet, flings back his chair, leaps lightly upon it, places his right foot on the table, raises his glass and pronounces these words:

Suas e, suas e, suas e!
Sios e, sios e, sios e!
A null e, a null e, a null e!
A nall e, a nall e, a nall e!
Na h'uile là gu math diut, mo charaid'.
Sguab as e!
Agus cha n'ol neach eile as a ghloine so gu brath![1]

He accompanies the words with appropriate gestures, emptying his glass after the 'Sguab as e!' Then, having spoken the last line, he flings the glass over his left shoulder on to the floor, where it is smashed to atoms.

6: *Old Scots Drinking Vessels*

'Of all the marvels related by the wise and learned Adamnan, who himself ruled in Iona as one of the successors of Columba, that which impressed me most', writes Neil Gunn, 'was his reference to the Picts having *drinking glasses.*'

That was thirteen hundred years ago, and, needless to say, no specimen of these remote Celtic and Nordic times survives. Passing on to a better authenticated period of Scottish domestic history, we find that the commonest drinking vessels were made of wood, more commonly known as 'timmer' or 'treen'. In Wilkie's famous painting of humble life, 'The Penny Wedding' (now in possession of H.M. the Queen), the vessels depicted are all of this material, with the exception of a fine 'tappit-hen' of pewter.

These traditional wooden vessels fall into two main groups— the bickers [beakers] and the quaichs. The bickers include the capacious cogs or coggies, the cap or cappie—a small bicker with

1. Up with it, up with it, up with it!
Down with it, down with it, down with it!
Out with it, out with it, out with it! [Away from me.]
In with it, in with it, in with it! [Towards me.]
May all your days be good, my friend!
Drink it up!
And let none ever drink from this glass again!

two handles—and the luggies. The luggie, however, is not strictly a drinking vessel, but rather a porringer. (It was sometimes constructed with a double bottom where a dry pea was confined and rattled when a second helping was desired.) All types of bicker are deep, with straight sides slightly tapered outwards.

'What makes even the humblest of these vessels attractive', writes Ian Finlay, who is a leading authority on the subject, 'is that as a rule they are constructed of cooper staves put together with a craftsmanlike cunning now unknown. The staves are of light and dark woods alternately, intricately 'feathered' into one another and bound with withies. In their original state they are perfectly watertight, although most have come loose with the passage of time. It is believed the craftsmen used nothing but a knife. The neatness and precision in construction reminds one of the best Japanese toys.'

The word *cap* occurs in such characteristic phrases as 'to drink cap out', to drink to the dregs; 'to kiss caps wi' ', to have a drink with [someone]; 'to drink frae a toom [empty] cappie', to be in want; and in the proverb, 'Better a timmer cap o ma ain than a siller [silver] cap that's borrowed'.

The quaich is of Highland origin, the name being a corruption of the Gaelic *cuach*, a cup. The shape is familiar to most of us, as it is being constantly reproduced, though seldom with the grace of the earlier specimens. In contrast with the bicker, the quaich is wide and shallow, with wedge-shaped horizontal handles which, to the convivially-minded, 'seem to invite a hearty grasp', and which certainly facilitate its being passed from hand to hand when circulated as a loving-cup. Like the bicker, the quaich was originally made of treen, but it was more elegant in appearance and, as a rule, more beautifully finished. When stave construction was used, plane was employed for the light staves, and laburnum, walnut, or mahogany for the dark. Some were mounted in silver, and before the end of the seventeenth century many were made entirely of that metal, the old stave construction being indicated by engraved lines radiating from the base, both inside and out. There are many types of quaich, some having three, and a few even four handles.

Long after cups and glasses came into general use, the smaller quaichs continued to be used for brandy or whisky. When Sir

Walter Scott was dispensing hospitality at Abbotsford, 'his Bordeaux', says Lockhart, 'was uniformly preceded by a small libation of the genuine *mountain dew*, which he poured with his own hand, *more majorum*, for each guest—making use for the purpose of such a multifarious collection of ancient Highland *quaighs* (little cups of curiously dovetailed wood, inlaid with silver) as no Lowland sideboard but his was ever equipped with—but commonly reserving for himself one that was peculiarly precious in his eyes, as having travelled from Edinburgh to Derby in the canteen of Prince Charlie. This relic had been presented to "the wandering Ascanius" by some very careful follower, for its bottom is of glass, that he who quaffed might keep his eye the while on the dirk hand of his companion.'

Long after Scott's time, at the Highland mess-table 'the most characteristic part of the Celtic entertainment was the silver-bound quaichs of old whisky which circulated simultaneously, and it was a gladsome moment when the pipe-major ... tossed off a scallop-shell at the president's elbow, saluted, and retired.'[1]

From the eighteenth century until well into the nineteenth, most of our drinking ware was made of pewter. Ranged on the shelf in the inn-parlour, these vessels reflected the firelight in a sombre glow. Chief among them all was the tappit-hen.

'I have seen one of these formidable stoups', says Sir Walter Scott in a note to *Guy Mannering*, 'at Provost Haswell's at Jedburgh in the days of yore. It was a pewter measure, the claret being in ancient days served from the tap, and had a figure of a crested hen upon the lid. In later times, the name was given to a glass bottle of the same dimensions. These are rare apparitions among the degenerate topers of modern days.'

'The tappit-hen', writes Ian Finlay, 'might be taken as the symbol of Scots conviviality, more typical even than quaich or tankard. Many is the pint of claret or steaming ale that must have been borne out in tappit-hens to passengers blue with cold on the outsides of coaches when horses were changed at the posting inns.'

The tappit-hen is, too, a symbol of the Auld Alliance and the old ties with France. The name was commonly believed to derive from the fancied resemblance of the knobbed lid to a crested hen, but it is in fact a corruption of *topynett*, an old French measure containing a quart. As the same writer points out: 'Claret came

1. Alexander Innes Shand: *Days of the Past.*

from France; so did the name of the vessel, like a score of other domestic things, such as ashets and tassies and serviettes. And with it came the name of its smaller relation, the chopin, which is simply the *chopine*, the French pint. Only the mutchkin is all-Scots—the little mutch—a pleasant pun.'

There are many references to the tappit-hen in our literature.

> Weel she loo'd a Hawick gill
> And leugh to see a tappit-hen,

runs an old anonymous song, and Burns commands,

> The tappit-hen, gae bring her ben!

In *Waverley*, Scott tells us how the Baron Brawardine entertained his guests at a primitive change-house:

'When they were seated under the sooty rafters of Lucky Macleary's only apartment, thickly tapestried with cobwebs, their hostess appeared with a huge pewter measuring-pot containing at least three English quarts, familiarly denominated a "Tappit Hen", and which, in the language of the hostess, reamed (mantled) with excellent ale just drawn from the cask.'

Of all our old pewter vessels, the most prized today is a graded set of thistle measures, which belong to the early nineteenth century. They had a brief life-span, for the shape, in itself attractive, had a snag; no matter how high the vessel was tipped, its bulging waist managed to retain some of the ale—a device which commended itself to the innkeeper, but hardly to the customer. So it was eventually banned. A set of five thistle measures is preserved in the Royal Scottish Museum.

During the sixteenth and seventeenth centuries, many of the drinking vessels in wealthier houses were made of silver. Scottish domestic silver was, on the whole, simple in style, its beauty depending less on the ornamentation, which was slight, than on good proportion, elegance of form, and the soft glow of the beaten silver. It attained a very high standard. The early Communion cups are modelled on the secular wine-cups of the period, the form being usually a shallow bowl set on a stem. Many of these remain the treasured possessions of various churches. A number of splendid silver tankards have also been preserved, among them one or two specimens of the rare peg tankards, which have small silver pegs on the inside to mark the diminishing contents—whence the saying, 'to drink a peg'.

Another type of drinking vessel is the mazer, a silver-mounted bowl which dates from the thirteenth to the end of the sixteenth century. The name derives from the Anglo-Saxon word, *maza*, spotted, its spotted appearance being a conspicuous feature of the bowl, which is made of wood—usually the burry excrescences of various trees. The burr was more suited than ordinary wood for a drinking bowl because it was harder and less liable to shrink, and maple was the most commonly used because it is especially resistant to liquids.

Whilst most of the English and Continental mazers are simple, silver-mounted bowls, the Scottish type (with one exception) is raised several inches on a finely wrought, sometimes trumpet-shaped, silver stem. Because of its rich appearance the mazer was particularly suited to ceremonious occasions, when it was frequently used as a loving-cup.

Only six of these Scottish standing mazers survive, but they constitute a very valuable group of native silverwork. One of them, the Watson mazer, has been acquired by the Royal Scottish Museum. The St Mary's Mazer belongs to St Andrews University, where it used to circulate at the college table on great occasions. The Fergusson mazer, now in the United States, is believed to have been the gift of James VI, when a small boy, to his tutor, David Fergusson. The remaining three—the Tulloch, the Craigievar and the Galloway—are, in Ian Finlay's view, the three finest standing mazers in existence.

'In the case of the Tulloch mazer', he writes, 'the mounts are of silver gilt, and the piece has faultless balance and symmetry. The baluster stem is enriched with acanthus leaves in a typical renaissance manner, while the mounts of the bowl are engraved with scroll-work and with figures.' On the 'print' or boss within the bowl are the arms of Tulloch of Tannochy, in whose possession it remained until after the first World War.

The Craigievar mazer is associated with Aberdeen, and is reputed to have been in the possession of the Forbes-Semphill family. It is the work of James Craufuird of Edinburgh, and the deacon who marked it was George Heriot, father of the celebrated 'Jinglin' Geordie', goldsmith to James VI.

Like the Tulloch, the Galloway mazer, which is considered the finest of them all, was made by James Gray of the Canongate, Master Coiner to James VI. It bears the arms of Archibald

Stewart (brother of the first Lord Doune and uncle of 'the Bonnie Earl o Moray' and the Admirable Crichton), Lord Provost of Edinburgh in 1579, and is also engraved with the Roses of Lennox and the Lion Rampant of the Earldom of Fife. Later it passed through marriage into the possession of the Earls of Galloway. This mazer came prominently into the limelight in 1954, when it changed hands at Sotheby's for the record sum of £11,000. Its destination appeared to be the United States, but, thanks to the intervention of the Reviewing Committee on the Export of Works of Art, it was saved for Scotland and is now in the National Museum of Antiquities in Edinburgh.

In a well-known song Burns writes,

> Gae bring to me a pint o wine,
> And fetch it in a silver tassie,

but the 'siller tassie' (cup or tankard) appears to have been largely superseded in the eighteenth century by drinking glasses. There were now many glass-works in the country—in Edinburgh and Leith, in the Glasgow district, and in Alloa and Fife. Our Scottish glassware, however, rarely reached the highest standards, with the exception of the very attractive and well-known Jacobite glasses. (After the 'Forty-five' many drinking customs were devised so that one might with impunity drink a toast to the King over the Water.) There appears, however, to be some uncertainty as to whether all of these are of native manufacture. Edinburgh was later to produce crystal famous for its purity and brilliance.

Another vessel that long held sway on every hospitable board was the punch-bowl. The majority were of crockery, and the Scottish potteries must have turned out thousands of painted bowls. Others were of fine china. One of these, which appeared on the dinner-table of a Glasgow merchant, is briefly described in *Peter's Letters to His Kinsfolk* (1819). 'The bowl itself was really a beautiful old piece of porcelaine. It was what is called a double bowl, that is, the coloured surface was cased in another of pure white network, through which the red and blue flowers and trees shone out most beautifully.' Others were of glass, frequently engraved with the owner's crest. A few were of silver, among them the splendid but rare 'menteiths'.

The 'menteith' is characterized by a fluted and scalloped rim, which had a definite purpose. When a cold punch, such as the

famous Glasgow punch, was to be made, the bowl was brought
in filled with cold water to cool the glasses, which rested with
their stems in the scallops of the rim, and were later removed for
the brewing of the punch. They were similarly heated for hot
punch.

One of these vessels is preserved by the Royal Company of
Archers, The Queen's Bodyguard in Scotland.

Punch-bowls varied considerably in size. Some were as much
as eighteen inches in diameter, with a four-gallon capacity. At
one time punch-bowls and racks of churchwarden pipes of Scottish clay were provided for regular customers at many country
inns.

The pleasant ritual of preparing a punch-bowl, or, in the old
phrase, 'handling the china', has left us with a host of beautiful
vessels and implements, notably the strainers to catch the lemon
pips and the long punch-ladles to serve the beverage, both exem-
plifying the graceful and delicate work of the Scottish silversmith.

Toddy, too, had its special equipage. This included a toddy-
kettle, usually made of copper, a spatula of glass or metal for
stirring, and a small deep ladle for serving the brew.

> The lads and lasses, blythly bent
> To mind baith saul and body,
> Sit round the table, weel content
> To steer about the toddy.

Thus Burns in *The Holy Fair*. The bard's own toddy-kettle
has been preserved and may be seen at his birth-place in Alloway.

On Hogmanay the toddy-kettle was used for the brewing of
Het Pint (hot ale, spiced and laced with whisky), of which more
anon.

On the farms, and particularly at the Harvest Home (known
variously as the Kirn, the Clyack and the Muckle Supper), the
homely 'grey-beardie' was in evidence. This was a large earthenware jar which usually held three gallons of whisky, though some,
with double 'lugs' (ears), held considerably more. In *Waverley*
Lucky Macleary manages to convey a grey-beard of brandy to
the Baron of Brawardine, 'for his comfort and solace'. Another
name for this vessel was the whisky-pig (Gael. *pige*, a crock).

The 'broun pig', like the 'little brown jug' of the song, was used
for carrying ale from the ale-house for home drinking.

Horn was a very useful material in the old days, for it is a sort of natural plastic and can be pressed and moulded into many shapes. Besides snuff-mulls, trinket-boxes, and spoons (some of which had a silver whistle at the end of the handle to summon a second helping), there were horn drinking-cups, some richly carved, and many silver-mounted. A ram's horn made a natural drinking vessel, and was often rimmed and lidded to hold whisky. The deeper scallop-shell, unadorned, was also useful. Boswell relates how, at a house on the Island of Coll where Dr Johnson and he were entertained 'with a primitive heartiness', 'whisky was served round in a shell, according to the ancient Highland custom'. Horn and shell appear in conjunction in *Waverley*, where Evan and his attendant enjoy an *al fresco* breakfast with the damsel of the caravan. After feasting on milk, eggs, a freshly caught salmon broiled in slices over a few withered fir branches, barley bread, fresh butter, honeycomb and wild cranberries, 'to crown the repast, Evan produced from the pocket of his short jerkin a large scallop-shaped shell, and from under the folds of his plaid a ram's horn full of whisky. Of this he took a copious dram.'

Among the treasures in the Castle of Dunvegan, the seat of Macleod of Macleod in Skye, is the drinking horn of Rory Mor, who was chief of the clan at the end of the sixteenth century. It is a long ox-horn, its mouth encircled with a deep silver band engraved with animals and a pattern of Celtic interlacing of twelfth-century style. When in use, it was firmly clasped near the mouth, whilst the horn was twined round the arm. In each generation the heir to the chiefship, on coming of age, was expected to give proof of his manhood by drinking its contents at one draught.

Another Macleod heirloom is a cup of ancient Irish workmanship. It is made of wood—to all appearance oak—but is most curiously wrought and embossed with silver work inset with coral, some of which has disappeared. In *The Lord of the Isles*, the lines occur:

> Fill me the mighty cup, he said,
> Erst owned by royal Somerled;

and in an explanatory note, Scott identifies the cup with that of Dunvegan.

In *Waverley*, we have a description of another curious drinking cup—that of the Baron of Brawardine. After the banquet, 'as the evening grew more late, the Baron ... produced a golden goblet of a singular and antique appearance, moulded in the shape of a rampant bear, which the owner regarded with a look of mingled reverence, pride, and delight. "It represents", he said, "the chosen crest of our family." He carefully decanted a cobwebbed bottle of claret into the goblet, which held nearly an English pint ... and devoutly quaffed the contents of the Blessed Bear of Brawardine.'

The goblet thereafter made the round of the company.

In a note to the novel Scott explains:

'The Poculum Potatorium of the valiant Baron, his Blessed Bear, has a prototype at the fine old Castle of Glammis, so rich in memorials of ancient times; it is a massive beaker of silver, double gilt, moulded into the shape of a lion, and holding about an English pint of wine. The form alludes to the family name of Strathmore, which is Lyon, and, when exhibited, the form must necessarily be emptied to the Earl's health. The author ought perhaps to be ashamed of recording that he has had the honour of swallowing the contents of the lion; and the recollection of the feat served to suggest the story of the Bear of Brawardine.

'In the family of Scott of Thirlestane (not Thirlestane in the Forest, but the place of the same name in Roxburghshire) was long preserved a cup of the same kind, in the form of a jack-boot. Each guest was obliged to empty this at his departure. If the guest's name was Scott, the necessity was doubly imperative.'

Another famous drinking vessel is (or was) the Cup of St Magnus, which was long preserved in Kirkwall. George Buchanan speaks of it and mentions its ample dimensions. It was presented, filled with strong ale—according to Hector Boece the Orkney ale was 'the starkest ale of Albion'—to each incoming Bishop of Orkney on his arrival at Scapa. Omens were deduced from the way in which he disposed of the drink. If he was able to quaff it in one draught—which, says Scott in a note to *The Pirate*, was a task for Hercules or Rorie Mhor of Dunvegan—the omen boded a crop of unusual fertility.

'What a blow at our craftsmen was the eclipse of the arts of hospitality!' writes Ian Finlay; 'what a stroke at the worker in silver or pottery or glass! One is forever criticized as a sentimentalist if one looks over one's shoulder nostalgically at some manner or custom of past ages, but progress is not leaving the past behind but keeping alive the best in it and blending it with the best we can do—which is little enough. . . . We look with horror at the toping of our ancestors, and we are quite right to do so; but in our virtuous aversion we are apt to forget we have lost their gargantuan hunger for life—a hunger which, crude as it was, carried with it a prolific culture ranging from the master-pieces of Burns and Scott and Raeburn down to the tankards and punch-bowls and ladles which still clutter our antique shops. How Dickens and Daumier would have fallen with glee on that institution of ours, the sherry party!—on its Miss Pecksniffian sipping and nibbling and arch giggling over thimble glasses brought from Czechoslovakia and chippolatas supplied ready skewered by the store round the corner! Even the Pecksniffs were hearty when they fell upon the punch.'

We have still good craftsmen in both silver and glass ware, but they are engaged chiefly in the reproduction of traditional designs and produce little that reflects contemporary taste or feeling. A few artists, however, are engaged in glass engraving and there are indications that the manufacture of glass ware in Scotland is likely to achieve greater importance than ever before. There are movements, too, for reviving silver, pottery and other hand-crafts, but the efforts of committees, however admirable, cannot alone dispel the inertia produced in the community by the dead routine of the factory and the office desk. 'I believe'—I quote Mr Finlay again—'there will always be an urge towards craftsman-ship where there is well-being and vitality, because it is in the nature of a healthy man to want to make things, and make them well.' In a word, if in the new Scotland we succeed in giving the people that 'fullness of life' to which they are entitled, the crafts will look after themselves.

A Note on the Choice and Care of Glasses

Fine glasses add considerably to the enjoyment of fine wines. Thick glasses should be avoided, and so should coloured ones, for only through clear glasses can one enjoy the beauty of colour —the pure gold, the tawny yellow, the ruby red of the wines. Glasses should not be too small, nor should they be filled to the brim. After use they should be carefully washed, dried with a spotlessly clean cloth, and polished with another dry one. They should not be left bowl downwards for any length of time, or they will acquire a musty smell which will communicate itself to the wine. So let your glasses be spotlessly clean, sweet-smelling and glittering.

Robert Louis Stevenson loved polishing glasses for his parties in Samoa. Gentlemen, please note!

7: *Convivial and Bacchanalian Songs and Poems*

'Let every good fellow now fill up his glass: *Vive la compagnie!*'

It is natural to love good company and the 'social glass', as Burns calls it, and it is fun to sing convivial songs in chorus; but the man who delights in such things must never sacrifice good sense to indulgence. Drinking songs are not to be sung on all occasions or in all companies—never, it has been wisely said, when they might add a spur where a rein is more necessary, or when they might be construed to fling a pseudo-halo on the vice of drunkenness.

John Stuart Blackie, Professor of Greek in the University of Edinburgh and founder of its Celtic chair, was a kenspeckle figure in Victorian Edinburgh with his clear-cut features, his silvery locks, his black wideawake hat, and the plaid of shepherd's tartan flung over his shoulder. Like so many Scots of his period, he was almost as much at home in a German as in a Scottish University. Now the singing of convivial songs is a tradition among the students of both countries, and Blackie, who loved songs and singing, used his opportunities to study the prevalence and social significance of the drinking songs in which Germany is so rich. Whilst some of the songs in this class are admittedly unedifying, many, he points out, are saved from cheapness and vulgarity by an element of philosophy, or by the portrayal of scene, situation or character, or again by sheer humour. There are songs that amuse us with an exhibition of human frailty which, if seriously treated would distress, and possibly even disgust us. As an admirable example of the humorous fashion of treating the drinker who 'has lost the sober use of his senses in the titillation of his nerves', or, in more homely phrase, 'has a drappie in his ee', he cites the well-known German student song *Gerad aus dem Wirtshaus*, in which the hero, on emerging from the tavern, is astonished to find the streets inverted, the moon making faces, the street lamps reeling, and only himself sober.

'Let us see', he writes, 'what crop of the same free revelry Scotland produces. And here, no doubt, one might be inclined to think, reasoning *a priori*, that a country of such severe religiosity and stern Sabbatic exercise [the period is the eighteen-eighties] would shrink from the exhibition of those purple blossoms of redundant vital enjoyment which drinking songs contain. But it is not so. Rather the contrary. Nature is mighty, and will leap forth on the Monday with a more violent bound in proportion as the repressive force of the Sunday had been severe. Of this we have an admirable example in the song, "Willie wi his Wig Agee".'[1]

Scotland has, for her size, a remarkable collection of drinking and convivial songs. Some, chiefly anonymous, date from at least the sixteenth century, and it is not surprising, considering the national flair for conviviality, that almost all our leading men of letters as well as many minor poets have contributed to the common stock.

'One of the strongest recurring strains in Scots poetry,' writes Mr Harvey Wood, 'is the poetry of revelry or of festive occasions —betrothals, bridals, fairs, and holidays, races and games. This is a natural theme in the literature of a small country, with a scattered and mainly rural population, where the community meets but seldom for such memorable occasions as these. The earliest surviving examples of this literature, the fifteenth-century "Peblis to the Play" and "Christis Kirk on the Green", though they commemorate popular celebrations, are, if tradition is to be believed, of royal authorship; but this is in no way exceptional or remarkable. It will be found that most of this popular Scots literature is of aristocratic origin—a pleasing testimony to the integrated character of Scots society before the Industrial Revolution. When what was in the main an agrarian population came to be centred in industrial areas, the significance of these local festivals disappeared, and the literature in which they were celebrated came to an end; but well into the nineteenth century the

1. *Scottish Song.*

K

theme survived. "The Blythsome Bridal" in Watson's *Choice Collection* (1706) revived the tradition, after the long and arid interval of the religious troubles, and thereafter in Fergusson's "Hallow Fair" and "Leith Races", Burns's "Holy Fair", and Tennant's "Anster Fair" (1811) it was continued and developed.'

Most of these poems are too long for inclusion in this brief anthology, and even of the shorter ones it has been possible to give only a selection. Among these are extracts from the work of Fergusson and Burns, which, as Sydney Goodsir Smith points out, is 'essentially bucolic and Bacchanalian in character' and 'immediately related to the contemporary folk festivals, fairs and rustic holidays which still expressed and renewed the essential jollity of a peasant folk in accord with the seasonal rhythms'.[1]

The stupidity, folly, and ludicrously human aspect of dram-drinking was never more tellingly displayed than in 'Tam o Shanter', where the heated imagination of a 'bletherin', blusterin', drunken blellum' runs riot, and 'there are no better bottle songs,' says John Buchan, 'than the three masterpieces of Burns.' These are, of course, 'Willie Brew'd a Peck o Maut', 'Contented wi' Little', and 'Gudewife, Count the Lawin' '. Buchan also finds 'a rich fescennine humour' in those 'deplorable ditties', 'Todlen Hame' and 'Hoolie and Fairly'; and adds, 'The moralists may shake their heads over "The Orgiasts", but Sir John Falstaff would have approved.'[2]

Curiously, there are comparatively few drinking songs in Gaelic, that is so rich in songs of love and labour and is concerned with practically all human interests and activities. Among the most notable are 'Oran Rioghail a' Bhotuil' (The Royal Convivial Song), by Alexander MacDonald (Alasdair MacMhaighstir Alasdair) and Duncan Ban MacIntyre's 'Oran a' Bhotuil' (Bottle Song). As Gaelic readers are few, I do not include any of them, but I give a list at the end, indicating where they are to be found.

The one Gaelic song I include (with music) is not a drinking song, but the well-known parting song, 'Oidhche Mhath Leibh' (Good Night to you), which in Gaelic circles, is sung as commonly as is 'Auld Lang Syne' elsewhere.

To quote John Stuart Blackie once again, 'The best drinking songs, where the social element prevails, are never sung by drunkards.'

1. *Robert Fergusson.*   2. *The Northern Muse.*

Here's to the Year that's awa

Words by John Dunlop

Here's to the year that's a-wa! We'll drink it in strong and in sma'! And here's to ilk bon-nie young lass-ie we lo'ed, While swift flew the year that's a-wa: And here's to ilk bon-nie young lass-ie we lo'ed, While swift flew the year that's a-wa.

Here's to the year that's awa!
We'll drink it in strong and in sma'!
And here's to ilk bonnie young lassie we lo'ed
While swift flew the year that's awa;
And here's to ilk bonnie young lassie we lo'ed
While swift flew the year that's awa.

Here's to the sodger who bled,
And the sailor who bravely did fa';
Their fame is alive, though their spirits are fled
On the wings o the year that's awa;
Their fame is alive, though their spirits are fled
On the wings o the year that's awa.

Here's to the friends we can trust
When the storms of adversity blaw;
May they live in our song and be nearest our heart,
Nor depart like the year that's awa;
May they live in our song and be nearest our heart,
Nor depart like the year that's awa.

John Dunlop (1755-1820)
(Lord Provost of Glasgow, 1796)

O Willie Brew'd a Peck o Maut

Words by Burns

O Willie brew'd a peck o maut,
    And Rob and Allan cam to pree;
Three blyther hearts, that lee-lang night,
    Ye wadna find in Christendie.

        We are na fou, we're nae that fou,
            But just a drappie in our ee;
        The cock may craw, the day may daw,
            And aye we'll taste the barley bree.

Here are we met, three merry boys,
    Three merry boys, I trow, are we;
And mony a night we've merry been,
    And mony mae we hope to be!

It is the moon—I ken her horn,
    That's blinkin' in the lift sae hie;
She shines sae bright to wyle us hame,
    But, by my sooth, she'll wait a wee!

Wha first shall rise to gang awa,
A cuckold coward loon is he!
Wha first beside his chair shall fa',
He is the king amang us three.

Robert Burns (1759–96)

Lee-lang, livelong; *fou*, drunk; *drappie*, little drop; *daw*, dawn; *bree*, brew;
mae, more; *lift*, sky; *wyle*, entice.

This song commemorates a merry meeting which Burns had at Moffat with
his old companion on his Highland tour, William Nicol, one of the masters at
the High School of Edinburgh, and Allan Masterton.

Contented wi' little

Contented wi' little, and cantie wi' mair,
Whene'er I foregather wi' sorrow and care,
I gie them a skelp as they're creepin' alang,
Wi' a cog o gude swats, and an auld Scottish sang.

I whyles claw the elbow o troublesome thought;
But man is a sodger, and life is a faught:
My mirth and gude humour are coin in my pouch,
And my freedom's my lairdship nae monarch dare touch.

A towmond o trouble, should that be my fa',
A night o gude fellowship sowthers it a'
When at the blythe end o our journey at last,
Wha the deil ever thinks o the road he has past!

Blind chance, let her snapper and stoyte on her way,
Be't to me, be't frae me, e'en let the jade gae:
Come ease, or come travail, come pleasure or pain,
My warst word is—Welcome, and welcome again!

Robert Burns

Cantie, jolly; *skelp*, whack; *cog o gude swats*, a pot of good new ale; *claw*, scratch;
sodger, soldier; *faught*, fight; *towmond*, twelvemonth; *fa'*, lot; *sowthers*, solders,
puts to rights; *snapper and stoyte*, stumble and stagger.

Blythe, blythe and merry are we,
  Blythe are we, ane and a';
Canty days we've aften seen,
  A nicht like this we never saw!

The gloamin' saw us a' sit doun,
  And meikle mirth has been our fa';
Then let the toast and sang gang roun'
  Till chanticleer begins to craw.
    Blythe, blythe and merry are we,
      Pick and wale o merry men;
    What care we though the cock may craw,
      We're masters o the tappit-hen!

The auld kirk bell has chappit twal'—
  Wha cares tho' she had chappit twa!
We're licht o heart and winna pairt
  Tho' time and tide may rin awa'.

Blythe, blythe and merry are we,
Hearts that care can never ding;
Then let time pass, we'll steal his glass,
And pu' a feather frae his wing.

Noo is the witchin' time o nicht
When ghaists, they say, are to be seen,
And fays dance to the glow-worm's licht
Wi' fairies in their gouns o green.
Blythe, blythe and merry are we—
Ghaists may tak their midnicht stroll;
Witches ride on brooms astride,
While we sit by the witchin' bowl.

Tut, never speir how wears the morn—
The mune's still blinkin' i' the sky,
And gif, like her, we fill our horn,
I dinna doubt we'll drink it dry.
Blythe, blythe and merry are we,
Blythe, out-owre the barley bree;
And let me tell, the mune hersel'
Aft dips her toom horn i' the sea!

Then fill us up a social cup,
And never mind the dapple dawn;
Just sit awhile, the sun may smile,
And syne we'll see the gait we're gaun.
Blythe, blythe and merry are we,
See, the sun is keekin' ben;
Gie time his glass—for months may pass
Ere sic a nicht we see again!

Charles Gray (Captain, R.M.)
(Written in 1814.)

Canty, cheerful; wale, choice; chappit, struck; ding, be cast down; speir, ask; gif, if; toom, empty; gait, way; keekin', peeping.

The deil cam fiddlin' throu' the toun,
  And danc'd awa wi' th' Exciseman;
And ilka wife cried, 'Auld Mahoun,
  I wish you luck o your prize, man!'
    The deil's awa, the deil's awa,
      The deil's awa wi' th' Exciseman;
    He's danc'd awa, he's danc'd awa,
      He's danc'd awa wi' th' Exciseman.

We'll mak our maut, we'll brew our drink,
  We'll dance, and sing, and rejoice, man;
And mony braw thanks to the meikle black deil
  That danc'd awa wi' th' Exciseman.
    The deil's awa, the deil's awa,
      The deil's awa wi' th' Exciseman;
    He's danc'd awa, he's danc'd awa,
      He's danc'd awa wi' th' Exciseman!

There's threesome reels, there's foursome reels,
There's hornpipes and strathspeys, man;
But the ae best dance e'er cam to the land
Was—the deil's awa wi' th' Exciseman.
The deil's awa, the deil's awa,
The deil's awa wi' th' Exciseman;
He's danc'd awa, he's danc'd awa,
He's danc'd awa wi' th' Exciseman!

Robert Burns

Deil, devil; *ilka*, every; *maut*, malt; *ae*, one.

Gudewife, count the lawin

Gane is the day, and mirk's the night,
But we'll ne'er stray for faut o light,
For ale and brandy's stars and moon,
And blude-red wine's the risin' sun.

Then, gudewife, count the lawin,
The lawin, the lawin;
Then, gudewife, count the lawin,
And bring a cogie mair.

There's wealth and ease for gentlemen,
And semple-folk maun fecht and fen';
But here we're a' in ae accord,
For ilka man that's drunk's a lord.

My cogie is a haly pool,
That heals the wounds o care and dool;
And pleasure is a wanton trout—
An ye drink but deep, ye'll find him out.

Robert Burns

Lawin, reckoning; *mirk*, dark; *faut*, lack; *cogie*, drinking cup; *semple*, simple;
fecht and fen', fight and fend for themselves; *haly*, holy; *dool*, sorrow; *an*, if.

HAPPY WE ARE A' THEGITHER

Anon.

Here around the ingle bleezin',
    Wha sae happy and sae free?
Tho' the northern wind blaws freezin',
    Frien'ship warms baith you and me.

        Happy we are a' thegither,
            Happy we'll be, ane an' a';
        Time shall see us a' the blyther
            Ere we rise to gang awa.

See the miser o'er his treasure
    Gloatin' wi' a greedy ee!
Can he feel the glow o pleasure
    That around us here we see?

Thus then let us a' be tassin'
    Aff our stoups o gen'rous flame;
And while roun' the board 'tis passin',
    Raise a sang in frien'ship's name.

Frien'ship maks us a' mair happy,
  Frien'ship gies us a' delight;
Frien'ship consecrates the drappie,
  Frien'ship brings us here the night.

Happy we are a' thegither,
  Happy we've been, ane an' a';
Time shall find us a' the blyther
  Ere we rise to gang awa.

Anon.

Advice to leesome merriness

When I have done consider
  This warldis vanitie,
Sa brukil and sa slidder,
  Sa full of miserie;
  Then I remember me
That here there is no rest;
  Therefore apparentlie
To be merrie is best.

Let us be blyth and glad,
  My friendis all, I pray.
To be pensive and sad
  Na thing it help us may.
  Therefore put quite away
All heaviness of thocht:
  Thoch we murne nicht and day
It will avail us nocht.

Sir Richard Maitland (1496-1586)

Leesome, lawful; *brukil*, uncertain, unreliable; *slidder*, deceitful; **thoch,** though.

Good Night an' Joy be wi' ye a'

Words by James Hogg

The year is wear-in' to the wane, An' day is fad-in' west awa! Loud raves the tor-rent an' the rain An' dark the cloud comes doun the shaw. But let the tem-pest tout and blaw, Up-on his loud-est win-ter horn, Good night and joy be wi' ye a', We'll may-be meet a-gain the morn.

The year is wearin' to the wane,
  An' day is fadin' west awa;
Loud raves the torrent an' the rain,
  An' dark the cloud comes doun the shaw.
But let the tempest tout an' blaw,
  Upon his loudest winter horn,
Good night, an' joy be wi' ye a'—
  We'll maybe meet again the morn.

O we hae wandered far an' wide,
  O'er Scotia's land o firth an' fell,
An' mony a simple flo'er we've culled,
  An' twined them wi' the heather-bell:
We've ranged the dingle and the dell,
  The hamlet an' the baron's ha';
Now let us tak a kind farewell—
  Good night, an' joy be wi' ye a'!

Ye hae been kind as I was keen,
 An' followed where I led the way,
Till ilka poet's lore we've seen
 O this an' mony a former day.
If e'er I led your steps astray,
 Forgi'e your minstrel ance for a';
A tear fa's wi' his partin' lay—
 Good night, an' joy be wi' ye a'!

James Hogg, The Ettrick Shepherd (1770-1835)

Shaw, thicket; *tout*, trumpet; *ilka*, every; *ance for a'*, once for all.

from *Will ye no come back again?*

Bonnie Charlie's noo awa,
 Safely owre the friendly main;
Mony a heart will brak in twa,
 Should he ne'er come back again.
  Will ye no come back again?
  Will ye no come back again?
  Better lo'ed ye canna be:
  Will ye no come back again?

Ye trusted in your Hielan' men;
 They trusted you, dear Charlie;
They kent your hidin' in the glen;
 Your cleadin' was but barely.
  Will ye no, etc.

Sweet the laverock's note an' lang,
 Liltin' wildly up the glen,
But aye to me he sings ae sang:
 Will ye no come back again?
  Will ye no, etc.

Lady Nairne (1766-1845)

Cleadin', clothing; *laverock*, lark.

This is commonly sung as a parting song for a well-loved guest.

Oidhche Mhath Leibh
(Good Night   A Parting Song)
Words by John MacFadyan

Soiridh leibh 'us oidhche mhath leibh,
Oidhche mhath leibh, beannachd leibh;
Guidheam slàinte ghnàth bhi mar ruibh;
Oidhche mhath leibh, beannachd leibh.

Cha'n 'eil inneal ciùil a ghleusar,
Dhuisgeas smuain mo chléibh gu aoibh,
Mar ni duan o bheòil nan caileag;
Oidhche mhath leibh, beannachd leibh.
      Soiridh leibh, etc.

'S guth gu m' chridhe pong nan òran,
Caidir sòlais òigridh 'seinn;
Aiteal ciùin air làithean m' òige;
Sonas a bhi 'n còmhnuidh leibh.
      Soiridh leibh, etc.

Mathair uisge 'n tobair fhìoruisg',
Cainnt ar sinnsir brìgh na loinn;
'S faochadh tlàth o ànradh m' inntinn,
'Nuair bheir rann na glinn a'm chuimhn',
    Soiridh leibh, etc.

Grian cha laidh an nochd air mìltean,
Leis am binn a fuinn 's a roinn,
'S do'm bi'n sgeul 'na mhòr thoil-inntinn
Dh'innseas dhaibh gu'n robh sinn cruinn.
    Soiridh leibh, etc.

Astar cuain cha dean ar sgaradh,
'S dùrachd daimh am bannaibh toinnt';
Gleidh an t-àgh na dh'fhàg a bheannachd;
Oidhche mhath leibh, beannachd leibh,
    Soiridh leibh, etc.

Thuit ar crann air saoghal carach;
'S coma sud, tha 'mhaitheas leinn;
'Bidh sinn béo an dòchas ra-mhath,'
Oidhche mhath leibh, beannachd leibh.
    Soiridh leibh, etc.

John MacFadyan

from *Maclean's welcome*

Come o'er the stream, Charlie,
Dear Charlie, brave Charlie,
Come o'er the stream, Charlie,
    And dine with Maclean;
And you shall drink freely
The dews of Glen-sheerly,
That stream in the starlight
    That kings do not ken;
And deep be your meed
Of the wine that is red,
To drink to your sire
    And his friend the Maclean.

(From the Gaelic)   *James Hogg, the Ettrick Shepherd*

Should auld acquaintance be forgot,
  And never brought to mind?
Should auld acquaintance be forgot,
  And days o auld lang syne?
      For auld lang syne my Dear,
      For auld lang syne,
      We'll tak a cup o kindness yet,
      For auld lang syne.

We twa hae run about the braes,
  An pu'd the gowans fine;
But we've wandered mony a weary fit
  Sin auld lang syne.

We twa hae paidl'd i' the burn,
  Frae morning sun till dine;
But seas between us braid hae roar'd
  Sin auld lang syne.

And there's a hand, my trusty fiere,
    An' gie's a hand o thine;
And we'll tak' a richt gude-willie waught
    For auld lang syne.

And surely ye'll be your pint-stoup,
    An' surely I'll be mine;
And we'll tak a cup o kindness yet,
    For auld lang syne.

Robert Burns

Auld lang syne, long ago; *braes*, hill-slopes; *gowans*, daisies; *burn*, brook; *braid*, broad; *fiere*, comrade; *gude-willie waught*, a hearty draught, drunk in friendship.

'Auld Lang Syne' was based on an anonymous verse which Burns took down from an old man's singing, and which so enchanted him that he wrote: 'Light be the earth on the breast of the Heaven-inspired poet who composed this glorious fragment.' Little did he think as he worked at the happy task of converting the fragment into a complete poem that he was writing what was destined to become the most widely sung song in the world. 'Auld Lang Syne' has been, and is still being translated into one language after another, including Russian and Japanese, and is fast becoming recognized as a sort of international anthem of good fellowship and good will.

It is to be deplored that the song is so often mumbled and messed up by a haphazard collection of people who do not trouble to learn the words of even the very simple chorus, which is, in fact, all they need to know. It is advisable to entrust the verses to a picked and reliable singer, or, better still, to four singing in parts, and let the company reserve its energies for the recurrent and final chorus, which breaks off into a vociferous 'three cheers'.

A word on the pronunciation. It is really extremely simple. *Auld Lang Syne* is *not* pronounced *Old Long Zyne*. *Auld* rhymes with *bald*; *lang* rhymes with *pang* (the *a* slightly broader); and the *s* in *syne* is sibilant, as in *since*. Three words of one syllable should not be hard to master!

Now a word on the simple ritual. The company form a circle, join hands, and remain thus, without swinging their arms, while the first three verses—or the first verse only, for the second and third are often omitted—are sung. On reaching the fourth verse, which begins, 'An' there's a hand, my trusty fiere', they advance a few steps (thus contracting the circle), unclasp hands, cross their arms in front and clasp the hands of their companions on either side. During the chorus, they move their hands rhythmically up and down, and when the climax is reached, unclasp them once more and give three hearty cheers.

To quote William Power: 'Fortune gave us the greatest of the world's songwriters, who gave the world its best convivial songs. Why not show ourselves worthy of the honour?'

L

Quha hes guid malt

Quha hes guid malt and makis ill drink,
   Wo mot be hir weird!
I pray to God scho rot and stink
   Sevin yeir abune the erd.
About hir beir na bell to clink,
   Nor clerk sing, lewed or leird,
Bot quik to Hell that scho may sink,
   The taptre quhile scho steir'd:
     This beis my prayer,
     For that man-slayer,
   Quhilk Christ in Hevin sal heird.

Quha brewis and givis me of the best,
   Sa be it stark and staill,
Baith quhyte and cleir, weil to digest,
   In Hevin meit hir that aill!
Lang mot scho leve, lang mot scho lest
   In lyking and gude saill;
In Hevin or erd that wife be blest
   Without barret or baill;
     Quhen scho is deid,
     Withouten pleid,
   Scho pass to Hevin all haill.

        Anon. (*Probably early sixteenth century*)

Quha, who; *wo mot be hir weird*, may woe be her destiny, ill befall her; *scho*, she; *abune*, above; *erd*, earth; *lewed or leird*, unlearned or learned; *taptre*, spiggot; *steir'd*, was pulling out; *quhilk*, which; *heird*, hear; *stark*, strong; *staill*, old; *baith*, both; *quhyte*, white; *meit*, meet; *leve*, live; *lest*, last; *lyking*, pleasure; *gude saill*, happiness; *barret*, tribulation; *baill*, sorrow; *quhen*, when; *pleid*, debate.

Gude ale hauds my hert abune

O gude ale comes and gude ale goes,
Gude ale gars me sell my hose,
Sell my hose and pawn my shoon,
Gude ale hauds my hert abune.
Gude ale keeps me bare and busy,
Brandy makes me dull and dizzy,
Gars me sleep and sough i' my shoon,
Gude ale hauds my hert abune.

O in the sweetest plumbs there's stanes,
And in the fairest beef there's banes;
Rum turns ye rude, wine makes ye pale,
There's life and love and soul in ale;
Gude ale's the medicine aften spae'd o,
The very stuff that life is made o,
Dropt in a receipt frae the mune,
To haud men's sinking herts abune.

May he rub shoulders wi' the gallows,
Wha wad keep gude ale frae gude fallows;
May he gape wide when suns are south,
And never drink come near his drouth;
But here's to him, where'er he roam,
Wha loves to see the flagons foam,
For he's a king o'er lord and loon—
Gude ale hauds my hert abune.

Anon.

Hauds my hert abune, keeps my heart up; *gars*, makes; *sough*, sigh; *spae'd*, prophesied; *drouth*, thirst.

Todlen hame

When I hae a saxpence under my thoomb,
Then I get credit in ilka toun,
But aye when I'm puir they bid me gang by;
O! poverty parts gude companie.
    Todlen hame, todlen hame,
    Cou'dna my luv come todlen hame?

Fair fa' the gudewife, and send her gude sale,
She gies us white bannocks to relish her ale;
Syne, if that her tippenny chance to be sma',
We'll tak a gude scour o't, and ca't awa.
    Todlen hame, todlen hame,
    As round as a neep come todlen hame.

My kimmer and I lay doun to sleep,
And twa pint-stoups at our bed's feet;
And aye when we waukened, we drank them dry:
What think ye o my wee kimmer and I?
    Todlen but and todlen ben,
      Sae round as my luv comes todlen hame.

Leeze me on liquor, my todlen doo,
Ye're aye sae good-humoured when weetin' your mou;
When sober sae sour, ye'll fecht wi' a flee,
That 'tis a blyth sicht to the bairns and me,
    When todlen hame, todlen hame,
      When round as a neep ye come todlen hame.

Anon. (From *The Tea-Table Miscellany*)

Todlen hame, toddling home; *fair fa'*, good luck befall; *tippeny*, twopenny ale;
scour, draught; *ca't awa*, drink it up; *neep*, turnip; *kimmer*, young woman;
todlen but and todlen ben, toddling through the house; *leeze me*, blessings; *doo*, dove
neep, turnip.

from *Hooly and fairly*

or *The drucken wife o Galloway*

Doun in yon meadow a couple did tarry:
The wife she drank naethin' but sack and canary;
The gudeman complained to her kimmers richt sairly—
Oh, gin my gudewife wad drink hooly and fairly!

    Hooly and fairly, hooly and fairly,
      Oh, gin my gudewife wad drink hooly and fairly!

First she drank Crummie and then she drank Gairie,
Syne she has drucken my bonnie grey mairie,
That carried me thro' a' the dubs and the glairie—
Oh, gin my wife wad drink hooly and fairly!

She has drucken her hose, she has drucken her shoon,
Her snawy white mutch and her bonnie new goun,
Her sark o the hollans that covered her rarely—
Oh gin my wife wad drink hooly and fairly!

Wad she drink but her ain things, I wadna much care,
But she drinks a' the claes that I canna weel spare;
When I'm wi' my gossips it angers me sairly—
Oh, gin my wife wad drink hooly and fairly!

My new Sunday's coat, she has laid it in wad,
And the gaucy blue bonnet that covered my heid;
To kirk or to mercat I'm forced to gang barely—
Oh, gin my wife wad drink hooly and fairly!

A pint wi' her kimmers I wad her allow,
But when she sits doun, she gets hersel' fou,
And when she is fou she is unco camstairie—
Oh, gin my wife wad drink hooly and fairly!

Hooly and fairly, hooly and fairly,
Oh, gin my gudewife wad drink hooly and fairly!

Anon.

Hooly and fairly, moderately and quietly; *sairly*, sorely; *gin*, if; *syne*, then; *dubs*, puddles; *glairie*, mud; *sark*, chemise; *claes*, clothes; *wad*, pawn; *gaucy*, comfortable; *camstairie*, unmanageable.

Andro wi' his cutty gun

Blyth, blyth, blyth was she,
  Blyth was she but and ben;
And weel she lo'ed a Hawick gill,
  And leugh to see a tappit-hen.
She took me in and set me doun,
  And hecht to keep me lawin-free;
But, cunnin' carline that she was,
  She gart me birl my bawbee.

We lo'ed the liquor weel eneuch,
  But, wae's my hert, the cash was dune
Before that I had quenched my drouth,
  And laith was I to pawn my shoon.
When we had three times toomed our stoop,
  And the neist chapin new begun,
Wha started in to heeze our hope
  But Andro wi' his cutty gun.

The carline brocht her kebbuck ben
   Wi' knuckled cakes weel brander'd broun;
Weel does the canny kimmer ken
   They gar the swats gae glibber doun.
We ca'd the bicker aft about,
   Till dawnin' we ne'er jee'd our bum,
And aye the cleanest drinker oot
   Was Andro wi' his cutty gun.

He did like ony mavis sing,
   And as I in his oxter sat,
He ca'd me aye his bonnie thing,
   And mony a sappy kiss I got.
I hae been east, I hae been west,
   I hae been far ayont the sun;
But the blythest lad that e'er I saw
   Was Andro wi' his cutty gun.

                         Anon.

Cutty gun, short clay pipe; *leugh*, laughed; *hecht*, promised; *lawin*, reckoning; *carline*, old woman; *gart*, made; *birl*, spin; *birl my bawbee*, spend my cash; *chapin*, quart; *heeze*, raise; *kebbuck*, cheese; *knuckled cakes*, cakes flattened out with the knuckles, without the use of a rolling-pin; *brandered*, fired on the brander, a barred girdle; *swats*, new ale; *glibber*, more smoothly; *jee'd our bum*, moved our seat; *mavis*, thrush; *in his oxter*, with his arm around me.

The Orgiasts

1. *The merry widower*

      O fare ye weel, my auld wife!
         Sing bum, biberry bum.
      O fare ye weel, my auld wife!
         Sing bum.
      O fare ye weel, my auld wife,
      Thou steerer up o sturt and strife!
      The maut's abune the meal the nicht
         Wi' some.

And fare ye weel, my pike-staff!
   Sing bum, biberry bum.
And fare ye weel, my pike-staff!
   Sing bum.
And fare ye weel, my pike-staff—
Nae mair wi' thee my wife I'll baff!
The maut's abune the meal the nicht
   Wi' some.

Fu' white white was her winding-sheet!
   Sing bum, biberry bum.
Fu' white white was her winding-sheet!
   Sing bum.
I was owre gladsome for to greet,
I danced my lane, and sang to see't—
The maut's abune the meal the nicht
   Wi' some.

Anon.

Steerer, stirrer; *sturt*, conflict; *baff*, beat; *greet*, weep; *my lane*, alone.

2. *Sic a parish*

Was there ere sic a parish, a parish, a parish,
   Was there ere sic a parish as Little Dunkeld?
They've stickit the minister, hanged the precentor,
   Dung doun the steeple, and drucken the bell!

Anon.

Stickit, stabbed; *dung*, knocked.

3. *We're a' dry*

We're a' dry wi' the drinkin' o't,
We're a' dry wi' the drinkin' o't,
The minister kissed the fiddler's wife,
And he couldna preach for thinkin' o't.

Anon.

The mautman

Bring a' your maut to me!
Bring a' your maut to me!
My draff ye'se get for ae pund ane,
    Tho' a' my deukies should dee.

Some say that kissing's a sin,
    But I think it's nane ava,
For kissing has wonn'd in this world,
    Since ever that there was twa.

O, if it wasna lawfu',
    Lawyers wadna allow it;
If it wasna holy,
    Ministers wadna do it.

If it wasna modest,
    Maidens wadna tak it;
If it wasna plenty,
    Puir folk wadna get it.

Bring a' your maut to me!
Bring a' your maut to me!
My draff ye'se get for ae pund ane,
    Though a' my deukies should dee.

> Anon. The chorus appears in a seventeenth
> century MS, the verses in Chambers's
> Scottish Songs (1829).

Draff, the refuse of malt that has been brewed from; *deukies*, ducklings; *ava*, at all; *wonn'd*, dwelt.

In praise of claret

The dull draff-drink maks me sae dowff,
A' I can do's but bark and yowff;
Yet set me in a claret howff
        Wi' folk that's chancy,
My muse may len' me then a gowff
        To clear my fancy.

Then Bacchus-like I'd bawl and bluster,
And a' the Muses 'bout me muster,
Sae merrily I'd squeeze the cluster,
    And drink the grape,
'T wad gi'e my verse a brighter lustre,
    And better shape.

William Hamilton of Gilbertfield (1665-1751)

Draff-drink, inferior whisky; *dowff*, dull, spiritless; *yowff*, give short, sharp barks; *howff*, a haunt, resort, tavern; *chancy*, lucky, bringing good luck; *gowff*, blow, cuff.

The tappit-hen

Vides ut alta stet nive candidum Soracte—Horace

Look up to Pentland's tow'ring tap,
    Buried beneath great wreaths of snaw,
Owre ilka cleugh, ilk scar and slap,
    As high as ony Roman wa'.

Driving their ba's frae whins or tee,
    There's no ae gowfer to be seen,
Nor doucer folk wysing a-jee
    The byass bouls on Tamson's green.

Then fling on coals, and ripe the ribs,
    And beik the house baith but and ben:
That mutchkin stoup it hauds but dribs,
    Then let's get in the tappit-hen.

Gude claret best keeps out the cauld,
    And drives away the winter soon;
It maks a man baith gash and bauld,
    And heaves his saul beyond the mune.

Let neist day comes as it thinks fit,
  The present minute's only ours:
On pleasure let's employ our wit,
  And laugh at Fortune's feckless powers.

Allan Ramsay (c. 1685-1758): From *To the Ph——*, *An ode*

Cleugh, cleft between rocks; *scar*, bare slope; *slap*, pass between hills; *gowfer*, golfer; *wysing a-jee*, inclining to one side; *byass bouls*, bowls (game of); *ripe the ribs*, rake the bars; *beik*, warm (v.); *mutchkin*, an Imperial pint; *hauds*, holds; *dribs*, driblets; *gash*, lively, talkative; *neist*, next; *feckless*, feeble, spiritless.

On a punch-bowl

Charge me with Nantz and limpid spring,
  Let sour and sweet be mixt;
Bend round a health, syne to the King,
  To Edinburgh's captains next,
Wha formed me in sae blyth a shape,
  And gave me lasting honours,
Take up my ladle, fill, and lape,
  And say, Fair fa' the donors.

Allan Ramsay

Lape, drink; *fair fa'*, good luck to.

from *Tullochgorum*

Come, gie's a sang, Montgomery cried,
And lay your disputes a' aside.
What signifies't for folks to chide
  For what's been done before them?
Let Whig and Tory a' agree,
Whig and Tory, Whig and Tory,
Let Whig and Tory a' agree
  To drop their Whig-mig-morum;
Let Whig and Tory a' agree
To spend the night in mirth and glee,
And cheerfu' sing alang wi' me
  The reel o Tullochgorum.

O Tullochgorum's my delight,
It gars us a' in ane unite,
And ony sumph that keeps up spite,
   In conscience I abhor him.
For blythe and cheerie we'se be a',
Blythe and cheerie, blythe and cheerie,
Blythe and cheerie we'se be a',
   And mak' a happy quorum.
For blythe and cheerie we's be a'
As lang as we hae breath to draw,
And dance, till we be like to fa',
   The reel o Tullochgorum.

There needs na be sae great a phraise
Wi' dringin' dull Italian lays,
I wadna gie our ain strathspeys
   For half a hundred score o 'em.
They're douff and dowie at the best,
   Douff and dowie, douff and dowie,
They're douff and dowie at the best,
   Wi a' their variorum:
They're douff and dowie at the best,
Their allegros, and a' the rest,
They canna please a Scottish taste
   Compar'd wi' Tullochgorum.

Let wardly minds themselves oppress
Wi' fears o want, and double cess,
And sullen sots themselves distress
   Wi' keepin' up decorum:
Shall we sour and sulky sit,
Sour and sulky, sour and sulky,
Shall we sour and sulky sit,
   Like auld Philosophorum?
Shall we sour and sulky sit,
Wi' neither sense, nor mirth nor wit,
Nor ever rise to shake a fit
   To the reel o Tullochgorum?

> Rev. John Skinner (1721-1807), Episcopal minister at
> Longside, Aberdeenshire

Sumph, surly fool; *phraise*, fuss, ado; *dringin'*, slow, lugubrious; *dowff*, dull;
dowie, sad, drooping; *cess*, tax.

Cauld kail in Aberdeen[1]

There's cauld kail in Aberdeen,
    An' custocks in Stra'bogie,
Whaur ilka lad maun hae his lass,
    But I maun hae my cogie.
For I maun hae my cogie, sirs,
    I canna want my cogie;
I wadna gie my three-girr'd cog
    For a' the wives in Bogie.

There's Johnnie Smith has got a wife
    Wha scrimps him o his cogie;
But were she mine, upon my life,
    I'd dook her in a bogie.
For I maun hae my cogie, sirs,
    I canna want my cogie;
I wadna gie my three-girr'd cog
    For a' the wives in Bogie.

An' twa-three toddlin' weans they hae,
    The pride o a' Strathbogie,
Whene'er the totums cry for meat,
    She curses aye his cogie;
Cryin', 'Wae betide the three-girr'd cog!
    O wae betide the cogie!
It does mair skaith than a' the ills
    That happen in Stra'bogie.'

She fand him aince at Willie Sharp's,
    An' what they maist did laugh at,
She brak the bicker, spilt the drink,
    An' tightly cuffed his haffet;
Cryin', 'Wae betide the three-girr'd cog!
    O wae betide the cogie!
It does mair skaith than a' the ills
    That happen in Stra'bogie!'

1. Mentioned by Burns as an old song.

Yet here's to ilka honest soul
　　Wha'll drink wi' me a cogie;
And for ilk silly, whingin' fule,
　　We'll dook him in a bogie.
For I maun hae my cogie, sirs,
　　I canna want my cogie;
I wadna gie my three-girr'd cog
　　For a' the wives in Bogie.

　　　　　　　　　　　　　　　Anon.

Custocks, cabbage stocks; *cogie*, drinking cup; *three-girred*, three-hooped; *dook*, duck; *bogie*, marsh, peat-bog; *weans*, children; *skaith*, damage; *haffet*, side of the face; *whinging*, whining.

from another version

There's cauld kail in Aberdeen,
　　And castocks in Stra'bogie;
Gin I hae but a bonnie lass,
　　Ye're welcome to your cogie.
And ye may sit up a' the nicht,
And drink till it be braid daylicht;
Gi'e me a lass baith clean and ticht,
　　To dance the reel o Bogie.

In cotillons the French excel,
　　John Bull loves country dances;
The Spaniards dance fandangoes well,
　　Mynheer an all'mande prances.
In foursome reels the Scots delight,
At threesomes they dance wondrous light,
But twaesomes ding a' oot o sight,
　　Danc'd to the reel o Bogie.

Come, lads, and view your partners weel,
　　Wale each a blythsome rogie;
I'll tak this lassie to masel',
　　She looks sae keen and vogie.
Now, piper lad, bang up the spring,
The country fashion is the thing,
To pree their mous ere we begin
　　To dance the reel o Bogie.

Now a' the lads hae done their best,
    Like true men o Stra'bogie;
We'll stop a while an' tak' a rest,
    And tipple out a cogie.
Come now, my lads, and tak your glass,
And try ilk ither to surpass,
In wishing health to every lass
    To dance the reel o Bogie.

Alexander, Duke of Gordon (1743-1821)

Braid, broad; *ding*, beat, excel; *wale*, choose; *vogie*, merry; *pree their mous*, kiss
them.

from *The daft days*

Auld Reekie! thou'rt a canty hole,
A bield for mony a cauldrife soul
Wha snugly at thine ingle loll
    Baith warm and couth,
While round they gar the bicker roll
    To weet their mouth.

When merry Yule-day comes, I trow,
You'll scantlins find a hungry mou;
Sma' are our cares, our stamacks fou
    O gusty gear,
And kickshaws, strangers to our view
    Sin' fairn-year.

Ye browster wives, now busk ye braw,
And fling your sorrows far awa;
Then come and gie's the tither blaw
    O reaming ale,
Mair precious than the well o Spa,
    Our hearts to heal.

Then, though at odds wi' a' the warl',
Amang oursels we'll never quarrel;
Though Discord gie a canker'd snarl
    To spoil our glee,
As lang's there's pith into the barrel
    We'll drink and gree.

Let mirth abound, let social cheer
Invest the dawning of the year;
Let blithesome innocence appear
    To crown our joy,
Nor envy wi' sarcastic sneer
    Our bliss destroy.

And thou, great god of *Aqua Vitae*!
Wha sways the empire of this city,
When fou, we're sometimes capernoity:
    Be thou prepared
To hedge us frae that black banditti,
    The City Guard.

O Muse, be kind and dinna fash us
To flee awa beyont Parnassus,
Nor seek for Helicon to wash us,
    That heath'nish spring!
Wi' Highland whisky scour our hawses,
    And gar us sing.

Robert Fergusson (1750-74)

Bield, shelter; *cauldrife*, chilly, feeling the cold; *couth*, friendly; *scantlins*, scarcely; *stamacks*, stomachs; *gusty*, appetising; *fairn-year*, last year; *browster wives*, ale-wives; *busk*, dress; *braw*, finely; *blaw*, a gorum of liquor; *reaming*, foaming; *gree*, agree; *capernoity*, peevish, bad-tempered; *hawses*, throats.

John Barleycorn

A Ballad

There was three kings into the east,
    Three kings both great and high,
And they hae sworn a solemn oath
    John Barleycorn should die.

They took a plough and plough'd him doun,
    Put clods upon his head,
And they hae sworn a solemn oath
    John Barleycorn was dead.

But the chearful spring came kindly on,
  And show'rs began to fall;
John Barleycorn got up again
  And sore surprised them all.

The sultry suns of summer came,
  And he grew thick and strong,
His head weel arm'd wi' pointed spears,
  That no one should him wrong.

The sober Autumn enter'd mild,
  When he grew wan and pale;
His bending joints and drooping head
  Show'd he began to fail.

His colour sickened more and more,
  He faded into age;
And then his enemies began
  To show their deadly rage.

They've ta'en a weapon long and sharp,
  And cut him by the knee;
Then ty'd him fast upon a cart,
  Like a rogue for forgerie.

They laid him down upon his back,
  And cudgell'd him full sore;
They hung him up before the storm,
  And turn'd him o'er and o'er.

They filled up a darksome pit
  With water to the brim,
They heaved in John Barleycorn,
  There let him sink or swim.

They laid him out upon the floor,
  To work him farther woe,
And still, as signs of life appear'd,
  They toss'd him to and fro'.

They wasted, o'er a scorching flame,
  The marrow of his bones;
But a Miller used him worst of all,
  For he crush'd him between two stones.

And they hae ta'en his very heart's blood,
    And drank it round and round;
And still the more and more they drank,
    Their joy did more abound.

John Barleycorn was a hero bold
    Of noble enterprise.
For if ye do but taste his blood,
    'Twill make your courage rise.

'Twill make a man forget his woe;
    'Twill heighten all his joy;
'Twill make the widow's heart to sing,
    Though the tear were in her eye.

Then let us toast John Barleycorn,
    Each man a glass in hand,
And may his great prosperity
    Ne'er fail in old Scotland.
                              Robert Burns

'This is partly composed on the plan of an old song known by the same name.'
R.B., 1787.

from *The Jolly Beggars*

When lyart leaves bestrow the yird,
Or wavering like the baukie-bird
    Bedim cauld Boreas' blast;
When hailstanes drive wi' bitter skyte,
And infant frosts begin to bite
    In hoary cranreuch drest;
Ae night at e'en a merry core
    O randie, gangrel bodies
In Poosie Nansy's held the splore,
    To drink their orra duddies:
        Wi' quaffing and laughing
            They ranted and they sang;
        Wi' jumping an' thumping
            The vera girdle rang.
                              Robert Burns

Lyart, grey, faded; *yird*, earth; *baukie-bird*, bat; *skyte*, a slanting blow; *cranreuch*,
frost; *core*, convivial company; *randie*, debauched; *gangrel*, vagabond; *splore*,
frolic; *orra*, odd, queer; *duddies*, rags; *ranted*, sang gaily.

M

from *Tam o Shanter*

When chapman billies leave the street,
And drouthy neebors neebors meet;
As market-days are wearin' late,
An' folk begin to tak the gate;
While we sit bousing at the nappy,
An' gettin' fou an' unco happy,
We think na on the lang Scots miles,
The mosses, waters, slaps and styles,
That lie between us and our hame,
Whare sits our sulky, sullen dame,
Gathering her brows like gathering storm,
Nursing her wrath to keep it warm.
   This truth fand honest Tam o Shanter,
As he frae Ayr ae nicht did canter
(Auld Ayr, wham ne'er a toun surpasses
For honest men an' bonny lasses.)

.   .   .   .

   But to our tale: Ae market night,
Tam had got planted unco right,
Fast by an ingle, bleezin' finely,
Wi' reamin' swats, that drank divinely;
An' at his elbow, Souter Johnie,
His ancient, trusty, drouthy crony;
Tam lo'ed him like a vera brither;
They had been fou for weeks thegither.
The night drave on wi' sangs an' clatter;
An' aye the ale was growing better:
The landlady and Tam grew gracious,
Wi' favours secret, sweet and precious;
The Souter tauld his queerest stories;
The landlord's laugh was ready chorus:
The storm without might rair and rustle—
Tam didna mind the storm a whistle.
   Care, mad to see a man sae happy,
E'en drown'd himsel' amang the nappy!
As bees flee hame wi' lades o treasure,
The minutes wing'd their way wi' pleasure:
Kings may be blest, but Tam was glorious,
O'er a' the ills o life victorious!

.   .   .   .

Nae man can tether time or tide;
The hour approaches Tam maun ride;
That hour, o night's black arch the key-stane,
That dreary hour he mounts his beast in;
An' sic a night he taks the road in
As ne'er poor sinner was abroad in.
    The wind blew as 'twad blawn its last;
The rattling show'rs rose on the blast;
The speedy gleams the darkness swallow'd;
Loud, deep and lang the thunder bellow'd;
That night, a child might understand
The Deil had business on his hand.
Weel mounted on his grey mare, Meg—
A better never lifted leg—
Tam skelpit on through dub and mire,
Despising wind, an' rain, an' fire;
Whiles holding fast his gude blew bonnet;
Whiles crooning o'er some auld Scots sonnet;
Whiles glow'ring round wi' prudent cares,
Lest bogles catch him unawares.

.   .   .   .

    Inspirin' bold John Barleycorn!
What dangers thou canst mak' us scorn!
Wi' tippeny, we fear nae evil,
Wi' usquabae, we'll face the Devil!

                                    Robert Burns

Chapman billies, pedlars; *drouthy*, thirsty; *gate*, road; *bousing*, boozing; *nappy*, ale; *slaps*, gaps in hedges; *fand*, found; *reaming swats*, foaming new ale; *souter*, shoemaker; *rair*, roar; *skelpit*, thrashed; *dub*, puddle; *glow'ring*, staring; *tippeny*, ale; *usquabae*, whisky.

Leeze me on drink

> Leeze me on drink, it gies us mair
>   Than either school or college:
> It kindles wit, it waukens lear,
>   It pangs us fu' o knowledge.
> Be't whisky gill or pennywheep
>   Or ony stronger potion,
> It never fails, in drinking deep,
>   To kittle up oor notion
>   By night or day.

Robert Burns

Leeze me on, I am grateful for (lief is me); *lear*, learning; *pangs*, crams; *penny-wheep*, very weak beer; *kittle*, tickle, stimulate.

Epitaph on John Dove

(The Innkeeper of Mauchline)

> Strong ale was ablution,
> Small beer, persecution,
>   A dram was *momento mori*;
> But a full-flowing bowl
> Was the saving his soul,
>   And port was celestial glory.

Robert Burns

The Greeks have no word for it

> Sages their solemn een may steek,
> Or raise a philosophic reek,
> And physically causes seek
>   In climes and season;
> But tell me whisky's name in Greek,
>   I'll tell the reason.

Robert Burns

Steek, shut.

from *A cogie o yill*

A cogie o yill
And a pickle aitmeal,
And a denty wee drappie o whisky,
  Was our forefathers' dose
  For to sweel doun their brose,
And keep them aye cheery and frisky.

    Then hey for the whisky and hey for the meal,
    And hey for the cogie and hey for the yill!
    Gin ye steer a' thegither they'll do unco weel,
      To keep a chiel cheery and brisk aye.

When I see our Scots lads
Wi' their kilts and cockades,
That sae aften hae loundered our foes, man,
  I think to masel
  On the meal and the yill,
And the fruits o the Scottish kail brose, man.

    Then hey, etc.

When our brave Highland blades,
Wi' their claymores and plaids,
In the field drove like sheep a' our foes, man,
  Their courage and pow'r
  Sprang frae this, to be sure—
They're the noble effects o the brose, man.

    Then hey, etc.

                    Andrew Sherriff (1762-1800)

Yill, ale; *loundered*, beaten; *unco*, very.

Neil Gow's fareweel to whisky

Ye've surely heard o famous Neil,
The man that played the fiddle weel;
I wat he was a canty chiel.
    An' dearly lo'ed the whisky, O.
An' aye sin he wore tartan hose,
He dearly lo'ed the Athole Brose;
An' wae was he, you may suppose,
To bid fareweel to whisky, O.

Alake, quo' Neil, I'm frail an' auld,
And find my bluid grows unco cauld,
I think it maks me blythe and bauld,
    A wee drop Highland whisky, O.
But a' the doctors do agree
    That whisky's no the drink for me;
I'm fleyed they'll gar me tyne my glee,
    Should they part me and whisky, O.

But I should mind on 'auld lang syne',
How paradise our friends did tyne,
Because something ran in their min'—
    Forbid, like Highland whisky, O.
While I can get both wine and ale,
And find my head and fingers hale,
I'll be content, though legs should fail,
    And though forbidden whisky, O.

I'll tak my fiddle in my hand,
And screw the strings up while they stand,
And mak a lamentation grand
    For guid auld Highland whisky, O!
O! a' ye pow'rs o music, come.
I find my heart grows unco glum;
My fiddlestrings will hardly bum
    To say, 'Fareweel to whisky, O'.

Agnes Lyon (1762-1840), wife of Dr Lyon,
Minister of Glamis

(Sung to an air by Neil Gow)

Fleyed, afraid; *tyne*, lose; *bum*, sound.

The piper o Dundee

The piper cam to oor toun,
To oor toun, to oor toun,
The piper cam to oor toun,
    And he played bonnilie.
He played a spring the laird to please,
A spring brent new frae owre the seas;
And then he ga'c his bags a wheeze,
    And played anither key.

        And wasna he a roguey,
            A roguey, a roguey,
        And wasna he a roguey,
            The piper o Dundee?

He played 'The welcome owre the main',
    And 'Ye'se be fou and I'se be fain',
And 'Auld Stuart's back again',
    Wi' muckle mirth and glee.
He played 'The Kirk', he played 'The Queir',
The 'Muilin Dhu', and 'Chevalier',
And 'Lang awa', but welcome here',
    Sae sweet, sae bonnilie.

        And wasna he a roguey,
            A roguey, a roguey,
        And wasna he a roguey,
            The piper o Dundee?

It's some gat swords, and some gat nane,
And some were dancin' mad their lane,
And mony a vow o weir was tane
    That nicht at Amulree!
There was Tullibardine and Burleigh,
And Struan, Keith and Ogilvie,
And brave Carnegie, wha but he,
    The piper o Dundee?

        And wasna he a roguey,
            A roguey, a roguey,
        And wasna he a roguey,
            The piper o Dundee?

                                    Anon.

Queir, choir of a church; *weir*, war.

from *Here's to the king!*

> Here's to the king, sir,
> Ye ken wha I mean, sir,
> And to ev'ry honest man
>   That will do't again!
>
> Fill, fill your bumpers high!
> Drain, drain your glasses dry!
> Out upon him, fye, fye,
>   That winna do't again!
>
> Here's to the chieftains
> O a' the Hielan' clans!
> They ha'e done't mair nor aince,
>   And will do't again.
>
> When you hear the trumpet sound
> Tuttie taittie to the drum,
> Up your swords and down your guns,
>   And to the rogues again!

Anon.

This song illustrates the artful manner in which the Jacobites sang their loyalty to the king over the water without laying themselves open to the charge of treason.

from *Carle, now the king's come*

> Carle, now the king's come!
> Carle, now the king's come!
> Thou shalt dance, and I will sing,
>   Carle, now the king's come!
>
> Cogie, now the king's come!
> Cogie, now the king's come!
> I'se be fou and ye's be toom,
>   Cogie, now the king's come!

Sir Walter Scott (1771-1832)

Carle, old fellow; *fou*, full; *toom*, empty.

A Toast

> Bring the bowl which you boast,
>   Fill it up to the brim;
> Here's to him we love most,
>   And to all who love him.
> Brave gallants, stand up,
>   And avaunt ye, base carls!
> Were there death in the cup,
>   Here's a health to King Charles!

Sir Walter Scott: *Woodstock*

from *Donald Caird*

> Donald Caird's come again,
> Donald Caird's come again!
> Tell the news in brugh and glen,
> Donald Caird's come again!

> Donald Caird can lilt and sing,
> Blithely dance the Highland fling;
> Drink till the gudeman be blind,
> Fleech till the gudewife be kind;
> Hoop a leglin, clout a pan;
> Or crack a pow wi' ony man;
> Tell the news in brugh and glen,
> Donald Caird's come again.

> Donald Caird can drink a gill,
> Fast as hostler-wife can fill;
> Ilka ane that sells gude liquor
> Kens how Donald bends a bicker:
> When he's fou he's stout and saucy,
> Keeps the kantle o the causey;
> Highland chief and Lawland laird
> Maun gi'e way to Donald Caird.

Sir Walter Scott

Brugh, burgh; *fleech*, coax, cajole; *leglin*, wooden milk-pail; *clout*, mend; *bends a bicker*, empties a drinking cup; *kantle o the causey*, middle of the pavement.

Willie wi' his wig a-gee

Oh, saw ye Willie frae the west?
    Oh, saw ye Willie in his glee?
Oh saw ye Willie frae the west,
    When he had got his wig a-gee?
There's 'Scots wha hae wi' Wallace bled',
    He towers it up in sic a key;
Oh, saw ye Willie, hearty lad,
    When he had got his wig a-gee?

To hear him sing a canty air,
    He lilts it o'er sae charmingly,
That in a moment aff flees care,
    When Willie gets his wig a-gee.
Let crones croon owre a winter nicht,
    A fig for them, whate'er they be,
For I could sit till morning licht
    Wi' Willie and his wig a-gee.

At kirk on Sundays, sic a change
    Comes owre his wig, and mou, and ee,
Sae douce—ye'd think a cannon-ba'
    Wad scarce ca Willie's wig a-gee.
But when on Mondays he begins,
    And rants and roars continually,
Till ilk owk's end, the very weans
    Gang daft—when Willie's wig's a-gee.

William Chalmers (1779-1843)

A-gee, awry; *ca*, drive; *owk*, week.

from *Sae will we yet*

Sit ye doun here, my cronies, and gie us your crack,
Let the wind tak' the care o this life on its back;
Our hearts to despondency we never will submit,
For we've aye been provided for, and sae will we yet.
    And sae will we yet, and sae will we yet;
    For we've aye been provided for,
        And sae will we yet.

Success to the farmer and prosper his plough,
Rewarding his eident toils a' the year through;
Our seed-time and harvest we ever will get,
For we've lippened aye to Providence, and sae will we yet.
    And sae will we yet, etc.

Then bring us a tankard o nappy brown ale,
It will comfort our hearts, and enliven the tale;
We'll aye be the merrier the langer that we sit;
We've drank wi' ither mony a time, and sae will we yet.
    And sae will we yet, etc.

Let the glass keep its course, and gae merrily roun',
For the sun it will rise tho' the mune has gaen doun;
Till the house be rinnin' roun' about it's time enough to flit;
When we fell we aye got up again, and sae will we yet.
    And sae will we yet, etc.

Walter Watson (1780-1854)

Crack, chat, gossip; *eident*, industrious; *lippened*, trusted; *nappy*, strong.

Song of a fallen angel over a bowl of rum punch

Heap on more coal there,
    And keep the glass moving,
The frost nips my nose,
    Though my heart glows with loving.
Here's the deep creature,
    No skylights—a bumper;
He who leaves heel-taps
    I vote him a mumper.
      With a hey cow rumble O,
      Whack! populorum,
      Merrily, merrily, men,
      Push round the jorum.

What are Heaven's pleasures
  That so very sweet are?
Singing from Psalters
  In short or long metre.
Planked on a wet cloud,
  Without any breeches,
Just like the Celtic[1]
  Met to make speeches.
    With a hey cow rumble O,
    Whack! populorum,
    Merrily, merrily, men,
    Push round the jorum.

Wide is the difference,
  My own boosing bullies,
Here round the punch bowl
  Heaped to the full is.
Then if some wise one
  Thinks that up 'yonder'
Is pleasant, as we are,
  Why—he's in a blunder.
    With a hey cow rumble O,
    Whack! populorum,
    Merrily, merrily, men,
    Push round the jorum.

John Wilson (Christopher North) (1785-1854)

Mumper, a contemptible creature.

Tak it, man, tak it

When I was a miller in Fife,
  Losh! I thought that the sound of the happer
Said, 'Tak hame a wee flow to your wife,
  To help to make brose to your supper.'
Then my conscience was narrow and pure,
  But somehow by random it rackit;
For I lifted twa nievefu' or mair,
  While the happer said, 'Tak it, man, tak it.'

1. The Celtic Society of Edinburgh University.

> Then hey for the mill and the kiln,
>   The garland and gear for my cogie;
> And hey for the whisky and yill,
>   That washes the dust frae my craigie!

Although it's been lang in repute,
  For rogues to mak rich by deceiving,
Yet I see that it disna weel suit
  Honest men to begin to the theiving.
For my heart it gaed dunt upon dunt,
  Oh, I thocht ilka dunt it wad crack it,
Sae I flang frae my nieve what was in't;
  Still the happer said, 'Tak it, man, tak it.'

> Then hey for the mill, etc.

A man that's been bred to the plough,
  Might be deav'd wi' its clamorous clapper;
Yet there's few that would suffer the sough,
  After kennin' what's said by the happer.
I whiles thought it scoffd' me to scorn,
  Saying, 'Shame, is your conscience no chackit?'
But when I grew dry for a horn,
  It chang'd aye to 'Tak it, man, tak it.'

> Then hey for the mill, etc.

The smugglers whiles cam wi' their pocks,
  'Cause they kent that I likit a bicker,
Sae I bartered whiles wi' the gowks,
  Gied them grain for a sowp o their liquor.
I had lang been accustomed to drink,
  And aye when I purposed to quat it,
That thing wi' its clappertie clink
  Said aye to me, 'Tak it, man, tak it.'

> Then hey for the mill, etc.

But the warst thing I did in my life,
  Nae doot but you'll think I was wrang o't;
Od! I tauld a bit bodie in Fife
  A' my tale, and he made a bit sang o't.

I hae aye had a voice a' my days,
    But for singin' I ne'er gat the knack o't;
Yet I try whyles, just thinking to please
    The greedy, wi' 'Tak it, man, tak it.'

       Then hey for the mill, etc.

Now, miller and a' as I am,
    This far I can see through the matter:
There's men mair notorious to fame,
    Mair greedy than me o the muter.
For 'twad seem that the hale race o men,
    Or, wi' safety, the hauf we may mak it,
Hae some speaking happer within,
    That said to them, 'Tak it, man, tak it.'

       Then hey for the mill, etc.

          David Webster (1787-1837)

Happer, hopper; *rackit*, suspended, strained; *nievefu'*, handful; *craigie*, throat; *nieve*, closed hand; *deav'd*, deafened; *sough*, whizzing sound; *chackit*, pricked; *gowks*, blockheads; *muter*, multure, miller's toll.

'Few songs have enlivened the ploughman's bothies of Scotland more frequently than this happily conceived and richly humorous ditty, which may occasionally be heard emanating, besides, from the village inns, the smiddies, or the cottage ingle-nooks in the land. The more popular and effective way of rendering it is for the singer to be seated on a chair or form, and to beat a mill-clapper-like accompaniment with his elbows and fists, or with an empty brose-caup, on a table before him.

'In Perthshire, to which county it particularly belongs, it has enjoyed, perhaps, the greatest popularity. Its author, David Webster, born in 1787, was a native of Dunblane. He was a weaver to trade, and died at Paisley in 1837.'—*Note* to Robert Ford's *Vagabond Songs and Ballads of Scotland*.

Nae mair a-roving
from *The Jolly Beggar*

      And we'll gang nae mair a-roving
        Sae late into the nicht;
      And we'll gang nae mair a-roving, boys,
        Let the mune sheen ne'er sae bricht.

          Trad. attr. James V (1512-42)

> So we'll go no more a-roving
>   So late into the night,
> Though the heart be still as loving,
>   And the moon be still as bright.

Lord Byron (1788-1824)

The deluge
From 'The Massacre of Macpherson'

> Phairson had a son
>   Who married Noah's daughter,
> And nearly spoiled the flood
>   By trinking up ta watter,
> Which he would haf done—
>   I, at least, pelieve it—
> Had ta mixture peen
>   Only half Glenlivet!

William Aytoun (1813-65)

Glenlivet

> Glenlivet it has castles three,
> Drumin, Blairfindy and Deskie,
> And also one distillery
> More famous than the castles three.
> Old Rhyme

A great distiller

> Lord grant gude luck to a' the Grants,
>   Likewise eternal bliss;
> For they should sit amang the san'ts
>   That mak a dram like this.
> Anon.

San'ts, saints.

(Lines written beneath the portrait of William Grant, distiller, that hangs in the London office of the firm—'a fine old warrior, in full uniform of a major'.)

Precentor's rhyme

> I wish I were a brewer's horse:
> Then when the coast was clear
> I'd turn my head where tail should be,
>   And drink up all the beer.

Anon.

Sung to the psalm-tune *Crimond* or other suitable metre.

NOTE.—In former times it was considered irreverent to sing the sacred words when practising the psalms and paraphrases, and innocuous doggerel verses were composed for the purpose. This custom gave the local wags an opportunity, and the above is a specimen of their efforts.

The tinkler's waddin'

> In June, when broom in bloom was seen,
> And bracken waved fu' fresh and green,
> And warm the sun, wi' silver sheen,
>   The hills and glens did gladden, O.
> Ae day, upon the Border bent,
> The tinklers pitched their gipsy tent,
> And auld and young, wi' ae consent,
>   Resolved to haud a waddin, O.

> > Dirrum dey, doo a day,
> >   Dirrim doo a da dee O,
> > Dirrim dey, doo a day,
> >   Hurrah for the tinkler's waddin', O.

> The bridegroom was wild Norman Scott,
> Wha thrice had broke the nuptial knot,
> And ance was sentenced to be shot
>   For breach o martial orders, O.
> His glecsome joe was Madge McKell,
> A spaewife, match for Nick himsel',
> Wi' glamour, cantrip, charm and spell,
>   She frichtit baith the Borders, O.

Nae priest was there, wi' solemn face,
Nae clerk to claim o crowns a brace;
The piper and fiddler played the grace
  To set their gabs a steerin', O.
'Mang beef and mutton, pork and veal,
'Mang paunches, plucks, and fresh cow-heel,
Fat haggises and cauler jeel,
  They clawed awa careerin', O.

Fresh salmon, newly taen in Tweed,
Saut ling and cod o Shetland breed,
They worried, till kytes were like to screed,
  'Mang flagons and flasks o gravy, O.
There was raisin kail and sweet-milk saps,
And ewe-milk cheese in whangs and flaps,
And they rookit, to gust their gabs and craps,
  Richt mony a cadger's cavie, O.

The drink flew round in wild galore,
And some upraised a hideous roar;
Blythe Comus ne'er a queerer core
  Saw seated round his table, O.
They drank, they danced, they swore, they sang,
They quarrelled and 'greed the hale day lang,
And the wranglin' that rang amang the thrang
  Wad matched the tongues o Babel, O.

The drink gaed dune before their drooth,
That vexed baith mony a maw and mooth;
It damped the fire o age and youth,
  And every breist did sadden, O.
Till three stout loons flew owre the fell,
At risk o life, their drouth to quell,
And robbed a neebourin' smuggler's stell,
  To carry on the waddin', O.

Wi' thunderin' shouts they hailed them back,
To broach the barrels they werena slack,
While the fiddler's plane-tree leg they brak
  For playin' 'Fareweel to Whisky', O.
Delirium seized the 'roarious thrang,
The bagpipes in the fire they flang,
And sowtherin' airns on riggins rang,
  The drink played siccan a plisky, O.

N

The sun fell laigh owre Solway banks,
While on they plied their roughsome pranks,
And the stalwart shadows o their shanks
   Wide owre the muir were spreadin', O,
Till, heids and thraws, amang the whins,
They fell wi' broken brows and shins,
And sair craist banes filled mony skins,
   To close the tinkler's waddin', O.

William Watt (1792-1859)

Joe, sweetheart; *spaewife*, fortune-teller; *Nick*, the Devil; *whangs and flaps*, large and small slices; *gabs a-steerin'*, mouths watering; *cauler*, fresh; *jeel*, jelly; *saut*, salt; *kytes*, stomachs; *screed*, rip; *rookit*, plundered; *to gust their gabs and craps*, to please their palates and stomachs; *cadger*, travelling hawker; *cavie*, hiding-place; *core*, convivial company; *thrang*, crowd; *stell*, still; *sowtherin' airns*, soldering irons; *riggin*, backbone; *siccan*, such; *plisky*, prank, mischief; *heids and thraws*, head over heels; *craist*, cracked.

This 'rarely humorous, graphic and rattling song' had formerly an immense vogue throughout the Scottish countryside, and, like the author's better remembered 'Kate Dalrymple' and Skinner's 'Tullochgorum', is set to an air with a spirited dancing rhythm.
   A weaver to trade, Watt cultivated poetry, painting and music as far as his circumstances allowed.

Captain Paton no mo'e

   Touch once more a sober measure,
     And let punch and tears be shed,
For a prince of old good fellows
     That, alackaday, is dead;
For a prince of worthy fellows,
     And a pretty man also,
That has left the Saltmarket
     In sorrow, grief and woe—
Oh! We ne'er shall see the like of Captain Paton no mo'e!

His waistcoat, coat and breeches
  Were all cut off the same web,
Of a beautiful snuff colour,
  Or a modest genty drab;
The blue stripe in his stocking
  Round his neat slim leg did go,
And his ruffles of the cambric fine,
  They were whiter than the snow—
Oh! We ne'er shall see the like of Captain Paton no mo'e!

His hair was curled in order,
  At the rising of the sun,
In comely rows and buckles smart
  That about his ears did run;
And before there was a toupee
  That some inches up did grow,
And behind there was a long queue
  That did o'er his shoulders flow—
Oh! We ne'er shall see the like of Captain Paton no mo'e!

And whenever we foregathered,
  He took off his wee three-cockit,
And he proffered you his snuff-box,
  Which he drew from his side-pocket;
And on Burdet or on Bonaparte
  He would make a remark or so,
And then along the planestanes
  Like a provost he would go—
Oh! We ne'er shall see the like of Captain Paton no mo'e!

In dirty days he picked well
  His footsteps with his rattan;
Oh! you ne'er could see the least speck
  On the shoes of Captain Paton!
And on entering the coffee-room
  About two, all men did know
They would see him with his *Courier*
  In the middle of the row—
Oh! We ne'er shall see the like of Captain Paton no mo'e!

Now and then, upon a Sunday,
  He invited me to dine
On a herring and a mutton-chop
  Which his maid dressed very fine;

There was also a little Malmsey
  And a bottle of Bordeaux,
Which, between me and the Captain,
  Passed nimbly too and fro—
Oh! I ne'er shall take pot-luck with Captain Paton no mo'e!

Or, if a bowl was mentioned,
  The Captain he would ring,
And bid Nelly to the Westport,
  And a stoup of water bring;
Then he would mix the genuine stuff,
  As they made it long ago,
With limes that on his property
  In Trinidad did grow—
Oh! We ne'er shall taste the like of Captain Paton's punch no
  mo'e!

And then all the time he would discourse
  So sensible and courteous,
Perhaps talking of the last sermon
  He had heard from Doctor Porteous;
Or some little bit of scandal
  About Mrs So-and-So,
Which he scarce could credit, having heard
  The *con*, but not the *pro*—
Oh! We ne'er shall see the like of Captain Paton no mo'e!

Or when the candles were brought forth,
  And the night was setting in,
He would tell some fine old stories
  About Minden-field or Dettingen;
How he fought with a French major,
  And dispatched him at a blow—
Oh! We ne'er shall hear the like from Captain Paton no mo'e!

But at last the Captain sickened,
  And grew worse from day to day,
And all missed him in the coffee-room,
  From which now he staid away;

On Sabbaths, too, the Wynd Kirk
  Made a melancholy show,
All for wanting of the presence
  Of our venerable beau—
Oh! We ne'er shall see the like of Captain Paton no mo'e!

And in spite of all that Cleghorn
  And Corkindale could do,
It was plain, from twenty symptoms,
  That death was in his view;
So the Captain made his testament,
  And submitted to his foe,
And we laid him by the Ram's-horn Kirk:
  'Tis the way we all must go—
Oh! We ne'er shall see the like of Captain Paton no mo'e!

Join all in chorus, jolly boys,
  And let punch and tears be shed
For this prince of good old fellows
  That, alack-a-day! is dead;
For this prince of worthy fellows,
  And a pretty man also,
That has left the Saltmarket
  In sorrow, grief, and woe—
For it ne'er shall see the like of Captain Paton no mo'e!

John Gibson Lockhart (1794-1854)

Three-cockit, three-cornered hat; *planestanes*, pavement.

NOTE.—Lockhart's 'superb comic elegy' first appeared in *Blackwood's Magazine*, September, 1819. The subject is a popular Glasgow worthy of the reign of George III.

Scotland yet

    Gae, bring my guid auld harp ance mair,
      Gae, bring it free and fast,
  For I maun sing anither sang
      E'er a' my glee be past;
  And trow ye as I sing, my lads,
      The burden o't sall be:
  Auld Scotland's howes, and Scotland's knowes,
      And Scotland's hills for me;
  I'll drink a cup to Scotland yet,
      Wi' a' the honours three.

  The heath waves wild upon her hills,
      And foaming frae the fells,
  Her fountains sing o freedom still,
      As they dash doun the dells;
  And weel I lo'e the land, my lads,
      That's girded by the sea:
  Then Scotland's dales, and Scotland's vales,
      And Scotland's hills for me;
  I'll drink a cup to Scotland yet,
      Wi' a' the honours three.

  The thistle wags upon the fields
      Where Wallace bore his blade,
  That gave her foeman's dearest blood
      To dye her auld grey plaid;
  And looking to the lift, my lads,
      He sang this doughty glee:
  Auld Scotland's right, and Scotland's might,
      And Scotland's hills for me;
  I'll drink a cup to Scotland yet,
      Wi' a' the honours three.

  They tell o lands wi' brighter skies,
      Where freedom's voice ne'er rang:
  Gie me the hills where Ossian lies,
      And Coila's minstrel sang;
  For I've nae skill o lands, my lads,
      That ken nae to be free:
  Then Scotland's right, and Scotland's might,
      And Scotland's hills for me;
  I'll drink a cup to Scotland yet,
      Wi' a' the honours three.

              Henry Scott Riddell (1798-1870)

from *A guid new year*

> A Guid New Year to ane an' a',
>   An' mony may ye see!
> An' durin' a' the years to come,
>   O happy may ye be!
> An' may ye ne'er hae cause to mourn,
>   To sigh or shed a tear!
> To ane an' a', baith great an' sma',
>   A hearty, Guid New Year!

Peter Livingstone (b. 1823)

A wish

> I wish I was a Bottle!
> O' brandy, rum, or what you please,
>   In some frequented hottle,
> Where gude souls tak their bread an' cheese;
>   To fill out a gill
> For some puir chiel' that wants a trade—
>   Or pass o'er the hass
> O some blythe, rantin', roarin' blade:
>   An' while unscrewed, I'd sit and brood,
>   An' think mysel weel blessed to ken
>   That when I dee'd I'd spend my bluid
>   To purchase joy for honest men!

George Outram (1805-56)

Chiel', fellow; *hass*, throat.

Drinkin' drams

> He ance was holy
> An' melancholy,
> Till he found the folly
>   O singin' psalms;
> He's now red's a rose,
> And there's pimples on his nose,
> And in size it daily grows
>   By drinkin' drams.

He ance was weak,
An' couldnae eat a steak
Wi' out gettin' sick
   An' takin' qualms;
But now he can eat
O ony kind o meat,
For he's got an appeteet
   By drinkin' drams.

He ance was thin,
Wi' a nose like a pen,
An haunds like a hen,
   An' nae hams;
But now he's round and tight,
And a deevil o a wight,
For he's got himsel' put right
   By drinkin' drams.

He ance was soft as dirt,
And as pale as ony shirt,
And as useless as a cart
   Wi'out the trams;
But now he'd race the deil,
Or swallow Jonah's whale—
He's as gleg's a puddock's tail
   Wi' drinkin' drams.

Oh! pale, pale was his hue,
And cauld, cauld was his broo,
An' he grumbled like a ewe
   Mang libbit rams;
But noo his broo is bricht,
An' his een are orbs o licht,
An' his nose is just a sicht
   Wi' drinkin' drams.

He studied mathematics,
Logic, ethics, hydrostatics,
Till he needed diuretics
   To lowse his dams;
But now, wi'out a lee,
He could mak' anither sea,
For he's left philosophy
   An' taen to drams.

He found that learnin', fame,
Gas, philanthropy and steam,
Logic, loyalty, gude name,
    Were a' mere shams;
That the source o joy below,
An' the antidote to woe,
And the only proper go,
    Was drinkin' drams.

George Outram

Gleg, brisk; *puddock*, frog; *broo*, brow; *libbit*, castrated; *lowse*, loosen; *lee*, lie.

The banks o the Dee

I met wi' a man on the banks o the Dee,
And a merrier body I never did see;
Though Time had bedrizzled his haffits wi' snaw,
An' Fortune had stown his luckpenny awa',
Yet never a mortal mair happy could be
Than the man that I met on the banks o the Dee.

When young, he had plenty o owsen an' kye,
A wide wavin' mailin, an' siller forbye;
But cauld was his hearth ere his youdith was o'er,
An' he delved on the lands he had lairdit before;
Yet though beggared his ha' an' deserted his lea,
Contented he roamed on the banks o the Dee.

'Twas heartsome to see the auld body sae gay,
As he toddled adoun by the gowany brae,
Sae canty, sae crouse, an' sae proof against care;
Yet it wasna through riches, it wasna through lear;
But I fand out the cause ere I left the sweet Dee—
The man was as drunk as a mortal could be!

George Outram

Haffits, temples; *owsen*, oxen; *mailin*, farm; *youdith*, youth; *crouse*, cheerful; *lear*, learning.

We're a' John Tamson's bairns

John Tamson was a merry auld carle,
 And reigned proud king o the Dee;
A braw laird, weel-to-dae i' the warl'
 For mony a farm had he,
And mony a servant-maid and man,
 Wham he met aft a year;
And fu' proud and jolly he wav'd his han',
 While they sang wi' richt gude cheer—
   O! we're a' John Tamson's bairns,
   We're a' John Tamson's bairns;
  There ne'er will be peace till the warld again
  Has learn'd to sing wi' micht and main,
   We're a' John Tamson's bairns.

John Tamson sat at the table heid,
 And supped the barley bree,
And drank success to the honest and gude,
 And heaven when they wad dee.
But the tyrant loon, the ne'er-dae-weel,
 The lee'ar, the rake and the knave,
The sooner they a' were hame wi' the deil,
 Lod! the better for a' the lave.
   O! we're a', etc.

Since Adam fell frae Eden's bow'r,
 And put things sair ajee,
There's aye some weakness to look owre,
 And folly to forgie.
And John wad sit and chat sae prood,
 And just before he'd gang,
He'd gie advice and blessings gude,
 Till roof and rafters rang
  Wi', we're a', etc.

Then here's to you, and here's to mysel',
 Sound hearts, lang life, and glee;
And if you be weel as I wish ye a',
 Gude faith, you'll happy be.
Then let us do what gude we can,
 Though the best are whiles to blame,
For in spite o riches, rank and lan',
 Losh man, we're a' the same.
   For w'ere a', etc.

The lave, the rest.   Dr Joseph Roy (Glasgow, b. 1841)

Heather ale

A Galloway Legend

From the bonny bells of heather
    They brewed a drink longsyne,
Was sweeter far than honey,
    Was stronger far than wine.
They brewed it and they drank it,
    And lay in a blessed swound
For days and days together
    In their dwelling underground.

There rose a king in Scotland,
    A fell man to his foes,
He smote the Picts in battle,
    He hunted them like roes.
Over miles of the red mountain
He hunted as they fled,
And strewed the dwarfish bodies
    Of the dying and the dead.

Summer came in the country,
    Red was the heather bell;
But the manner of the brewing
    Was none alive to tell.
In graves that were like children's
    On many a mountain head,
The Brewsters of the Heather
    Lay numbered with the dead.

The king in the red moorland
    Rode on a summer's day;
And the bees hummed, and the curlews
    Cried beside the way.
The king rode, and was angry,
    Black was his brow and pale,
To rule in a land of heather
    And lack the Heather Ale.

It fortuned that his vassals,
    Riding free on the heath,
Came on a stone that was fallen
    And vermin hid beneath.

Rudely plucked from their hiding,
    Never a word they spoke:
A son and his aged father—
    Last of the dwarfish folk.

The king sat high on his charger,
    He looked on the little men;
And the dwarfish and swarthy couple
    Looked at the king again.
Down by the shore he had them;
    And there on the giddy brink—
'I will give you life, ye vermin,
    For the secret of the drink.'

There stood the son and father
    And they looked high and low;
The heather was red around them,
    The sea rumbled below.
And up and spoke the father,
    Shrill was his voice to hear:
'I have a word in private,
    A word for the royal ear.

'Life is dear to the aged,
    And honour a little thing;
I would gladly sell the secret,'
    Quoth the Pict to the king.
His voice was as small as a sparrow's,
    And shrill and wonderful clear:
'I would gladly sell my secret,
    Only my son I fear.

'For life is a little matter,
    And death is naught to the young;
And I dare not sell my honour
    Under the eye of my son.
Take *him*, O king, and bind him,
    And cast him far in the deep:
And it's I will tell the secret
    That I have sworn to keep.'

They took the son and bound him,
    Neck and heels in a thong,
And a lad took him and swung him,
    And flung him far and strong,

And the sea swallowed his body,
　　Like that of a child of ten;—
And there on the cliff stood the father,
　　Last of the dwarfish men.

'True was the word I told you:
　　Only my son I feared;
For I doubt the sapling courage
　　That goes without the beard.
But now in vain is the torture,
　　Fire shall never avail:
Here dies in my bosom
　　The secret of Heather Ale.'

Robert Louis Stevenson (1850–94)

'Among the curiosities of human nature this legend claims a high place. It is needless to remind the reader that the Picts were never exterminated, and form to this day a large proportion of the folk of Scotland, occupying the eastern and the central parts, from the Firth of Forth, or perhaps the Lammermoors, upon the south, to the Ord of Caithness on the north. . . . Is it possible the chronicler's error was merely nominal? that what he told, and what the people proved themselves so ready to receive, about the Picts, was true or partly true of some anterior and perhaps Lappish savages, small of stature, black of hue, dwelling underground —possibly also the distillers of some forgotten spirit?' See Campbell's *Tales of the West Highlands*.

Atholl brose

Willie and I cam doun by Blair
　　And in by Tullibardine;
The Rye were at the riverside,
　　An' bee-skeps in the garden;
I saw the reek o a private still—
　　Says I, 'Gude Lord, I thank ye!'
As Willie and I cam in by Blair,
　　And out by Killiecrankie.

Ye hinny bees, ye smuggler lads,
　　Thou Muse, the bard's protector,
I never kent what Rye was for
　　Till I had drunk the nectar!
And shall I never drink it mair?
　　Gude troth, I beg your pardon!
The neist time I come doun by Blair
　　And in by Tullibardine.

Robert Louis Stevenson

A mile and a bittock

A mile and a bittock, a mile or twa,
Abune the burn, ayont the law,
Davie an' Donal' an' Cherlie an' a',
   An' the mune was shinin' clearly!

Ane went hame wi' the ither, an' then
The ither went hame wi' the ither twa men,
An' baith wad return him the service again,
   An' the mune was shinin' clearly!

The clocks were chappin' in hoose an' ha',
Eleeven, twal, an' ane an' twa;
An' the gudeman's face was turnt to the wa',
   An' the mune was shinin' clearly!

A wind got up frae affa the sea,
It blew the stars as clear's could be,
It blew in the een of a' o the three,
   An' the mune was shinin' clearly!

Noo, Davie was first to get sleep in his head;
'The best o frien's maun twine,' he said;
'I'm weariet, an' here I'm awa' to my bed.'
   An' the mune was shinin' clearly!

Twa o them walkin' an' crackin' their lane,
The mornin' licht cam' grey an' plain,
An' the birds they yammert on stick an' stane,
   An' the mune was shinin' clearly!

O years ayont, O years awa',
My lads, ye'll mind whate'er befa'—
My lads, ye'll mind on the bield o the law,
   When the mune was shinin' clearly.

                Robert Louis Stevenson

Bittock, little bit; *law*, hill; *chappin'*, striking; *twine*, part; *crackin'*, talking; *their lane*, alone; *yammert*, chattered; *bield o the law*, shelter of the hill.

from *The wedding of Shon Maclean*

A Bagpipe Melody

To the wedding of Shon Maclean,
    Twenty pipers together
Came in the wind and rain,
    Playing across the heather;
Backward their ribbons flew,
Blast upon blast they blew,
Each clad in tartan new,
    Bonnet and blackcock feather:
And every piper was fou,
    Twenty pipers together!

At the wedding of Shon Maclean
    They blew with lungs of leather,
And blythesome was the strain
    Those pipers played together!
Moist with the mountain-dew,
Mighty of bone and thew,
Each with the bonnet of blew,
    Tartan and blackcock feather:
And every piper was fou,
    Twenty pipers together!

At the wedding of Shon Maclean,
    Twenty pipers together,
Blowing with might and main,
    Through wonderful lungs of leather!
Wild was the hullabaloo!
They stamped, they screamed, they crew!
Twenty strong blasts they blew,
    Holding the heart in tether;
And every piper was fou,
    Twenty pipers together!

The small stars twinkled over the heather,
As the pipers wandered away together,
But one by one on the journey dropt,
Clutching his pipes, and there he stopt!
One by one on the dark hillside
Each faint blast of the bagpipes died,
    Amid the wind and the rain!

And the twenty pipers at break of day
In twenty different bogholes lay,
Serenely sleeping upon their way
    From the wedding of Shon Maclean.

Robert Buchanan (1841-1901)

Hughie's winter excuse for a dram

Frae whaur ye hing, my cauldrife frien',
    Your blue neb owre the lowe,
A snawy nichtcap may be seen
    Upon Benarty's pow;
An' snaw upon the auld gean stump,
    Wha's frostit branches hang
Oot owre the dyke abune the pump
    That's gane clean aff the fang.
The pump that half the toun's folk ser'd,
    It winna gie a jaw,
An' rouch, I ken, sall be your beard,
    Until there comes a thaw!

Come, reenge the ribs, an' let the heat
    Doun to oor tinglin' taes;
Clap on a gude Kinaskit peat
    An' let us see a blaze;
An' since o watter we are scant,
    Fess ben the barley-bree—
A nebfu' baith we sanna want
    To wet oor whistles wi'!
Noo let the winds o Winter blaw
    Owre Scotland's hills and plains,
It maitters nocht to us ava—
    We've simmer in oor veins!

The pooers o Nature, wind and snaw,
    Are far abune oor fit,
But while we scoog them, let them blaw;
    We'll aye hae simmer yet.

An' sae wi' Fortune's blasts, my frien',—
    They'll come an' bide at will,
But we can jink ahint a screen
    An' jook their fury still.
Then happy ilka day that comes,
    An' glorious ilka nicht;
The present disna fash our thoombs,
    The future needna fricht!

Hugh Haliburton (James Logie Robertson, 1846-1922)

Cauldrife, shivery; *lowe*, flame, glow; *gae aff the fang*, cease to grip; *jaw*, gush (of water); *reenge*, rake; *fess*, fetch; *scoog*, shelter from; *jook*, dodge.

A cheery guid-nicht

Noo I've sattled the score, an' the gig's at the door,
    An' the shaltie is kittle to ca',
Aye the langer we sit we're the sweirer to flit,
    Sae it's time to be wearin' awa.
A douce eller like me an example maun be,
    An' it wouldna be seemly ava
Stottin' hame in daylicht, an' jist think o the sicht
    Supposin' we happened to fa'.
Ye're weel-slockened noo, an' afore ye get fou
    Be guided by me an' say 'Na';
By my tongue ye can tell I've had plenty mysel',
    Sae a cheery guid-nicht to ye a'.

A cheery guid-nicht, ay, a cheery guid-nicht,
    A cheery guid-nicht to ye a',
By my sang ye can tell I've had plenty mysel',
    Sae a cheery guid-nicht to ye a'!

Rowe graavits weel roun, an' your bonnets rug doon,
    Syne set the door wide to the wa',
An' the gig that's in front is the safest to mount,
    Gin the dram gars you trow there is twa.
O it's little we care gin the furth it be fair,
    Or mochie or makin' for snaw,

Gin it's frosty an' clear we can lippen the mear,
  Gin it's dubby the safter the fa'.
Noo roadit for hame there's some I could name
  Nae freely sae croose i' the craw,
For they've wives like mysel' an' the lees we maun tell
  Blauds the tail of a nicht for us a'.

    It blauds a guid-nicht, ay, it blauds a guid-nicht,
      When the wives winna swallow them a',
    Though for peace ye may tell a bit lee like mysel',
      Here's a hindmost guid-health to them a'.

Charles Murray (1864-1941)

Shaltie, pony; *kittle*, ticklish; *ca'*, drive; *sweir*, disinclined; *eller*, elder; *stot*, bounce; *slocken*, quench thirst; *rowe*, roll; *graavits*, scarves; *rug*, pull; *the furth*, out of doors; *mochie*, muggy; *lippen*, trust; *dubby*, muddy; *nae sae croose i' the craw*, not so ready to talk big; *blauds*, spoils.

A stirrup-cup

Lines written on meeting the granddaughter of Cameron of Lochiel

Lady whose ancestor
  Fought for Prince Charlie,
Met once and nevermore,
  No time for parley!

Yet drink a glass with me
  'Over the water';
Memories pass to me,
  Chieftain's granddaughter!

'Say, will he come again?'
  Nay, Lady, never.
'Say, will he never reign?'
  Ay, Lady, ever.

Ay, for the heart of us
  Follows Prince Charlie;
There's not a part of us
  Sways not as barley

> Under the breeze that blew
> Up the Atlantic,
> Wafting the one, the true
> Prince, the romantic,
>
> Back to his native land
> Over the water:
> Here's to Prince Charlie and
> Lochiel's granddaughter.

Douglas Ainslie (1865-1950)

Hogmanay

Oh, it's fine when the New and the Auld Year meet,
An' the lads gang roarin' i' the lichtit street,
An' there's me an' there's Alick an' the miller's loon,
An' Geordie that's the piper oot o Forfar toon.
      Geordie Faa! Geordie Faa!
Up wi' the chanter, lad, an' gie's a blaw!
For we'll step to the tune while we've feet intill oor shune,
Tho' the bailies an' the provost be to sort us a'!

We've three bonnie bottles, but the third ane's toom,
Gin the road ran whisky, it's mysel wad soom!
But we'll stan' while we can, an' be dancin' while we may,
For there's twa we hae to finish, an' it's Hogmanay.
      Geordie Faa! Geordie Faa!
There's an auld carle glow'rin' oot ahint yon wa',
But we'll sune gar him loup to the pipin' till he coup,
For we'll gie him just a drappie, an' he'll no say na!

My heid's dementit an' my feet's the same,
When they'll no work thegither it's a lang road hame;
An' we've twa mile to travel, or it's mair like three,
But I've got a grip o Alick, an' ye'd best grip me.
      Geordie Faa! Geordie Faa!
The morn's near brakin', an' we'll need awa',
Gin ye're aye blawin' strang, then we'll mebbe get alang,
An' the deevil tak the laddie that's the first to fa'!

Violet Jacob (1863-1946)

Soom, swim

A braw Scots nicht

When the last big bottle's empty and the dawn creeps grey and cold,
And the last clan-tartan's folded and the last damned lie is told;
When they totter down the footpaths in a braw unbroken line,
To the peril of the passers and the tune of 'Auld Lang Syne',
You can tell the folk at breakfast as you watch the fearsome sicht,
They've only been assisting at a braw Scots Nicht!

                                        Will Ogilvie (1869-1939)

from *Just a wee deoch-an-doris*

            Just a wee deoch-an-doris,
                Just a wee yin, that's a';
            Just a wee deoch-an-doris
                Before we gang awa.
            There's a wee wifie waitin'
                In a wee but an' ben;—
            If ye can say, 'It's a braw
                bricht moonlicht nicht',
            Ye're a' richt, ye ken.

                            Harry Lauder (1870-1950)

Deoch-an-doris, drink at the door.

from *I belong to Glasgow*

            I belong to Glasgow—
                Dear old Glasgow town!
            But what's the matter wi' Glasgow?
                For it's going round and round.
            I'm only a common old working-chap,
                As anyone can see,
            But when I get a couple of drinks on a Saturday,
                Glasgow belongs to me!

                            Will Fyffe (1885-1947)

A song after sunset

We have no beer, and we are very dry.
    We have no beer.
Though day is past, and ten o'clock is nigh,
    We have no beer.
Across the west old Sol has long since gone,
Rosy with nut-brown ale, and we've had none.

We were not always thus, nor could avow
    We'd had no beer.
Even as the owl we oft were screwed; but now
    We have no beer.
All day we have been sober; from our slate
Previous convictions, Lord, obliterate.

So long we have been thirsty, and so long
    We've had no beer,
We need a glass or two at evensong,
    Sad hearts to cheer.
And with the moon we shall go rolling home
To the same tavern as we started from.

Robert Browning (Scotus)
(Glasgow University Magazine, 1905-6)

To be sung to the air of *Lead, Kindly Light*.

Fragment

I remember, I remember
    Nothing further after that,
But I wakened in the morning
    On an alien lobby mat,
And I felt not unpersuaded
    (Though my reasons were not clear)
That I'd spent a merry Christmas
    And a prosperous New Year.

George Fletcher (Caurnie)
(Glasgow University Magazine, 1905-6)

from *A drunk man looks at the thistle*

I am na fou' sae muckle as tired—deid dune.
It's gey and hard work coupin' gless for gless
Wi Cruivie and Gilsanquhar and the like,
And I'm no juist as bauld as aince I wes.

The elbuck fankles in the coorse o time,
The sheckle's no sae souple, and the thrapple
Grows deef and dour: nae langer up and doun
Gleg as a squirrel speils the Adam's apple.

Forbye, the stuffie's no the real Mackay.
The sun's sel' aince, as sune as ye began it,
Riz in your vera saul: but what keeks in
Noo is in truth the vilest 'saxpenny planet'.

And as the worth's gane doun the cost has risen.
Yin canna thow the cockles o yin's hert
Wi'oot ha'en' cauld feet noo, jalousin' what
The wifc'll say (I dinna blame her fur't).

It's robbin' Peter to pay Paul at least . . .
And a' that's Scotch aboot it is the name,
Like a' thing else ca'd Scottish nooadays
—A' destitute o speerit juist the same.

> .   .   .   .

Rabbie, wad'st thou were here—the warld hath need,
And Scotland mair sae, o the likes o thee!
The whisky that aince moved your lyre's become
A laxative for a' loquacity.

Hugh MacDiarmid (b. 1892)

Coupin', emptying; *elbuck*, elbow; *fankles*, becomes, unsteady; *sheckle*, wrist; *deef*, deaf, unimpressionable; *dour*, intractable; *gleg*, eager; *speils*, climbs; *thow*, thaw.

Toddlin hame

> They're a' hame but Watty Pratt,
> Wha hauds the croon o the causey:
> They're a' hame but Watty Pratt
> And a mune that glaiks sae gaucy.
>
> Ding! gangs the muckle toun-bell
> And dirls a while as it dwinnels:
> Ding, gangs the muckle toun-bell
> And dwines awa through the vennels.
>
> A braw nicht; says Wattie Pratt,
> And his fit plays diddle-doddle:
> A braw nicht; says Wattie Pratt,
> And his heid gaes niddle-noddle.

> William Soutar (1898-1943)

Croun o' the causey, middle of the road; *glaiks*, shines; *gaucy*, jolly; *dirls*, tingles, vibrates; *dwinnles*, dwindles; *dwine*, fade; *vennel*, alley; *fit*, foot.

Riddle

> It maks a body cheerie
> Or maks a body greet:
> It maks a body steerie
> Or ca's ye aff your feet.
>
> It maks a body canty
> Or maks a body glum:
> It maks a body ranty
> Or maks ye unco mum.
> (Drink)

> William Soutar

Greet, weep; *steerie*, obliged to keep moving; *ca's*, drives; *ranty*, talkative.

Ballade of Better Living

I have seen trouble now and then
Come driving up from here and there,
From distant zones beyond my ken,
Or out of gardens lately fair;
But yet, however grim its lair,
However great might be the row,
I still pulled in a cheerful chair
—I had not seen a Purple Cow.

I'd seen great loch or mighty ben
By midnight matches eerie flare,
Go skipping like a heedless hen
In ways for which I do not care.
These visitations were but rare,
And I returned with open brow
The candid comrade's closest stare
—I had not seen a Purple Cow.

But I went out to see some men
With vagrant vine-leaves in my hair,
And crawled at daybreak to my den,
The *Evening News* my only wear.
In fact, I went upon the tear
With Pleasure at the gilded prow,
Till Heaven's avenging wrath stood bare:
For I have seen a Purple Cow.

Friend, this blue ribbon badge I wear
Friends cannot ravish from me now;
All that a man may risk, I dare—
But I have seen a Purple Cow.[1]

Walter Elliot (Parvus)
Glasgow University Magazine, c. 1910

1. I never saw a Purple Cow,
      I never hope to see one,
   But I can tell you anyhow,
      I'd rather see than be one.
                    Gelett Burgess in *The Lark*, San Francisco

RECIPES

1: *Traditional Drinks*

HEATHER ALE

> From the bonny bells o heather
> They brewed a drink langsyne,
> Was sweeter far than honey,
> Was stronger far than wine.

Robert Louis Stevenson: 'Heather Ale'

Across the western tip of the Mull of Galloway runs an entrenchment called The Double-Dykes, which, according to an ancient tradition, was the scene of the tragedy whereby the secret of preparing the true, the indigenous heather ale was lost for ever. The Galloway legend has been immortalized by Robert Louis Stevenson in one of his *Ballads*; by Neil Munro in a story included in the volume, *The Lost Pibroch*; and by Sir Herbert Maxwell in his book, *A Duke of Britain*.

In the fourth century Niall of the Nine Hostings led an expeditionary force from Northern Ireland into Galloway and exterminated the Pictish inhabitants—all but that staunch patriot, Trost of the Long Knife, with his father and brother, who alone knew the secret of heather ale, and Sionach, the archdruid, a traitor who had deserted the Picts and joined the enemy. To the three loyal survivors Niall offered their lives in exchange for the coveted receipt. Trost conveyed to the King that if the others were first put to death, his desire should be granted. Having heroically sacrificed his father and brother, he told the King that he could reveal the secret only to one of his own race, namely to

Sionach, and that out of hearing of the Scots. The King agreed.
' "Sionach, we will withdraw a space. Keep your sword in
hand. This man is unarmed: he cannot hurt you." He motioned
back the crowd. Sionach and Trost were left standing alone.
Trost, with hands behind his back, turned to walk along the brow
[of the cliff]; the Druid followed him warily. But not warily
enough for the old hunter. Where the cliff was steepest, the
brink almost abrupt, Trost turned like a flash, wrapped his sinewy
hands around the Druid, crying out, "The secret dies!"; and both
men disappeared over the edge.'

This is Sir Herbert Maxwell's version. The others differ in
detail. And so countless generations of Scots have mourned the
passing of heather ale. But did it die? Assuredly it did not. When
making researches into old Scottish fare, the present writer found
clear proof of that. The legend, like so many others, was in all
probability founded on fact, but would certainly have the usual
accretions. It may well be that an appalling slaughter of the Picts
by the Scots did take place in Galloway, but it is highly impro-
bable that the whole race was extirpated, even in that region.
And even so, there remained Northern Pictland, which stretched
from the Pictland or Pentland Hills to the Pentland Firth.

Pennant, who visited the Hebrides in 1774, tells us that in Islay
they made ale from 'the tops of young heath, mixed with a third
part of malt and a few hops'. It is said to have been made in
Rannoch (Perthshire) as late as 1840, the tops of the heather being
cut, steeped, boiled, and fermented. Again, in an article in *The
Gallovidian* we read that 'contrary to other legends ... down to
comparatively recent times it was brewed locally in the pear-
shaped kilns, notably in the parishes of Minigaff and Kirkma-
breck'.[1] Darnel (tares), the writer adds, was grown with the bear
(a kind of coarse barley) and used to give a strong narcotic quality
to the ale.

There is no mention of heather ale in Ossian, but the Fingalians
appear to have drunk deeply of ale or mead, which may or may
not have been the traditional Pictish beverage. 'If so,' writes Neil
Gunn, 'it was brewed out of more than heather-tops, for though
the bees suck there to make their finest honey, no purplest bloom
offers in sufficient degree the necessary basis of alcohol. At any
rate, such a mildly fermented drink as would have been concocted

1. B. J. Williams: *Galloway Fare.*

would certainly be classed today for revenue purposes as non-alcoholic. Heather ale was not so simple as all that if the Picts had a hand in it! And we do know that in some of the Western Isles a very potable liquor was still being brewed from two parts heather-tops to one part malt in the eighteenth century. From the malt is got the saccharine basis without which alcohol cannot be obtained. It is important to remember that. Honey or mead has got that saccharine basis and alcohol could have been distilled from it.'

In *The Curiosities of Ale and Beer*, a fascinating and comparatively rare book, John Bickerdyke writes on the traditions of Pictish beer and suggests that the heather was used primarily for flavouring:

'The blossoms of the heather are carefully gathered and cleansed, and then placed in the bottom of vessels; wort of the ordinary kind is allowed to drain through the blossoms, and gains in its passage a peculiar and agreeable flavour, known to all familiar with heather honey.'

Now let the present writer lapse for a little into the first person singular.

Some years ago (between the Wars), when staying in a village in Moray, I came across, in an old coverless book of cottage cookery, a recipe for heather ale, and although it was obviously a good deal removed from the Pictish original—witness such modern ingredients as ginger and golden syrup—it was definitely an exciting find, definitely something to work on. An opportunity came on my next visit to that part of Northern Pictland. I was staying in a country house near Findhorn, on the shores of the Moray Firth. Behind us were pinewoods, before us the sea, and all around was moorland. My hostess, Jean Smith, a modern young woman who drove a car, played golf, and the rest, had also most of the accomplishments beloved of our grandmothers: she could make barley broth, bake bannocks, and brew ale; she knew all there was to know about a dairy; and she kept a goat, hens and bees—and at that very moment those little busy bees were out on the heather improving the shining hour. Heather bells, heather honey, and a brewer all to hand!

On the last morning of my brief visit we set off, Jean, her sister Nan and I, each with a basket on her arm. The sun shone; down on the pebbly beach the wavelets danced and curtsied and broke into a white lacework of foam; the bees, flitting among the red-purple heather-bells, hummed continuously. The air was like wine—I had almost said like heather ale. All too soon we had filled our baskets, and presently we emptied them on to the table in the big, flag-floored kitchen. We trimmed off the withered blooms and the longer stalks, and 'couped' the heather croppings into the muckle black pot that stood on the range in readiness. The pot was then filled with cold water and set on the fire. 'I'll see to the rest,' said Jean.

Unluckily I had to leave that day for Inverness, but Jean promised that as soon as the ale was ready for use she would 'run in' with a bottle or two for us to taste.

Inverness is, of course, the capital of ancient Pictland. Here, in the sixth century, St Columba was entertained by Brude, King of the Picts and regaled—who can doubt it?—with the *vin du pays*. And now, nine centuries later, heather ale was to be drunk once more in the Pictish capital. Obviously it was an occasion—even though our fair brewer had written to say that the result of her experiment had proved disappointing. So to my brother Duncan's house we summoned Neil Gunn, John MacCormick, Robin MacEwan, and other selected Picts and Scots (for now we are happily amalgamated).

'Now, don't expect too much. It's bitter stuff,' Jean warned us, as, seated round the table, we raised our reaming glasses. Bitter we had to admit it was, but in spite of that it was agreeably exhilarating, and behind the bitterness was a faint, heather-scented sweetness. We had not yet discovered the secret, but we definitely had a hint of it.

What was amiss with our experiment? I talked it over later with Jean. For one thing, we decided, we had left too much stalk on the heather. Again, we were possibly wrong in using bell heather in place of ling. After all, when Stevenson wrote of 'the bonnie bells of heather' he knew no more about the kind of heather used than I did. Pennant had written that in Islay the 'tops of young heath' were used. Then the Picts were said to have steeped their heather. We hadn't. And what about the darnel, and what did the Picts use in place of hops? And so forth.

The next experiment was carried out in Orkney, with the help of a crofter's wife in Harray. There is lots of home brewing in Orkney, and Nell Hourston, my kind friend, remembered an old woman who lived up on the hill, who was reputed to have made ale from heather—a potent brew from all accounts—but it was no longer made in the Islands. I carried a bottle over to Merkister for Eric and Marjorie Linklater to pree. The old bitterness had gone, but we had spoiled the ale with too much ginger! No ginger at all next time, I vowed. But the second war broke out and one way or another there has been no next time—yet. (Jean married and moved to a city, and Nell, alas, is dead.) But I have collected some more oddments of information. For instance, a very intelligent policeman, a native of the Isle of Lewis, told me there was a tradition of heather ale in Uig, the most north-westerly point of that Island; but so far I have been able to trace only an infusion—of a very special kind of heather, of which he kindly gave me a specimen. What kind? I am not going to say until I have experimented again, or induced a trusty home brewer to do so.

Meanwhile I give here the modern cottage recipe with the recommendation that heather honey be substituted for golden syrup; that ground ginger, if used at all, should be used very sparingly; and that the recipe be regarded mainly as a basis for experiment.

Heather Ale

Crop the heather when it is in full bloom—a good large quantity. Put the croppings into a large-sized pot, fill up with water, set to boil. Boil for one hour. Then strain into a clean tub. Add one ounce of ground ginger, half an ounce of hops, and a pound of golden syrup for every dozen bottles. Set to boil again and boil for twenty minutes. Strain into a clean cask. Let it stand until milkwarm, then add a teacupful of good barm (brewer's yeast). Cover with a coarse cloth till next day. Skim the barm from the top and pour gently into a tub so that the barm may be left in the bottom. Bottle and cork tight. It will be ready for use in two or three days. This makes a very refreshing and wholesome drink as there is a good deal of spirit in heather.

ATHOLL BROSE

Atholl Brose emerged from the Highland mists in the year 1475 but it may well be centuries older. We do not know whether the

Murrays should be credited with the invention of this famous beverage, but it was certainly an incident in the annals of that clan, of whom the Duke (at that time Earl) of Atholl is the Chief, that brought the celebrated beverage into the light of day. This incident was the decoying and capture of the rebel Lord of the Isles by means of the Atholl Brose.

The Lords of the Isles, as all students of Scottish history know, were for long virtual monarchs in their own domains, with their fleet of galleys, their Parliament in Islay, and all the rest. In short, they were a continuous menace to the authority of the Scottish kings. In 1475 a rebellion broke out, headed by Iain Macdonald, Earl of Ross and Lord of the Isles. The Earls of Crawford and Atholl were sent out upon a punitive expedition, Crawford commanding the sea forces and Atholl those on land. The expedition was successful, Ross being captured by a ruse of which the tradition is preserved in the Atholl family. The Earl of Atholl received information that Ross, who was in hiding in the hills, was in the habit of drinking from a certain small well in a rock, and he gave instructions that this well should be filled with a compound of honey, whisky and meal. Alas for the Lord of the Isles! Enchanted by the nectar that so mysteriously emanated from a hidden source, he dallied by the well too long! The compound has ever since borne the name of Atholl Brose. As a reward for his services, Atholl was granted the land and forests of Clunie. In the Charter, which is dated 1480, it is expressly stated that the grant was made 'for the said Earl of Atholl's singular service and expenses in suppressing John [Iain], Lord of the Isles, of old Earl of Ross'.

Another legend was recorded by R. Macdonald Robertson in a gamekeeper's cottage in Glen Tilt, when spending a fishing holiday in the district, and was kindly passed on to the present writer.

Some time before 1600 the young and lovely heiress of Tulli-bardine (the Duke of Atholl's family) had a favourite walk along the richly wooded banks of the Tay from Dunkeld to Blair of Atholl. In the adjacent forest, however, there lurked a man of wild aspect and savage nature, known as Ruraidh Mor, who would appear from nowhere and attack and rob the passer-by. More than once the Maid and her attendants had been intimidated, but all efforts to capture him had ended in the death or forced flight of the man who challenged the cateran to combat. At last the Maid of Tullibardine pledged her hand and a portion of her land to any young unmarried man who could rid the countryside of its tormentor.

Of the youths who came forward there was one who possessed good looks, intelligence and courage, and the wit to devise a scheme to ensnare the wild man of the woods. He discovered that Big Rory (that was his name in English) used to drink daily at a certain well, a cup-shaped stone filled by the cool waters of a small burn and surrounded by a dense thicket of oak trees. One morning the youth diverted the stream from the stone and emptied the basin, which he re-filled with a mixture of whisky and honey, adding sufficient water to avert suspicion. Then he climbed into an adjacent tree and waited.

In due course the wild man appeared and, falling flat on his stomach, began to drink; nor did he raise his head until he had drunk the well dry; then, completely intoxicated, he fell into a profound sleep. Warily the young man got down from the tree and fettered his victim; then, summoning two colleagues, he trailed him to the feet of the Maid, who joyfully welcomed the hero as her future husband.

Ever after, the nectar composed of whisky and honey was known as Atholl Brose, and it is said that the fettering of the half-naked savage inspired the armorial bearings of the ducal family of Murray and its motto—*Furth and fill the fetters*.

Ordinary brose is normally made by pouring boiling liquid over oatmeal in sufficient quantity to make a fairly substantial mixture; but Atholl Brose is unique in that the liquid employed required no heating, for whisky, as every wise man's son doth know, engenders its own heat. Strictly, Atholl Brose is not brose, but crowdie, for that is the generic name for any mixture of meal and cold liquid. But Atholl Brose it has been called for centuries, and Atholl Brose it is likely to remain.

Atholl Brose appears to have developed out of a simple concoction of whisky and oatmeal—a glass of whisky into which a little oatmeal was stirred—and in this form it is still known in the remoter Highlands and Islands. Then some one was inspired to sweeten the mixture with heather honey, which is rich in nectar. In the Highlands, hunting for wild bees' nests was one of the great ploys for boys in the autumn months.

'Cameron [one of his estate workers] tells me', says Osgood Mackenzie, 'that as a young boy, before he left his home, there was an island in Loch Bhad A Chreamha where there was no necessity for hunting for bees' nests, as the whole island seemed under bees, the nests almost touching each other in the moss at the roots of tall heather.'[1]

Although, thanks to our degenerate climate, these nests are everywhere far less plentiful than formerly, heather honey remains part of the pride of Scotland, and it seems quite in the nature of things that the addition of nectar should convert brose into ambrosia. Anyhow, that is what happened.

Atholl Brose is mentioned by Scott in *The Heart of Midlothian*, and Robert Louis Stevenson describes in *Kidnapped* how David Balfour and Alan Breck Stewart are regaled with it at Balquhidder:

'Duncan Dhu made haste to bring out the pair of pipes that was his principal possession, and to set before his guests the mutton-ham and a bottle of that drink which they call Athole Brose, and which is made of old whisky, strained honey and sweet [fresh] cream, slowly beaten together in the right order and proportion. ... Maclaren pressed them to taste his mutton-ham and "the wife's brose", reminding them the wife was out of Athole and had a name far and wide for her skill in that confection.'[2]

The recipes vary. That preserved in the ducal family of Atholl contains no cream, and in Edinburgh the original Brose went through a process of refinement which was eventually carried to the point of omitting the oatmeal altogether.

Atholl Brose
(Meg Dods's Recipe 1826)

Put a pound of dripped honey into a basin and add sufficient cold water to dissolve it (about a teacupful). Stir with a *silver* spoon, and when the water and the honey are well mixed, add gradually one and a half pints of whisky, alias mountain dew. Stir briskly till a froth begins to rise. Bottle and keep tightly corked.

Sometimes the yolk of an egg is beat up in the brose.

1. *A Hundred Years in the Highlands* (1921).
2. In some Highland houses Atholl Brose, with a basis of whipped cream, adequately thickened with toasted oatmeal, is served as a sort of mousse, for dessert.

Atholl Brose (with Cream)
(As made by the late Williamina Macrae at her angling-inn in Lochailort)

Beat one and a half teacups of double cream to a froth; stir in a teacup of very lightly toasted oatmeal; add half a teacup of dripped heather honey and, just before serving, two wine-glasses of whisky. Mix thoroughly and serve in shallow glasses.

Atholl Brose (without Cream)
(Traditional Recipe)

Mix half a pound of run honey and half a pound of fine oatmeal together with a little cold water, then pour in very slowly a quart of well-flavoured malt whisky. Stir the whole vigorously (using a silver spoon) until a generous froth rises to the top; then bottle and cork tightly. Keep for two days, and serve in a silver bowl.

Some years ago, the late Duke of Atholl generously made public the traditional recipe in use at Blair Castle. This is probably the identical beverage of which the author of *The Laird of Logan* writes that, when entertaining Sheridan, the Duke of Atholl of that day 'ordered some Atholl Brose, which the dramatist relishing, partook of rather freely'. Queen Victoria and Prince Albert, too, partook, let us hope rather less freely, of this 'giant's drink', when they visited Blair Atholl in September 1844.[1]

Atholl Brose
(The Late Duke of Atholl's Recipe)

'To make a quart, take four dessertspoonfuls of run honey and four sherry glassfuls of prepared oatmeal; stir these well together and put into a quart bottle; fill up with whisky; shake well before serving.

To prepare the oatmeal, put it into a basin and mix with cold water to the consistency of a thick paste. Leave for about half an hour, pass through a fine strainer, pressing with the back of a wooden spoon so as to leave the oatmeal as dry as possible. Discard the meal and use the creamy liquor for the brose.

On Hogmanay, the Atholl Brose, carried by two subalterns and preceded by a piper, is carried into the sergeants' mess of the

1. See Queen Victoria's *Leaves from the Journal of our Life in the Scottish Highlands.*

P

Argyll and Sutherland Highlanders, where a quaich is filled for every officer and man: and in other Highland regiments—as in many a Highland home—the New Year is welcomed in with this delectable compound. Needless to say, it should be drunk with Highland Honours.

A golden rule in making Atholl Brose, laid down by a young gentleman of Edinburgh is, 'Keep tasting and proceed empirically!'

HET PINT

In Edinburgh and elsewhere until well into the nineteenth century, the great Hogmanay beverage was Het Pint, a sort of wassail bowl, which was carried through the streets in scoured copper kettles (commonly known as toddy-kettles) an hour or more before 'the chappin' o the twal' '. The carrier of the kettle had always a cup-bearer in attendance, and a noggin of the steaming beverage was pressed on all and sundry. The invariable toast was, 'a gude New Year to ane an' a', and a merry Handsel Monday!' He who declined to quaff his noggin was reckoned a churlish fellow by his hospitable companions.

The whole of the ancient ceremonial of the *Daft Days*, as they are called in Scotland, obtained respect at Abbotsford. 'He [Scott] said it was *uncanny* and would certainly have felt it very uncomfortable, not to welcome the New Year in the midst of his family, and a few old friends, with the immemorial libation of a het pint.'

J. G. Lockhart: Life of Scott

Het Pint
(Meg Dods's Recipe)

Grate a nutmeg into two quarts of mild ale and bring it to the point of boiling. Mix a little cold ale with sugar necessary to sweeten this[1] and three eggs well beaten. Gradually mix the hot ale with the eggs, taking care that they do not curdle. Put in half a pint of whisky and bring once more nearly to boiling-point. Then briskly pour it from one vessel to another till it becomes smooth and bright.

'In Edinburgh,' we read in the Annals of the Cleikum Club,

1. Say 4 oz. or according to taste.

'in her bright and palmy state—her days of "spice and wine", while she yet had a court and Parliament, while France sent her wines, and Spain, Italy and Turkey fruits and spices—a far more refined composition than the above was made by substituting light wine for ale, and brandy for whisky.'

THE HOGMANAY WASSAIL BOWL

Simmer the following spices in a teacupful of water—mace, cloves, cardamoms, cinnamon, nutmeg, ginger, coriander seed, allowing for each bottle of wine

10 grains mace	28 grains cinnamon
46 grains cloves	48 grains ginger
37 grains cardamoms	49 grains coriander seed

Add the mixed spices to two, four, or six bottles of port, sherry, or Madeira, allowing one and a half pounds of pounded loaf sugar for four bottles, and set all on the fire in a clean, bright saucepan. Meanwhile have the yolks of twelve and the whites of six fresh eggs well whisked up separately and put into the wassail bowl. When the spiced, sugared wine is warm, take out one teacupful at a time till you have a third, and add it to the eggs. Add the remaining two-thirds when it comes to the boil, but without letting it actually boil, pouring it in very gradually and whipping all the time to get a good froth, partly mixed through but mainly on the top. When all the wine is in, toss in twelve fine, soft-roasted apples. Send the whole up hot with a ladle.

from *The Scots Week-end*, edited by Catherine and Donald Carswell

HOGMANAY DRINKING-SOWANS
(Aberdeen and North-East Scotland)

Procure a quantity of sids (the inner husks of the oats) from the miller. Put this into a wooden tub or jar (the sowans-bowie) and cover well with lukewarm water. Using a wooden spoon, press down the sids that rise to the surface, and leave for about a week, or up to ten days in cold weather, till they are quite sour. Empty the contents of the bowie into a sowans-sye or sieve placed over another vessel, squeezing the sids by hand to get all the goodness out of them. (This process is called 'the syeing o the so'ans'.) Throw out the sids for the hens to peck at, and let the liquid stand for two days longer to allow the starchy matter to sink to the bottom.

When required, pour the clear liquid off the top and put some of the sediment into a flagon or wide-mouthed jar standing in a pan of boiling water. Add warm water gradually until it is of the consistency of cream. Cook gently for about ten minutes. Add a little salt, sweeten to taste with heather honey or treacle, and lace with whisky.

Sowans is often eaten thick, like gruel, lightly salted but not sweetened, and accompanied with milk or single cream.

WHIPKULL

(An Ancient Shetland Yule Beverage)

> 'Was it whipkull that Brynhild presented in her golden cup to
> Sigurd when he woke her from her long sleep?'—Jessie Saxby.

In Shetland, the Scandinavian blood is purer and the Scandinavian traditions are stronger than anywhere else in Scotland, and it is not surprising to find that Yule is better preserved there, both in form and in spirit, than in any other part of the British Isles. So strong, indeed, is the tradition, that Yule, the feast of the winter solstice, has never been identified with Christmas, the feast of the Nativity, the latter being kept (where it is kept at all) on December 25 and the former on January 6—that is, December 25, Old Style. It is not, then, surprising to find in the Islands a Yule beverage of ancient and noble lineage. Its name is Whipkull, or Whipcol—the derivation is unknown—and it has always been the crowning glory of the great Yule breakfast served in the homes of the Shetland Udallers or lairds. Here is a boyhood memory (mid-nineteenth century) of a Shetlander, the Rev. Biot Edmonston, who always spent Yule with his uncle, the laird.

After describing the gargantuan feast, 'At the end of the meal,' he goes on, 'from the sideboard are now brought and set before our host a large old china punch bowl kept expressly for the purpose; a salver with very ancient, curiously shaped glasses . . . and a cake basket filled with rich crisp shortbread. The bowl contains whipcol. I do not know whether there is any truth in the tradition that it was the favourite drink of the dwellers in Valhalla, gods and heroes, when they kept their high Yule festival. But this I know, there was never a festival in the old house without it.'

Whipkull
(The Edmonston Family Recipe)

The yolks of a dozen eggs are vigorously whisked for half an hour with about a pound of softed loaf sugar (castor sugar); nearly half a pint of old rum is added, and then about a quart of rich, sweet (fresh) cream.

A bumper of this, tossed off to many happy returns of Yule Day, together with a large square of shortbread, always rounded off our Yule breakfast.

HIPPOCRAS

Hippocras or Ypocras was one of the most popular aromatized and spiced wines during the Middle Ages and long after. It was found in many countries, though the recipe naturally varied. 'There is every reason to believe', writes M. André Simon, 'that the basis of Hippocras was sour or pricked wine, of which there must have been an embarrassingly large quantity at a time when wine was kept on ullage, in casks, or in ill-stoppered bottles, before the use of cork for stoppers. Such wine being heavily sweetened with honey and flavoured with herbs and spices was then filtered through a woollen bag known as a Hippocrates sleeve, hence the name *Hippocras*, often written *Ipocras* or *Ypocras*.'

In sixteenth-century Edinburgh, the burgess family, on returning from early mass on Yule Day, regaled themselves with hot spiced claret called Ypocras, and gilded gingerbread baked in fantastic shapes—dragons, horses, demons and so forth.

Hippocras
(Traditional Recipe)

Simmer one ounce of cinnamon and one of cloves in three gills of water for ten minutes. Strain, and add a wineglassful,

together with a wineglassful of port, to each bottle of claret.
Make very hot, sweeten to taste with honey or pounded loaf
sugar, and serve in a tappit-hen or other vessel with three or four
slices of lemon floating on top.

MEAL-AND-ALE

Ale-Crowdie, or Meal-and-Ale, is a dish traditionally associated
with the Kirn, or feast of Harvest Home. So popular was it in
Aberdeenshire and the north-east that it gave its name to the
festival. It was invariably made with the first of the grain to be
returned from the mill, to commemorate the renewal of the food
supply.

In the morning, some of the meal was placed in a small wooden
tub or a large earthenware bowl—a handful or so sufficed for each
person—and over this was poured a quantity of home-brewed
ale. The crowdie had to be of drinking consistency, but there
was a superstition that if it were made too thin the next year's
crops would be thin. It was sweetened with treacle and handsomely
laced with whisky, and then left to 'lithe' or mellow until the
arrival of the guests in the evening. The matrimonial ring was
put in, and occasionally other charms. Sometimes the bowl was
placed in the middle of the kitchen table, and the company
gathered round with spoons; if, however, there were too many
present to allow of their all getting round, the meal-and-ale was
divided and served in large bowls, six or seven persons sharing a
bowl. A ring was placed in each, and the crowdie was supped in
rounds of spoonfuls until the dish was empty.

This ceremony is probably of very great antiquity.

'In the gruel of oatmeal and ale which the harvesters sup with
spoons as an indispensable part of the harvest-supper, have we
not', asks Sir James Frazer, 'the Scottish equivalent to the gruel
of barley-meal and water, flavoured with penny-royal, which the
initiates at Eleusis drank as a solemn form of communion with
the Barley Goddess, Demeter? May not that mystic sacrament
have originated in a simple harvest supper held by the Eleusian
farmers at the end of the reaping?'[1]

1. *The Golden Bough.*

AULD MAN'S MILK

(Meg Dods's Recipe)

1 quart new milk or single cream	6 eggs
½ pint whisky, brandy or rum	Nutmeg or lemon zest (to taste)
	Sugar (to taste)

Beat the yolks and whites of the eggs separately. Put to the beat yolks the sugar, milk or cream. Add to this rum, whisky or brandy to taste (about a half-pint). Slip in the whipped whites, and give the whole a gentle stir-up in the china punch-bowl, in which it should be mixed. It may be flavoured with nutmeg or lemon zest.

This is described as a 'morning drink'. It is reputed to be a wonderful pick-me-up. It is sometimes mixed by being poured from one vessel to another until a deep froth appears on the surface.

2: Punch and Toddy

GLASGOW PUNCH

A hundred years ago and more, the signal toast at the Glasgow clubs was 'The Trade of Glasgow and the outward bound!' Jamaica is the home of the world's finest rum, and as the trade with the West Indies developed, rum grew in popularity. It is recorded that: 'Rum punch was the universal beverage of the members of the Pig Club, as it was of those of all the jovial fraternities in the city.'[1]

'We have it on the authority of Mr J. G. Lockhart', writes James Bertram, 'that much of the rum which reached the Clyde from the West India Islands went back thither in stout earthenware jars transmuted.

1. Dr John Strang: *Glasgow and Her Clubs.*

'... Not a few of the Glasgow men of the olden time,' he adds, 'looked upon the "furnishing" of their china and silver bowls as an important duty—brewing the punch, by some of them, indeed, was treated as a solemn function—a kind of fine art not lightly to be gone about. It was a treat to see some of the old city fathers at this congenial work—how tenderly they dedicated the bowl by running cut limes round the inside. And when the "browst" was deemed complete, but before it began to be ladled out, some good judge who might be at table was called upon to "pree" the compound and give his opinion, and that being favourable, the work of distribution commenced. . . . In some Glasgow houses of olden time the recipe for the making of the punch was a secret which descended from sire to son, and was never betrayed.'

In *Peter's Letters to his Kinsfolk* (1819) we have a description of the ritual of punch-making in the manner of the Glasgow burgesses. The ingredients are rum, sugar, water, limes and lemons.

'The sugar being melted with a little cold water, the artist squeezed about a dozen lemons through a wooden strainer, and then poured in water enough almost to fill the bowl. In this state, the liquor goes by the name of sherbet, and a few of the connoisseurs in his immediate neighbourhood were requested to give their opinion of it—for in the mixing of the sherbet lies, according to the Glasgow creed, at least one half of the whole battle. This being approved by an audible smack of the lips of the umpires, the rum was added to the beverage, I suppose, in something about the proportion of one to seven. Last of all, the maker cut a few limes, and running each section rapidly round the rim of his bowl, squeezed in enough of this more delicate acid to flavour the whole composition. In this consists the true *tour de maître* of the punchmaker.

'Glasgow punch should be made of the coldest spring water newly taken from the spring. The acid ingredients above mentioned will suffice for a very large bowl.'

The proportions per tumblerful should be approximately:

1 tablespoon sugar	1 wineglass rum
1 lemon	¾ tumbler water

Icing-sugar dissolves more readily than the ordinary kind. The bowl may be placed on ice, or chipped ice may be added.

RUM PUNCH (HOT)

1 quart rum	1 lb. sugar
1 quart tea	1 lemon

Grate the lemon rind, remove all pith, cut the fruit into slices and remove all seeds. Place the rind and pulp in a mixing bowl, add the sugar, and over this pour the hot tea, which should be freshly and well infused. Cover and let it stand until the sugar is dissolved. Strain and add the rum. Re-heat, but do not let it boil. Serve in a punch-bowl or in large stemmed wine glasses.

P.E.N. PUNCH

(The late W. G. Burn-Murdoch's recipe, which has been greatly appreciated by foreigners, Sassenachs and others, and, not least, by members of the Scottish P.E.N. visiting his house on festive occasions.)

1 bottle old rum	5 lemons
½ lb. sugar lumps	Piece of cinnamon stick
Water (to strength desired)	

Rub the lemons with the sugar lumps until you have removed all the yellow rind. Put the lemony sugar into a bowl, add the rum, then the strained juice of the lemons. Put in a piece of cinnamon stick, and over all pour on boiling water to the strength required, stirring all the time. Remove the cinnamon stick when the beverage is sufficiently spiced. Serve very hot, ladling it from the punch-bowl into glasses.

COLD WHISKY PUNCH

1 bottle Scotch whisky	½ lb. loaf sugar
1 quart boiling water	3 lemons

Pare the rind of the lemons finely and strain the juice. Place these in a jug with the sugar, and pour the boiling water over all. Leave till cold; then strain into a punch-bowl. Add the whisky, mixing well. Place the bowl in a large vessel; surround with ice; cover, and leave for an hour.

TODDY

'Although whisky in the Highlands at any rate, is still regarded as a spirit not to be adulterated or tampered with, I must admit there were and are receipts for its use as a medicine and also for the final glory of a feast, receipts far more ancient than the blended whisky which we drink today. Of these the best known are toddy and Athole Brose.' Sir Robert Bruce Lockhart

> Sit roun' the table weel content,
> An' steer about the toddy.
>
> Burns

Toddy which, unlike punch, contains no acid, is excellent both as a cure for a cold and as an elixir of life. It requires careful preparation. The ingredients are loaf-sugar, boiling water, and preferably a well-matured malt whisky. (An inferior quality may have unpleasant fumes.)

First half-fill the tumbler with hot water, and when the glass has reached a comfortable temperature pour it out. Put in three or four pieces of loaf-sugar and pour over them a wineglassful of boiling water. When the sugar is dissolved, add a wineglassful of whisky and stir with a silver spoon; add another glassful or so of boiling water and then a second glass of whisky. Stir again, and sip the toddy 'with slow and loving care'.

The quantity of whisky may be reduced by one half. It is a matter of taste.

When a company is to be served, heat the punch-bowl and multiply the above quantities by the number to be served. 'And, of course, you do not "swig" it brutally from runner or tumbler,' writes Professor Saintsbury, quoting the Morayshire rules, 'but ladle it genteely, as required, with a special instrument made and provided for the purpose, into a wineglass which has been brought again, specially inverted beforehand in the runner or tumbler itself.'[1]

Toddy[2] is excellent both as a stimulant and as a cure for a cold. For a cold, drink it in bed.

1. *Notes on a Cellar-Book.*
2. In his poem, 'The Morning Interview' (1721) Allan Ramsay speaks of 'some

BLUE BLAZER

>   3 liquid ounces Scotch whisky
>   3 liquid ounces boiling water
>   1 teaspoonful powdered sugar
>   Twist of lemon peel

Take two metal mugs, and place the whisky and sugar in one and the boiling water in the other. Touch a match to the whisky, and when it is blazing pour it rapidly into the boiling water, then back and fore between the mugs in one running flame of fire, five or six times, until the blaze dies down. Serve in a small thick glass and twist a tail of lemon over for zest.

SCOTCH HIGHBALL

Put a good-sized piece of ice into an ordinary tumbler; then pour in a cocktailglassful of Scotch whisky and fill up with soda-water. Stir, and float a thin slice of lemon on the surface.

3: Liqueurs and Whisky Compounds

CALEDONIAN LIQUEUR
(Mrs Dalgairns's Recipe)

>   1 oz. oil of cinnamon   2½ lb. loaf sugar
>   1 gallon best whisky

Bruise the sugar lumps, place in a jar, and drop the oil of cinnamon over them. Pour the whisky over this, cover, and leave until the sugar is dissolved; then filter and bottle.

kettles full of Todian spring', and appends the note: 'The Todian spring, i.e. Tod's well, which supplies Edinburgh with water. Tod's Well and St Anthony's Well, on the side of Arthur's Seat, were two of the wells which very scantily supplied the wants of Edinburgh, and when it is borne in mind that whisky derives its name from water, it is highly probable that Toddy in like manner was a facetious term for the pure element.'

CARAWAY WHISKY

1 gallon old malt whisky	8 oz. caraway seeds
¼ oz. thin yellow rind of Seville oranges	2 sticks cinnamon
	Sugar to taste

Place in a bottle or jar the caraway seeds, cinnamon sticks (bruised) and orange rind, and pour the whisky over them. Mix, and leave, closely covered, for a month; then filter through a jelly-bag. Sweeten slightly with powdered white sugar-candy or with syrup of sugar and water clarified as for preserves.

GINGER CORDIAL

2 quarts whisky	1 oz. ground ginger
3 lemons	3 oz. sweet almonds
1 lb. raisins	1 oz. bitter almonds
3 lb. lump sugar	½ oz. caraway seeds

Slice the lemons and put all the ingredients into a crock. Cover with a cloth, and stir every day for three weeks. Strain through filtering paper or three folds of blotting-paper, and bottle.

GEAN (WILD CHERRY) WHISKY

12 lb. cherries	2 blades mace
12 cherry kernels	8 peppercorns
3 bitter almonds	3 lb. sugar
1 nutmeg	3 quarts whisky

Stalk and stone, then bruise the cherries, which must be sound and ripe, and put them into a jar. Crack the kernels and add, along with the sugar and spices, and pour the whisky over all. Cover and stir every day for a week; then seal and cork. After it has stood for a year, strain and bottle.

HIGHLAND BITTERS

'Every year [my grandmother] made gooseberry and currant wines, balm ditto, raspberry vinegar, spruce and ginger beer. I remember they were celebrated, and liqueurs numberless included magnums of camomile flowers and orange-peel and gentian root bitters for old women with indigestion pains.'

Osgood Mackenzie: *A Hundred Years in the Highlands*

1¾ oz. gentian root	½ oz. cloves
1 oz. coriander seed	¼ oz. cinnamon stick
½ oz. bitter orange peel	¼ oz. camomile flowers
2 bottles whisky	

The orange peel should be freed from all white pith before it is weighed. Cut it and the gentian root into small pieces and put them into a mortar together with the coriander seed, cloves, cinnamon stick and camomile flowers. Bruise all together. Place in an earthenware jar and empty the two bottles of whisky over all. Cover so that the jar is air-tight, and leave for about ten days; then strain and bottle.

More whisky may be added to the flavouring materials, which remain good for a considerable time.

HIGHLAND CORDIAL

1 pint white currants	1 teaspoonful essence of
1 lb. loaf sugar	ginger
1 lemon	1 bottle whisky

Strip the currants off the stalks. Peel the lemon thinly, discarding all white pith. Put the currants, lemon rind and essence of ginger into a wide-mouthed bottle or jar, and pour the whisky over them. Mix and cover so that it is air-tight, and leave for forty-eight hours. Strain, add the loaf sugar, and leave for a day to dissolve. Bottle and cork. It will be ready for use in three months.

SLOE WHISKY

Sloes (the blue-black fruit of the blackthorn), white sugar, whisky

Put into a gallon jar two pounds of sloes, one and a half pounds of white sugar, and half a gallon of whisky. Cover so that it is air-tight. Shake daily for a month; then strain off and bottle.

ROWANBERRY LIQUEUR

Rowanberries, loaf sugar, brandy

Gather ripe, red rowanberries and dry them in the sun till quite shrivelled. Place them in brandy, allowing a handful of berries to each pint. Cover so that it is air-tight, and leave for a week or ten days. Strain and mix with an equal quantity of thick, very clear syrup made with loaf sugar in a brass boiler. Bottle for use.

GEAN (WILD CHERRY) BRANDY

Wild cherries, sugar candy, best pale French brandy

Select ripe wild cherries when perfectly black. Fill a large prune-bottle or wide-mouthed jar three-quarters full with the fruit, then fill up the bottle with bruised sugar candy, and pour in as much brandy as the bottle will hold. When the sugar is melted, it is fit for use.

HAWTHORN LIQUEUR
(Mrs Dalgairns's Recipe)

Hawthorn blossoms, French brandy, clarified sugar or capillaire

The full blossoms of the white hawthorn are to be picked dry and clean from the leaves and stalks, and as much put in to a large bottle as it will hold lightly without pressing it down; it is then to be filled up with French brandy, and allowed to stand two or three months, when it must be decanted off, and sweetened with clarified sugar, or with capillaire. Without the sweetening, it is an excellent seasoning for puddings and custards.

LOUDON'S ADMIRABLE[1]

Peaches, greengages, magnums (a kind of large yellow cooking-plum), sugar, water, brandy or whisky

1. John Claudius Loudon (1783-1843), the son of a Lanarkshire farmer, achieved fame as a landscape gardener and horticultural writer. This recipe is preserved in Meg Dods's *Manual of Cookery* (1826).

Skin two dozen ripe peaches; then quarter them and take out the stones. Add to this the pulp of two dozen ripe greengages and one dozen ripe magnum plums. For every four pounds of pulp allow six pounds of sugar and two quarts of water. Boil these together slowly for half an hour or more. Skim, strain, and when cool add three quarts of brandy or flavourless whisky.[1]

SCOTS NOYAU
'A very pleasant compound'—Meg Dods

Proof-spirit, syrup, almonds (sweet and bitter), water

Two quarts of proof-spirit, a pint and a half of water, a pound and a half of syrup, six ounces of sweet almonds and four bitter almonds, blanched and chopped. Infuse for a fortnight, shaking the compound occasionally, and filter.

N.B.—Lemon juice or grate is sometimes added, but Meg maintains that the nutty or almond flavour does not harmonize well with acid or citrus flavours.

4: *Whisky Cocktails*

CAMERON'S KICK

| ⅓ Scotch Whisky | ⅙ Lemon Juice |
| ⅓ Irish Whisky | ⅙ Orgeat Syrup |

Shake well and strain into cocktail glasses.

ROB ROY

One of the very best whisky cocktails and a fast mover on St Andrew's Day at the Savoy Hotel.

½ Scotch Whisky ½ Italian Vermouth
2 dashes Angostura Bitters

Shake well with cracked ice and strain into cocktail glasses.

1. Patent still whisky, before blending, is almost pure alcohol, flavourless. Pot still whisky does not blend well with fruit. Anyhow, it is a wicked waste of good whisky!

ROBBIE BURNS

Robbie, not Bobbie, please!

½ Scotch Whisky　　　　½ Italian Vermouth
3 dashes Benedictine

Shake well and strain into cocktail glasses.

FLYING SCOTSMAN

3 glasses Scotch Whisky　　2½ glasses Italian Vermouth
1 tablespoon bitters　　　　1 tablespoon sugar syrup

HIGHLAND FLING

⅔ Scotch Whisky　　　　⅓ Italian Vermouth
2 dashes orange bitters

Serve with an olive

TAM O SHANTER

3 glasses Whisky　　　　2 glasses French Vermouth
½ glass Orange Juice

Shake well, add a little nutmeg, and serve with an olive.

SOUTAR JOHNNY

½ Scotch Whisky　　　　¼ Italian Vermouth
¼ Kina Lillet

CROW

⅔ Scotch Whisky　　　　⅓ Lemon Juice
1 dash Grenadine

DEWAR'S DRINK[1]

⅗ Scotch Whisky　　　　⅖ Ginger Wine

1. Named after the author's uncle, Dr James Dewar, Orkney, who, after exposure to high gales and wild seas when visiting patients in his island group, would concoct this drink as a restorative.

HIGHLAND MILKMAID

$\frac{2}{3}$ Scotch Whisky $\frac{1}{3}$ Cream

AULD ALLIANCE

$\frac{2}{3}$ Scotch Whisky   2 dashes Absinthe
$\frac{1}{3}$ French Vermouth   2 dashes Grenadine
            2 dashes Orange Bitters

CLYDE

1 glass Scotch Whisky   1 dash Absinthe
2 dashes Jamaica Rum   2 dashes Lemon Juice
            1 dash Orange Bitters

DRAMBUIE COCKTAILS

Prince Charlie
  $\frac{1}{3}$ Drambuie
  $\frac{1}{3}$ Cognac
  $\frac{1}{3}$ Lemon Juice

Flora Macdonald
  $\frac{1}{4}$ Drambuie
  $\frac{1}{4}$ Dry Gin
  $\frac{1}{2}$ French Vermouth

Isle of Skye
  $\frac{1}{3}$ Drambuie
  $\frac{1}{3}$ Gin
  $\frac{1}{3}$ Lemon Juice

Golden Heath
  $\frac{1}{3}$ Drambuie
  $\frac{1}{3}$ Calvados
  $\frac{1}{3}$ Lemon Juice

Mystic Marvel
  $\frac{1}{4}$ Drambuie
  $\frac{1}{4}$ Brandy
  $\frac{1}{4}$ Calvados or Apple Jack
  $\frac{1}{4}$ Lime Juice
Stir, strain into glass,
Squeeze Orange Peel on top.

Deansgate
  $\frac{1}{4}$ Drambuie
  $\frac{1}{4}$ Lime Juice
  $\frac{1}{2}$ Bacardi
Squeeze Orange Peel on top.

Auld Nick
  $\frac{1}{4}$ Drambuie
  $\frac{1}{2}$ Whisky
  $\frac{1}{8}$ Orange Juice
  $\frac{1}{8}$ Lemon Juice

Ecstasy
  $\frac{1}{3}$ Drambuie
  $\frac{1}{3}$ Cognac
  $\frac{1}{3}$ French Vermouth
Squeeze Lemon Peel on top.

Q

5: *Ale Cups*

EDINBURGH ALE PUNCH

2 pints Scotch Ale	A pinch of cinnamon
3½ oz. rum	A pinch of ground cloves
3½ oz. gin	A little grated nutmeg
½ pint boiling water	½ lemon
Sugar to taste	A few quarter-slices oranges and lemons

Pour the ale into a large porcelain-lined pan and add the rum, gin and boiling water. Slice the half lemon thinly, place it in the pan, sweeten the mixture to taste, and add the spices. Turn on the flame to effect a slow heating, but do not let boil.

As soon as the mixture begins to simmer, remove it from the fire, allow to cool a few minutes, then strain through muslin into your punch-bowl. Add the quarter-slices of orange and lemon and serve immediately in punch glasses.

The quantities indicated here should be enough for six people.

KING'S CUP

1 quart Strong Scotch Ale	A little ground cloves
½ pint brandy	A little cinnamon
1 pint water	A little ground ginger
4 oz. brown sugar	A little grated nutmeg
1 lemon	2 slices toast

Dissolve the sugar in the water; slice the lemon into it and let it stand for fifteen minutes or so. Add the cloves and cinnamon, pour in the brandy and the ale, and stir the mixture well. Put in the toast and stir, sprinkle the nutmeg and ginger over it.

This may be drunk warmed or iced. It is drunk chiefly at dinner.

ROYAL TOAST

1 bottle Scotch Ale	2 lemons
1 glass sherry	1 handful mint
2 tablespoonfuls sugar	A little nutmeg
1 pint cold water	

Put the juice of 2 lemons and the rind of 1 into a bowl. Add the water, sugar, sherry and mint, grate in a little nutmeg, and let it stand for fifteen minutes. Remove the mint, add the ale and serve in tankards.

SUMMER CUP

2 pints Scotch Ale	¼ oz. cinnamon
4 bottles ginger beer	2 cloves
1 gill sherry	1 allspice
A little grated nutmeg	

Soak the cinnamon, cloves, nutmeg and allspice in the sherry, and let it stand for two hours. Strain, with pressure, into a jug. Pour in the ale and ginger beer, and add a little ice.

LEMON ALE

3 pints Scotch Ale	1 tablespoon sugar
Juice of 1 lemon	1 sprig mint
1 glass sherry	A little grated nutmeg

Add the lemon juice to the ale, stir in the sugar, pour in the sherry, and add the nutmeg and mint.

TWEEN-DECK CUP

2 quarts Scotch Ale	A little cinnamon
1 pint rum	A little ginger
1 pint lime-juice	A little nutmeg
6 crushed cloves	

Put all the spices into the rum and let it stand for one hour. Strain with pressure, and add the lime juice and ale.

JACK FROST

1 bottle Scotch Ale	1 slice cucumber
2 bottles ginger beer	1 pint shaven ice
½ gill syrup from preserved ginger	

Pour the ginger beer into the ale. Add the syrup, cucumber and ice. Mix together, stirring well, and pour into thin glasses.

SCOTCH ALE SANGAREE

1 large tumbler Scotch Ale   1 teaspoon icing sugar
1 small lump ice   A little grated nutmeg
1 tablespoon water

Put the icing sugar into a large tumbler and dissolve in the water. Add the ice, fill up with ale, dust with nutmeg and serve.

SCOTCH SHANDYGAFF

1½ pints Scotch Ale   1 wineglassful liqueur
3 bottles ginger beer   or brandy
A few lumps of ice

Put the ice into a jug and pour the ale over it. Add the liqueur or brandy, pour in the ginger beer, and stir well.

A PARTING CUP

1 quart Scotch Ale   A little grated nutmeg
⅔ bottle of sherry   Small quantity syrup
1 bottle soda-water   2 slices well-browned toast

Put the toast into a bowl; add the ale, pour in the sherry, add the nutmeg and sweeten to taste with the syrup. Just before serving, add the soda-water.

6: Miscellaneous Drinks

CIDER CUP

I

1 quart bottle cider   1 oz. castor sugar
1 quart bottle soda-water   7 or 8 thin slices cucumber
2 wineglassfuls sherry   1 sprig mint or small bunch
   or Marsala   borage

Put all the ingredients into a large jug and mix well. Stand on ice or in cold water for two hours. (If borage is used, remove after ten minutes.) Pour into a tureen or wide-mouthed jug and add some table ice. Garnish with a few slices of lemon and cucumber, or with little bunches of red currants, cherries, or any small fruits in season.

II

1 quart bottle cider	1 liqueur glass maraschino
1 quart bottle soda-water	Juice of half lemon
1 wineglass sherry	1 oz. castor sugar

Make and garnish as above.

CLARET CUP
I

1 bottle claret	1 dessertspoonful castor sugar
1 bottle soda-water	A few thin strips of lemon rind
2 glasses curaçao	A few thin strips of cucumber rind

Put the claret into a glass jug; add the lemon and cucumber rind, cover, and let the jug stand in ice for an hour. Before serving, add the curaçao and soda-water, and sweeten to taste.

II

1 bottle claret	1½ wineglassfuls port
1 bottle soda-water	1 liqueur-glassful curaçao
1 bottle lemonade	One or two sprigs of borage

Mix the ingredients well and chill.

MULLED CLARET

1 bottle claret	Rind of ½ lemon
1 wineglassful port	12 cloves
1 tablespoonful sugar	A pinch of grated nutmeg

Put the spices into a small saucepan with a gill or so of water and simmer for half an hour. Strain, and add a wineglassful to the claret. Add the port and sugar, and make the beverage very hot, without letting it boil. Serve with thin slices of lemon rind.

A small piece of cinnamon stick may be substituted for the lemon rind.

ST RONAN'S NEGUS

Mr Winterblossom, a guest at the little Border spa immortalized by Sir Walter Scott in *St Ronan's Well*, prepares his negus:

' "Dinah—my bottle of pale sherry, Dinah—place it on this side—there's a good girl;—and, Toby—get my jug with the hot water—and let it be boiling. . . . And, Dinah, bring the sugar—the soft East Indies sugar, Dinah—and a lemon, Dinah, one of those which came fresh today—Go fetch it from the bar, Toby—and don't tumble downstairs if you can help it. And Dinah—stay, Dinah—the nutmeg, Dinah, and the ginger, my good girl. . . . . I do not think I want anything else.

' " . . . Will your ladyship honour me by accepting a glass of negus?—I learned to make negus from old Dartineuf's son.—He always used East India sugar, and added a tamarind—it improves the flavour intimately.—Dinah, see your father sends for some tamarinds." '

Here is a reconstruction of the recipe:

1 pint sherry	4 oz. sugar (soft East
1 quart water	Indies or loaf)
1 lemon	Grated nutmeg and ground
	ginger to taste

Put the wine into a jug. Rub the sugar lumps on the lemon rind until all the yellow part is absorbed; then squeeze out and strain the juice. Add the lemony sugar and the lemon juice to the wine, and also the spices. Pour the boiling water over; then cover the jug, and when the negus has cooled slightly it is ready for use.

If East India sugar is used, add grated lemon rind separately.

BRAMBLE CORDIAL

4 lb. brambles	A few cloves
1 lb. sugar	Some root ginger
	1 pint malt vinegar

Bring the vinegar to boiling-point. Put the fruit into a crock, mash well with a wooden spoon, and pour the boiling vinegar over it. Let it stand for twenty-four hours. Strain well, measure the liquid, and put into the preserving-pan with the sugar. To each pint of liquid allow 6-8 cloves, 2-3 oz. root ginger and, if desired, a small piece of cinnamon stick, all tied in muslin. Boil for thirty minutes, remove the spices, cool and bottle.

The cordial will be ready to use in forty-eight hours, and is delicious in soda-water, or as a hot winter drink with water to taste.

RASPBERRY VINEGAR

3 lbs. ripe raspberries   2½ lb. preserving sugar
          1 quart white wine vinegar

One pound of raspberries should be gathered on three successive days. Remove the stalks of the first lot and place the berries, which must be perfectly dry, in a large bowl, and bruise them slightly with the back of a wooden spoon. Pour all the vinegar (which should be of the best quality) over them, cover, and leave for twenty-four hours. Next day strain off the vinegar, replace the raspberries with fresh ones, pour the vinegar over them, cover, and leave for another twenty-four hours. Repeat the process on the third day, and on the fourth, strain the vinegar through a cotton cloth or jelly-bag. It should be a clear, brilliant red. Measure it and pour into an enamel lined pan. Add the sugar, allowing a pound for each pint of vinegar. Leave it for a little until the sugar has started to dissolve; then bring it to the boil and let it simmer for five minutes, carefully removing all scum that rises.

Next day bottle the vinegar, corking it lightly; after four or five days cork it down securely.

Two tablespoonfuls of raspberry vinegar in a glass of iced water makes a refreshing drink.

In Meg Dods's sweet-sour sauce for venison, a glass of claret is added to three times the quantity of venison or mutton stock, which is then boiled until it is reduced to half its volume; lastly a small glass of raspberry vinegar is added.

7: Country Wines and Ales

HOME-MADE or British wines, as the products of our domestic
stills are commonly called, are of ancient lineage, but since the
dawn of the industrial era they have declined in popularity, and
are now as unfamiliar to most of us as are vodka or Chianti.
Happily there are quite a few country houses and farmhouses
scattered over the country where the secrets of the still-room
have been preserved, and there are signs of a renewed interest in
this admirable domestic art.

In England, until the middle of the eighteenth century, even
the wealthiest classes commonly drank home-made wines and
beers, reserving the 'real' wines—those imported from the grape-
growing countries—for festive occasions, and the custom of
home-brewing lingered among what may be called the middle
sort of folk until well into the nineteenth century, when it was
largely ousted by the vogue for tea.

In Scotland, on the other hand, thanks to the Auld Alliance
and the free and untrammelled wine trade with France, home-
made wines played a much smaller part in the national economy;
but for all that the women of Scotland, and particularly those of
Lowland Scotland, were great brewers and distillers in their day.
Tibbie Shiels, whose inn on St Mary's Loch was well-known to
the Edinburgh *literati* of Scott's day, was noted for her green-
grozet (gooseberry) wine, which is commemorated by Christopher North in the *Noctes Ambrosianae*:

'Now, sir, you have tasted Tibbie's green-grozet. St Mary,
what are the vine-covered hills and gay regions of France to the
small, yellow, hairy gooseberry-gardens of your own Forest!'

Mrs Gentle's primrose wine is also mentioned in the same
work. The lady presents some bottles of it to the Ettrick Shepherd.

'Mr Hogg, Mr North requested me to take charge of the making of his primrose wine this season, and I used the freedom of
setting aside a dozen bottles for your good lady at Altrive.'

And we all know that when the Laird o Cockpen came a-wooing
the 'penniless lass wi' the lang pedigree',

> Mistress Jean she was makin' the elderflo'er wine:
> 'An' what brings the Laird at sic a like time?'
> She put aff her apron and on her silk goun,
> Her mutch wi' reid ribbons, an' gaed awa doun.

Meg Dods's famous *Manual of Cookery*, published in Edinburgh in 1826, gives a number of recipes for home-made wines, liqueurs and cordials popular in her day. Almost everything that grows ferments, and the materials employed include flowers, leaves, berries, vegetables, grain, and even the sap of certain trees, notably the birch and the spruce. The domestic cellar could easily be filled from the garden and the adjacent hedgerows, the home brewer starting with the sap in the early spring and continuing with flowers in the later spring and summer months, berries in the autumn, and root vegetables in the winter months. When bread is made outside the home, the quality inevitably deteriorates, thanks to the methods of mass production and the consideration of profits, and the same is true of our traditional wines. There is genuine satisfaction to be had in picking the flowers and fruit in the sun, digging the vegetables from the soil, and fetching water from the spring; and once the skill is acquired, home brewing becomes a fascinating occupation.

Connoisseurs of wine are apt to wax sarcastic on the subject of the home-made varieties.

'They are said to be appreciated by pickle-fanciers', writes Mr Morton Shand. 'Nervous mistresses often give the cook two or three bottles of "a British wine" for a servant's party on the supposition that it is less dangerously alcoholic than a "foreign one". I know a country house where excellent Blackberry Wine, mistaken by the curate for Port, is made every year, though it is far from being the teetotal tipple that those who make and consume it fondly imagine. Once or twice I have found home-made Cowslip Wine delicious (who could resist the temptation of tasting something which promises to capture in its flavour the scent of the most fragrant of all wild flowers?) and once or twice it has constrained me to a most unmannerly expectoration. Sheen has a story of an old lady who, after dinner, offered him a glass of "Hock" which, she said, she could assure him was genuine ... because she had made it from holly-hocks grown in her own garden.'[1]

The moral is, if you make wines at all, take the trouble to make them with care, and above all, do not make the far too common mistake of offering them to your guests before they have sufficiently matured. That is what is apt to cause an 'unmannerly expectoration'.

1. *A Book of Food*

Those who desire to make wine in any quantity should consult an approved treatise on home-made wines.

A useful quantity for a small household is five gallons, which can be matured in a small cask called a demi-firkin. This holds four and a half gallons, to which quantity the five gallons is usually reduced by the time the straining and 'topping up' (filling up the cask when the contents are diminished by fermentation) is completed. But even five gallons is a formidable quantity for an inexperienced brewer, and it would be wise to experiment with a gallon, which can be matured in a large jar.

The equipment required is simple—a large preserving-pan for the boiling; a gallon jar to hold the liquor when strained from the fruit; with one or two bowls, strainers (hair or nylon), wooden spoons and a funnel (not metal) for bottling. Do not use a saucepan of aluminium or iron, as these metals spoil the colour of the fruit; and do not use a metal jar, for wine should not come into contact with metal when in a state of fermentation.

Both flowers and fruit should be gathered in dry, sunny weather. The flowers should be fully open, and their perfume at its strongest and sweetest. Only the blossoms are used, and all stalks should therefore be removed. The fruit should be fully ripe, but not over-ripe. All unripe or spoiled berries must be discarded, as one ill-flavoured berry will taint the juice of many good ones.

The flavour of the wines is improved if the fruit or flowers used are well crushed by hand before straining.

Do not add spices that are liable to destroy the true flavour of the wine. Try to capture, retain and intensify the natural goodness, flavour and scent of the berries, flowers or other main ingredient employed.

Some fruits contain natural ferments, and do not require the use of yeast; but yeast can be used to hasten the process of fermentation. Brewer's yeast is preferable to baker's compressed yeast, but the latter may be used. Before the yeast is added, a little of the wine should be put aside for 'topping up'. Yeast must always be added when the liquid is lukewarm (70°-85° F), and may either be spread on a piece of toast and floated on the wine in the cask, or creamed with a little of the lukewarm liquid and stirred in immediately. (This is the more usual method with smaller quantities of wine.) The mouth of the cask or jar is then covered with a piece of thick blanket or several thicknesses of cotton. This allows the gases generated by the fermenting wine to escape, whilst excluding all contact with the air.

During the period of the first or 'tumultuous' fermentation, which usually lasts from four to seven days, the excess of yeast will ooze out and run down the sides, and the jar should be placed in some receptacle to catch it. The more the waste matter exuded, the clearer the wine. The jar should be 'topped up' or replenished every morning, in order to avoid the formation of an air pocket, which may sour the wine. Let it ferment in a warm room, at an even temperature of 65°-80° F.

When the first ferment is over, the 'tumult' will cease and the working of the wine will not be apparent unless one puts one's ear to the mouth of the jar, when what has been described as 'a low, contented, sizzling sound, like a hive of orderly bees', can be heard. The jar may now be put aside so that the wine may finish its peaceful ferment. It should be lightly corked at first to exclude air, for if too tightly corked before fermentation has finally ceased, it is liable to explode. Leave to mature—in most cases for not less than six months, and preferably for a year, before bottling. Store in a cool place (50°-60° F). A cask should lie on its side, six inches off the ground. Decant carefully into clean, dry bottles, discarding all the sediment that lies at the bottom of the jar (or cask). Fill the bottles full, cork tightly with new corks, and store at the same cellar temperature, letting the bottles lie on their side.

Green or brown bottles should be used for red wine, which loses its colour if exposed to the light.

Mrs McLennan, Port Appin, comments, 'The amount of yeast mentioned in most of those old country recipes errs on the side of being too much. I have found that a small teaspoonful creamed with a little of the lukewarm liquor and thoroughly stirred into the whole is best.'

BARLEY WINE

1 lb. pot barley	4 lb. white sugar
1 lb. potatoes	1 oz. yeast
1 lb. raisins	1 gallon water

Pot, not pearl, barley should be used and old, not new potatoes.

Scrub, but do not peel the potatoes and cut into small chunks. Put barley, potatoes, raisins and sugar into a jar and cover with hot, but not boiling water. When reduced to tepid, use a little to dissolve the yeast and add to the rest. Leave for twenty-one days, stirring daily. Strain and bottle. Leave the corks loose for a week, then fasten securely. Keep for at least six months before use.

This makes a lovely golden wine.

Some home brewers add a sliced orange and lemon to the barley, etc., before pouring on the hot water.

BEE'S WINE

This is a different drink from bee-ale, which is a kind of mead. In the 'thirties the present writer received a letter from a friend enclosing a newspaper cutting, a query from an anonymous correspondent in Forres:

'Sir,—I should be obliged if any of your readers would be kind enough to tell me the name of, and where to procure, a plant for making treacle ale. It resembles a kind of seaweed, and is placed in a large glass or earthenware receptacle with treacle and water added. As time goes on, the plant increases and multiplies so much that part of it must be removed and either placed in other vessels or thrown away.'

The covering letter ran: 'Have you heard of this beverage? (I hadn't.) I cannot see any reference to it in *The Scots Kitchen*. It is made from a sort of fungus or wort found amongst the froth you see where a river meets the sea, and where salmon are found. A few pieces are put into a bottle and a brew is made of two tea-spoonfuls of treacle and two teaspoonfuls of sugar. Mix with warm water and let it get cold before adding the brew to the bottle containing the fungus. Cork the bottle and leave for twenty-four hours. The fungus grows very quickly. The taste is quite good.'

I have been unable to verify the statement that the fungus, which, incidentally, is a yeast-plant, is found near the mouth of a salmon river or, indeed, that it is indigenous to Scotland. Its origin is unknown, but the general idea is that it was introduced into Britain from the Continent about the mid-nineteenth century, when its cult spread rapidly. In England it is known as the ginger-beer plant, the brew being flavoured with ginger instead of treacle, as in Scotland.

The name Bee's Wine derives from the resemblance of the fungus, while it is 'working', to a cluster of bees on a comb.

A Barra friend tells me that the fungus was introduced there by Shetland fishermen, and also that the brew, when used in place of milk, makes excellent treacle scones.

BEETROOT WINE

4 lb. beetroot	12 cloves
6 pints water	1 oz. root ginger

Allow to each gallon of juice:

1 lemon	$\frac{1}{2}$ oz. yeast (spread on toast)
2$\frac{1}{4}$ lb. sugar	$\frac{1}{4}$ oz. isinglass (to clear)

$\frac{1}{2}$—1 gill brandy (optional)

Wash the beets thoroughly, and slice or chop them without removing the skin. Put into a pan with the cold water, cloves and ginger, bring to the boil, and simmer until all the juice is extracted (from one to one and a half hours). Strain through a cloth, pressing well. Return the juice to the rinsed pan with the sugar and lemon rind. Stir until the sugar is dissolved, bring to the boil and simmer for fifteen minutes. Remove the rind, pour the liquor into a crock, and when lukewarm add the lemon juice and the yeast spread on a piece of toast or frothed in a little of the warm liquor. Cover lightly and leave in a warm place to ferment. When the bubbling has ceased, stir, let it settle for three days, then filter into the cask. If it appears very cloudy, put in the isinglass; and if desired, add the brandy. Then bung down tightly and put into a cool dark place for a year.

The wine may be strained into bottles after fermentation has ceased, and left for six months to mature.

BIRK WINE

The birch tree grows plentifully in the Highlands. Pennant, writing of the Aberdeenshire Highlands in 1796, speaks of the many uses the tree was put to, such as for roofing, for the making of agricultural implements, for tanning with its bark; and mentions that 'quantities of excellent wine are extracted from the live tree by tapping'. Actually the sap was extracted and converted by fermentation into a beverage with some power of stimulation.

The sap should be drawn in March, when it is rising, before the leaves begin to shoot. 'Bore a hole in a tree', says Mrs Dalgairns, 'and put in a faucet, and it will run for two or three days together without hurting the tree; then put in a pin to stop it, and next year you may draw as much from the same hole.' The faucets or pipes used for draining were commonly of elder.

Birk Wine
(Mrs Dalgairns's Recipe)

To every gallon of juice from the birch tree, three pounds of sugar, one pound of raisins, half an ounce of crude tartar, and one ounce of bitter almonds are allowed: the juice, sugar and raisins are to be boiled twenty minutes, and then put into a tub, together with the tartar; and when it has fermented some days, it is to be strained, and put into the cask, and also the almonds, which must be tied in a muslin bag. The fermentation having ceased, the almonds are to be withdrawn, and the cask bunged up, to stand about five months, when it may be fined and bottled.

Birk Wine
Meg Dods's Recipe

To every gallon of the sap of the birch tree, boiled, put four pounds of white sugar, and the thin paring of a lemon. Boil and skim this well. When cool, put fresh yeast to it. Let it ferment for four or five days; then close it up. Keep the bung very close, and in four months rack it off, and bottle it.

NOTE.—The sap should be used when freshly drawn, or else must be carefully corked up till required. Less sugar will do, says Meg. One recipe allows as little as two pounds to the gallon.

BLAEBERRY (Bilberry) WINE

1 gallon blaeberries	4 lb. sugar
1 gallon water	1 oz. yeast

Pour the water (cold) over the crushed blaeberries. Stir and mash daily for six days, then strain, add the sugar, and stir till dissolved. Spread the yeast on a slice of toast and put in to float on the liquid (made luke-warm). Leave in a warm place to ferment for fourteen days. Skim and bottle, corking lightly until all fermentation has ceased, then cork securely.

Blaeberry Wine
(Another way)

4 lb. blaeberries	4 lb. sugar
4 lb. apples	½ lb. raisins
1 gallon water	

The apples must be steeped for four days before the blaeberries are gathered.

Wash the apples and cut them up without peeling or coring. Pour half a gallon of water over them. Squeeze and stir every day for eight days. When they have stood for four days, gather your blaeberries, cover with another half gallon of water, and stir and squeeze each day for four days until all the juice is extracted. Strain both apple and blaeberry juice and mix them. Add the sugar and chopped raisins and stir until the sugar is dissolved. Let it ferment for three weeks, then skim, strain and bottle. Keep for a year before use.

BRAGWORT or BEE-ALE

Bragwort,[1] or bee-ale, as it is known in the north-east, or mead, is a mild alcoholic beverage of great antiquity, and is made by fermenting honied water.

'After the bees are *smuiked* (smoked) in the *hinharrest* time (at the end of the harvest), the *gude wife* takes the *kaimes* (honeycombs) out of the *skep* (hive), and lets the *hinny* (honey) drop out of them before the fire; when this is done, she takes these combs or *kaimes* and steeps them in water. This water, warmed and quickened with barm, composes *bragwort*. It is an extremely sweet and

1. The name is probably of Pictish origin: O. Scots *brogat*, akin to the Welsh *bragod*, *-ydd*, a malt liquor (from *brag*, malt). Wort was probably added through the erroneous association of the suffix *wort* with *et*.

pleasant drink . . . when put in bottles it is apt to break them.[1] That person is a favourite in that house, when, by making a call, he is treated with a draught of *bragwort*. If he be a young man of fair character, looking out for a wife, and this house be a place where fair dames are, he is sure to taste bragwort. It may be called with propriety "the lovers' drink".'[2]

Bragwort
(Here is a more explicit recipe)

Having drained the honey from the combs, place these in an earthen vessel and cover with cold water. Let this stand for a week or ten days. Strain, make lukewarm, and allow an ounce of compressed yeast to the gallon of honied water. Spread the yeast on a piece of toast and float on top; let the liquor ferment, and when it has done working, bottle it.

Bragwort may be spiced if desired. Ginger and clove, or cinnamon and clove may be used, either in equal quantities or with rather less clove in proportion. Add the spices (to taste) after straining the liquor, and boil until the desired flavour is obtained. Allow to cool to lukewarm before adding the yeast.

BRAMBLE WINE

1 gallon brambleberries   1 gallon water
2 lb. sugar to each gallon of juice
A little brandy (optional)

The berries should be gathered on a fine day and must be ripe and dry. Pick them over carefully and place in an earthenware crock. Bruise the fruit with a wooden spoon and pour the boiling water over it. Cover and allow to stand for six days, stirring every day. Skim, and strain through linen or fine muslin.

Measure the juice and the proportionate amount of sugar. Return the juice to the rinsed crock, add the sugar, and stir until it has dissolved. Cover the crock lightly and leave until fermentation ceases (a week or longer). Add the brandy if desired. Pour into bottles, corking them loosely at first; then tighten up and

1. 'Will ye hae a drink o bee-ale? It's aye blawin' the corks.' Aberdeen, 1933 (quoted in the *Scottish National Dictionary*).
2. Mactaggart's *Gallovidian Encyclopedia*.

leave for not less than six months, and preferably for twelve to mature.

The wine may be spiced by adding half a teaspoonful apiece of ground cloves, ginger, cinnamon and mixed spice along with the sugar to each gallon of liquid.

CAIRM

This beverage seems to be peculiar to the Highlands. The name is derived from the Gaelic *carmeal*, the wild liquorice. The roots of both carmeal and orobus-tuberosis were used for ale. They were pounded and infused, and yeast was added in the usual way.

Martin Martin, who visited the Hebrides in 1691, tells us that the natives of Mull chew a piece of the root (carmeal), which they find aromatic, to prevent drunkenness.

COWSLIP WINE

1 gallon cowslip flowers (yellow corollas only)	3 lb. loaf sugar
1 lemon	1 oz. yeast
1 Seville orange (optional)	1 gallon water
	1 gill brandy (optional)

The cowslips, which are to be had only in spring, should be freshly gathered and must be perfectly dry. They should be stripped of all stalks and traces of green before they are measured.

Simmer the water and sugar together for half an hour, carefully removing all scum. Meanwhile pare the rind of the lemon and orange very thinly and squeeze out the juice. Put the rinds into a large crock and pour the boiling syrup over them. When it has cooled to lukewarm, stir in the flowers and the fruit juices and add the yeast frothed up with a little of the lukewarm liquor. Cover with a cloth or flannel and leave for three days, stirring three or four times a day; then strain the liquor into a cask, reserving a little for later use. Leave the bung loose until all working has ceased; then fill up with the remaining liquor and bung up tight. Bottle in three months.

Cowslip wine is strongly narcotic and makes an excellent soporific since it forms no injurious habit.

R

CRAB-APPLE WINE

1 gallon crab-apples   1 gallon water
3 lb. brown sugar

Wash but do not peel the apples; pour the water over them, and leave for two or three days, till soft and swollen; then break to mush with the hand. Leave for twenty-one days, stirring daily; then strain, add the sugar, and stir till dissolved. Leave to ferment for another twenty-one days. Skim, turn into a jar and cork up; or bottle straight away, leaving the corks loose for a time.

Another method is to make as above, adding a pound of wheat and a pound of raisins along with the sugar, and sprinkling a tablespoonful of yeast on the top. Complete as above.

DAMSON WINE

10 lb. damsons   1 gallon water
4 lb. sugar   ½ pint brandy (optional)

Bruise or pound the fruit, place in a large bowl and pour the boiling water over it. Cover with a cloth and leave for four days, stirring and pounding well once or twice every day. Strain into another vessel, put in the sugar, and stir vigorously. In a few days, when the sugar is dissolved, turn the liquor into a clean, dry cask. Cover the bung-hole with a folded cloth, and when fermentation ceases bung tightly and store for twelve months, when the wine may be racked off into bottles.

DANDELION WINE

3 quarts dandelion flowers 8 oz. raisins
3 lb. moist sugar   1 oz. yeast
2 sweet oranges   1 gallon water
1 large lemon

Only the heads of the flowers are used, so nip off the stalks before measuring. Place the flowers in an earthen crock or bowl and pour the boiling water over them. Cover and leave for ten days, stirring occasionally.

Peel the oranges and lemon as thinly as possible, discarding the white pith. Strain the dandelion liquor into a pan; add the yellow rinds and the sugar, and simmer for twenty minutes. Return to the crock and allow to cool, but while still lukewarm add the juice of the oranges and lemon and the yeast. Let the crock stand, covered, for two or three weeks, until fermentation ceases; then strain through muslin. Put into a cask with the stoned raisins, or into bottles. If bottles are used, divide the raisins equally among them and put them in before filling up with wine. The bottles should not be quite filled. Cork very loosely at first, but as soon as it is safe to do so, cork down tightly and lay the bottles on their sides. Leave for six months. If made in May or June, the wine will be ready for Christmas.

Dandelion wine is a reputed blood purifier and diuretic.

ELDERBERRY WINE

In the late autumn elderberries hang in shining black bunches on every twig of the wild elder bushes that grow in profusion in the country, and often within easy reach of the town. It is advisable to gather them in a pail, not a basket, for the juice is penetrating and the dye hard to remove. Always use the black-berried wild elder for your wine, and not the red-berried garden variety.

Elderberry Wine
(A Galloway Recipe)

7 lb. elderberries	3 gallons water

To each gallon of liquid obtained after steeping allow:

3 lb. sugar	½ oz. ground ginger
1 lb. raisins	½ dozen cloves
1 gill brandy (optional)	1 oz. yeast

Strip the berries from the stalks, discarding any unripe or withered ones. Pour the boiling water over them and leave them to steep for twenty-four hours; then crush them well and strain into your preserving-pan. Add the other ingredients (except the brandy), bring to the boil, and boil gently for an hour, skimming as required. Allow to cool to lukewarm, stir in the yeast, and put into a clean cask. Cover the bung-hole with a folded cloth, leave for fourteen days, then stir in the brandy. Bung firmly, and bottle in six months, or not earlier than February.

Elderberry has always been one of the most popular of our home-made wines.

Elderberries have diuretic and aperient qualities, but their taste is unpleasant without the addition of cloves and other spices. Drunk hot and spiced—mulled, or as negus—this is a very pleasant and comforting winter drink.

Elderberry Wine
(An Argyll Recipe)

By using 3½-4 lb. berries and 3½ lb. sugar to the gallon of water, fermenting in the usual way, omitting all spices and spirits, and leaving for two years to mature, you get a really nice wine with no trace of elderberry flavour, but more like Burgundy.

ELDERFLOWER CHAMPAGNE

3 large heads of elderflower	1 lemon
1½ lb. sugar	2 tablespoonfuls white
1 gallon spring water	wine vinegar

Gather the flowers on a hot summer day, when they are in full blossom and richly scented. Strip or shake the flowers lightly from their stalks. Empty them into a crock, add the juice and thinly peeled rind of the lemon (carefully avoid all white pith), the sugar, and the vinegar. Pour over this a gallon of cold spring water, and leave to steep for forty-eight hours or longer. Strain into strong bottles, such as beer or champagne or mineral water containers, and cork firmly, for this wine is strongly effervescent. It should be ready in a fortnight.

ELDERFLOWER WINE

1 quart elderflowers	3 lb. loaf sugar
1 lb. raisins	1 tablespoonful yeast
1 lemon	1 gallon water

The elderflowers should be gathered when in full bloom or just about to fall, and should be quite dry. Shake or strip the flowers lightly from their stalks, fill a quart measure (packing it loosely) and empty it into a crock.

Meanwhile have a hot syrup in readiness made thus:

Put into a pan the water, sugar, and thinly peeled lemon rind and boil for an hour, removing the scum as it rises. Pour, scalding hot, over the flowers and stir well. When it has cooled to rather more than lukewarm, add lemon juice and yeast. Cover the vessel with a cloth, and stir every day until fermentation ceases (about a week). To every gallon of liquor allow a pound of large fleshy raisins. Put these into a cask and strain the wine over them. Next day fix the bung tightly into the cask. Keep in a cool cellar for six months before bottling.

A pint or more of Rhenish wine may be added along with the raisins to each gallon of liquor, if desired.

GEAN (WILD CHERRY) WINE

> 12 lb. cherries   ½ pint sugar to each quart of juice
> Pinches of ground cloves and mace (optional)

The small, wild black cherries make delicious wine. Gather them when fully ripe, wipe them and remove the stalks. Put them into a large bowl and bruise them with a mallet to break the skins. Cover and set aside for twenty-four hours, then drain off the juice through a hair or nylon sieve. Measure the juice and add the sugar, with the spice if desired. Stir well, and stand undisturbed for another twenty-four hours until the sugar is quite dissolved. Strain into a clean dry cask to ferment. When all working has ceased, bung closely, store, and bottle off after six months, filtering first.

This wine should be drunk within eighteen months, as the bouquet of the cherries is evanescent.

The wine may be enriched by adding ½ pint brandy to every quart of wine.

GINGER BEER

> 1¼ lb. white sugar   ½ oz. cream of tartar
> 1½ oz. root ginger   ½ oz. yeast
> 2 lemons   1 gallon water

Peel the lemons thinly, discard pith and seeds and cut into thin slices. Bruise the ginger. Put the sugar into a large bowl, add the ginger and cream of tartar with the rind and pulp of the lemons. Pour the boiling water over this and stir to dissolve the sugar. When it has cooled to lukewarm, add the yeast creamed with a teaspoonful of sugar. Cover with a cloth and leave in a moderately warm atmosphere for twenty-four hours. Skim, strain and bottle immediately. Cork and tie down securely, or use screw-top bottles. It will be ready for use in two or three days' time.

GINGER WINE

(Old Midlothian Recipe)

4 oz. best root ginger	3 gallons water
8 lb. brown sugar	3 egg-whites
3 Seville oranges	½ teacupful fresh yeast
3 lemons	2 bottles whisky

Bruise the ginger. Squeeze the juice from the oranges and lemons. Beat the egg-whites to a froth. Put the water, sugar and egg-whites on to boil. Remove the scum, add the ginger, and boil for forty-five minutes. Leave to cool, and when lukewarm add the strained juice of the oranges and lemons and stir in the yeast. Leave it for three days to ferment. Now put it into a cask with the whisky and bung up—not very tight at first. It may be bottled in eight or ten weeks, and is good after six months, but may be kept much longer.

GORSE or WHIN WINE

(Ayrshire Recipe)

½ gallon gorse flowers	3 lb. Demerara sugar
2 oz. root ginger	1 oz. compressed yeast
1 orange	1 gallon water
1 lemon	

Always pick these flowers when warm from the sun's rays. The wine has then a richer bouquet.

Simmer the flowers, water and ginger together for fifteen

minutes; add the sugar and stir till dissolved. Slice the orange
and lemon and add to the cooling liquid, and when just warm
add the yeast. Cover with a folded blanket, leave undisturbed
for a week, then skim off the head. Strain into a jar; allow to
work for another week before corking tightly. A few raisins and
a lump of sugar-candy keep it lively. Bottle off in November, or
not less than three months after fermentation ceases.

GREEN-GROZET (GOOSEBERRY) WINE

> 8 lb. green gooseberries   2 gallons water
> 3 lb. sugar to each gallon of juice

The gooseberries should be ripe, but not over-ripe—that is,
they should not have begun to change colour. Wash, top and
tail them, and bruise them well, but not sufficiently to bruise the
seeds. Now measure them and place in a crock or wooden tub.
Pour the cold water over them and mix and mash well. Cover
with a cloth and leave for two days. Strain and measure the
liquid, return to the crock and add the sugar. Stir well, and let
it stand until the sugar has dissolved, stirring frequently. Turn
into a cask and leave in a warm place until the fermentation has
ceased—about three weeks; then bung up securely. Fit a peg
into the vent hole, and every day pull it out to allow any gas to
escape. When the wine is quite still, close up tightly and leave in
a cool place for eight months, when it will be ready for bottling.
Half a pint of brandy may be added to every gallon of wine
when it is put into the cask.

HAWTHORN WINE

> 1 gallon hawthorn flowers   2 lemons
> 6 lb. rhubarb   4 lb. sugar
>   1 gallon water

Cut up the rhubarb very small and cover with the water (cold).
Peel the lemon thinly, discarding all pith, and slice it, removing
all pips. Add to the rhubarb, together with the hawthorn flowers.
Stir well and leave, lightly covered, for fourteen days, stirring
daily. Strain and add the sugar. Stir till dissolved and leave to

ferment (about a week); then skim, strain and bottle. Leave for at least eight months, and preferably for twelve, before use.

HERB ALE

In Georgian times, it was customary for members of Glasgow's Morning Club to foregather in Currie's Close before breakfast.

'In the comfortable tavern, with its blazing fire, situated in the then fashionable locality, the members were always sure of getting either a tankard of hot herb-ale, whose medicinal qualities were considered no bad antidote to the rather uneasy effects produced by the previous evening's heavy potations—or that beverage which was then well-known by the designation of a "baurie", which consisted of a half-mutchkin of rum, with a due proportion of hot water and sugar, poured out and *skinked* in a quart mug. With either placed on the board, and with a newspaper in hand, each member felt himself quite in his element.

'. . . The practice of drinking hot herb-ale in the morning existed till about the year 1820. At that time there was a peripatetic club, composed of a number of respectable manufacturers, who took their early walk round the Public Green—like the ancient Greeks in their Arcadia—and who, on their return about 8 or 9 o'clock, wound up their morning's pleasure with a tankard of this potation, in a famous herb-ale house, nearly opposite the Old Gate, which led into the Green at the north end of the Saltmarket.'[1]

Herb Ale
(Traditional Recipe)

Take three pounds of watercresses, twenty ounces of dandelion roots, twelve ounces of juniper berries, and twenty-four drops of wormwood; mince all together quite small, and put them in a brown linen bag, which place in six pints of beer-wort to steep for forty-eight hours. Strain; then take a four-gallon cask of ale and draw off as much as will leave room for the infusion; when quite fine, bottle it, and in each bottle place a piece of orange peel. This is very wholesome, and very pleasant to drink.

1. John Strang, LL.D.: *Glasgow and Her Clubs.*

MALT WINE or SCOTTISH MALMSEY

(Meg Dods's Recipe)

6 gallons worts (unfermented beer must)	4 lb. muscatel raisins
	12 oz. bitter almonds
6 lb. sugar and 6 lb. honey or 12 lb. sugar	1 oz. isinglass
	Some brewer's yeast
6 gallons water	1 quart whisky

Get from the brewer, or make, the required quantity of strong, fresh, sweet worts, or get the same quantity of 'pot ale' from the distiller. To this add first the water and then the sugar and honey. Take a pint of the mixture, warm it a little, and add to it the brewer's yeast (say two ounces). When it is well working, stir it into the rest. Leave the cask for one month to ferment, keeping it well filled. While the wine is working, let the almonds and raisins (both chopped) soak in the whisky, and when the first ferment is finished and the liquor has cleared, strain the whisky (reserving the almonds and raisins for cakes and other culinary purposes) and add it to the cask, together with the isinglass dissolved in a little wine. Bottle the wine in from four to six weeks' time.

MARIGOLD WINE

1 peck marigold petals	2 tablespoonfuls yeast
6 lb. sugar or honey	$\frac{1}{2}$ oz. isinglass
1 lb. raisins	2 oz. sugar-candy
2 Seville oranges	$2\frac{1}{2}$ gallons water
1 egg-white	1 pint French brandy

The marigolds should be gathered at midday when the sun is at full strength. The calyxes must be stripped away, and only the petals used. Measure a peck of these and place them in a crock with the raisins. Boil the water with the sugar or honey for half an hour; then stir in the beaten egg-white and skim quite clear. Pour the hot liquid upon the flowers and cover the vessel closely. Leave for twenty-four hours, then stir for twenty minutes consecutively and leave for another twenty-four hours. Strain into a cask over the juice and thinly peel rind (no white pith) of the oranges, with the sugar-candy broken up very small. Take about a pint of the marigold liquor, make it lukewarm, and add the yeast. When it is fermenting rapidly, add it to the cask and cover the vent with a piece of thick cloth. As it works and the level falls fill up the cask. When the fermentation ceases, add the brandy and the isinglass dissolved in a little warm water. Bung tightly and leave for at least nine months—preferably twelve—before bottling.

The monks of old used the marigold as a remedy for all weaknesses of the heart and as a specific against cancer.

MEAD

1 lb. fresh honey	$\frac{3}{4}$ oz. dried hops
1 gallon water	1 oz. yeast

Put the hops and honey into a pan with the water, bring to the boil and boil gently for an hour. Turn into a crock, and when the liquor has cooled to lukewarm add the yeast, either spread on toast or stirred into a little of the liquor. Leave for three or four days; then strain into a cask, but do not bung tightly until the fermentation has ceased. Store for a year, then draw off and bottle.

NETTLE BEER

4 lb. tops of young nettles	2 oz. root ginger
1 pint dandelion petals	1 oz. yeast
1 lb. Demerara sugar	1 gallon water

The common or stinging kind of nettle is used, the young tops only. Wash them and place in a large enamel-lined saucepan with the dandelion (loosely packed when measured), the sugar, ginger (bruised) and water. Bring to the boil, stirring frequently until the sugar is dissolved; then strain into a crock. When the liquor is tepid, add the yeast. Cover and leave to ferment, then skim and strain through a hair sieve. Pour into dry beer bottles and screw down the corks. This beer needs no keeping and will be ready for use in a day or two.

The first brewing is made when the young shoots appear in

spring, and bunches of young nettles are hung from the rafters to dry for use later in the year.

The nettle used to be regarded as a universal panacea. Taken in spring, it purifies the blood and clears the system of colds and rheums, and counteracts the general sluggishness and lassitude that so often succeed a long winter.

ORANGE WINE

12 Seville oranges	1 gallon water
2 lemons	2 lb. sugar to each gallon of liquor

Wipe and slice the fruit, removing all pips. Place in a crock and pour the boiling water over it. Cover lightly and leave for a week, stirring as often as you like. Strain through a jelly-bag, measure the liquid and add sugar in proportion. Stir well, and when the sugar has dissolved pour the liquor into a cask and leave to ferment. When fermentation has ceased, bung up, and leave for four months before bottling. A dessertspoonful of whisky may be added to each bottle.

Meg Dods writes: 'This wine may be improved to some tastes by substituting honey for one-third of the sugar. It may be enriched by the addition of some of the high-flavoured wines, and perfumed with ginger, bitter almonds, bermagot, citron, peach-leaves, etc. etc.'

ORKNEY ALE

1 stone malt	1½ lb. sugar
2 oz. hops	8 gallons water
2 tablespoonfuls brewer's barm *or*	
1 oz. baker's yeast	

See that the kirn or cask is spotlessly clean (or the barm won't work satisfactorily) and put in the malt. Bring the water almost to boiling-point, but it must not be actually boiling when used. (You may add two or three pints of cold water to take it off the boil.) Pour the hot water over the malt, cover lightly, and let it mask for three hours. Strain into a pan, add the hops (which may be tied in a muslin bag to save straining) and a pound of sugar, and boil for an hour. Return the liquor to the kirn, and when it has cooled to blood heat, add the barm, which may be 'started' by sprinkling with a little sugar or by frothing in a little of the warm liquor, some more liquor being added before it is put into the kirn.

When fermentation has ceased (usually after two or three days), skim off any surface barm, allow to settle, and bottle. Half a teaspoonful of sugar may be added to each bottle. See that well-fitting corks are used.

Let the ale stand in a cool place until it recovers a little 'life'.

Some Orkney housewives add double the quantity of hops or more; others, half the quantity of water. It is a matter of taste. In one recipe given to the present writer, half the sugar is put into the kirn with the malt, and the remainder is boiled up with the hops. There are always minor variations, but the method is basically the same.

Mask, infuse.

PARSLEY WINE

1 lb. parsley	3 lb. sugar
2 oranges	$\frac{1}{2}$ oz. yeast
2 lemons	1 gallon water
1 oz. root ginger	

Remove all the stalks from the parsley before weighing. Wash it and place in a large crock. Pour the boiling water over it, cover and stand for twenty-four hours. Strain the liquor into a pan, add the ginger and yellow rinds (thinly pared) of the oranges and lemons. Return to the crock, add the sugar and the juice of the oranges and lemons, and stir until the sugar is dissolved. Allow to cool, and when lukewarm float toast spread with the yeast on top. Leave for five days; then strain and bottle, corking loosely at first, and tightly when the fermentation ceases.

Kept sealed and undisturbed for five years, this wine has been found 'delicious, smooth and mellow, the flavour delicate, and the colour a clear sparkling golden tint.'

Parsley wine is light, refreshing, and delicately flavoured. It is said to be good for rheumatism if taken regularly and over a long period.

PARSNIP WINE

5 lb. parsnips	½ oz. yeast
3 lb. Demerara sugar	1 gallon water
½ oz. bruised ginger	

It is preferable to dig parsnips when autumn is advanced and lay them out to get well frosted. This increases the sugar content.

Clean the parsnips but do not peel them, and slice them not too thinly. Put them in the cold water, bring to the boil, and boil gently for about half an hour till they are soft but not broken. (If they are over-boiled the wine will be cloudy.)

Strain the liquor through muslin into an earthen crock or wooden tub. Measure it and return to the pan, allowing the above quantities of Demerara sugar and ginger for each gallon. Bring to the boil again and boil for half an hour. Pour it back into the crock, and when it has cooled to lukewarm add the yeast. Stir vigorously, then leave the crock in the warmth of the kitchen to assist fermentation. After two days, remove any scum and pour the wine into a cask or jar. Keep back a little wine to add daily to the cask or jar as the waste works over the bung-hole. When fermentation has ceased, bung down tightly. Leave for at least six months before bottling.

This is one of the pleasantest of cordial wines, light and delicate, tasting of anything but parsnip, and creaming in the glass in a manner most agreeable to the eye.

Parsnip wine has decided laxative and diuretic properties.

Carrot Wine is made in precisely the same way.

POTATO WINE

5 lb. small potatoes	2 oranges
2½ lb. sugar	2 lemons
1 gallon water	

Scrub the potatoes thoroughly and boil them whole in the

measured water for ten to fifteen minutes, taking great care that they do not break in the boiling. Put the sugar, preferably Demerara, into a large crock with the sliced oranges and lemons, and pour over this the strained potato liquor. Cover lightly and leave to soak overnight. Empty the crock into the preserving-pan, bring to the boil, stirring well; then boil steadily for thirty minutes, stirring occasionally. Strain back into the crock, and when it is quite cold, bottle and cork securely. (No yeast is required.)

A first-class wine is made by combining potatoes with wheat. See *Wheat Wine*.

PRIMROSE WINE

8 quarts primroses, *or*	1½ lb. stoned raisins
6 quarts primroses and	3 lemons
2 quarts cowslips	1 tablespoonful yeast
8 lb. loaf sugar	3 gallons spring water
½ oz. powdered ginger	½ pint brandy
A few cloves	A little isinglass

Only the yellow corolla of the flower is used. (The calyx would embitter the wine and spoil the scent.) Measure the flowers and empty them into a crock. Boil together the water, sugar, ginger and cloves. Skim frequently until the liquor is clear, allow to cool, and strain over the flowers. Stir well; then add the raisins and the juice of the lemons. Cover the crock and leave for three days; then strain into a cask. Take a little of the infusion, warm it to blood heat, no more; beat in the yeast and when it is frothing add it to the liquor in the cask. When the wine has ceased to ferment pour in the brandy and add a little isinglass dissolved in water. Bung the cask down and keep it for at least a year before bottling, and for another six months before using.

Primrose wine is very delicate and light, but lacks the soporific quality of cowslip wine.

RAISIN WINE

5 lb. large, fleshy raisins	1 gallon water
½ pint brandy	

The quality of the wine depends largely on the quality of the raisins. Malaga or Belvidere are recommended.

Boil the water and allow it to get perfectly cold. Remove all stalks from the fruit and pull each raisin in two. Place the raisins in a crock and pour the water over them. Cover lightly, and let them steep for a fortnight, stirring them every day. Strain, squeezing the juice out of the raisins. Put the liquor into a cask that will just hold it, for it should be quite full. Lay the bung lightly over, stir the wine every day, and keep the cask full by adding, as required, more water that has been boiled and allowed to get quite cold. As soon as the fermentation has ceased, which may be from six to seven weeks, add the brandy, bung up the cask, and leave the wine untroubled for six months before bottling. It is seldom drinkable in less than twelve months and is the better for being kept two years or longer.

The first quarter of the year is the best time for making raisin wine, and March is said to be the best month of all.

RASPBERRY WINE

> 1 gallon raspberries   1 gallon water
> 4 lb. sugar

Choose sound, ripe raspberries, put them into a suitable vessel, crush them and pour the water (cold) over them, stirring well. Cover lightly and leave for twenty-four hours. Strain the juice through a jelly-bag, measure it, and to each quart add a pound of sugar. Stir until the sugar is dissolved, then pour into a jar or cask and leave, lightly covered, until fermentation has ceased (about a fortnight). Bung or cork tightly, and leave for three months before bottling. It is the better for being kept two years.

RED CLOVER WINE

> 2 quarts red clover flowers 2 oranges
> 4 lb. white sugar   3 lemons
> 1 oz. yeast   1 gallon water

Gather the clover on a dry day. If it is at all dewy, leave it to dry in the sun. Remove the flowers from the stalks, discarding those that are not yet in full bloom and those that are past their best. Measure them, put them into a crock, and pour over them the boiling water. While the liquor is cooling, slice the oranges and lemons, and when it is lukewarm put them in, together with the sugar and the yeast spread on toast, or frothed up in a little of the warm liquor. Leave for five days, stirring twice daily; strain, and leave for another five days; strain again, and leave for three days longer. Bottle, leaving the corks loose for ten days; then cork up. The wine will be ready for use in a month.

RED CURRANT WINE

1 gallon red currants	1 gallon water
3 lb. sugar	

Strip the berries of their stalks, bruise them, add the sugar and cover with the boiling water. Leave for four or five days, stirring every day. Then strain through a hair sieve, squeezing out all the juice. Add the sugar and stir till dissolved. Set aside to ferment (about fourteen days). When this is completed, skim, strain into a cask and bung tightly. Leave for at least six months before bottling. It is the better for being kept for two years.

The seventeenth-century herbalist, Gerard, recommends the use of the red currant 'to extinguish or mitigate fevers, repress choler, temper the over-hot blood, and to resist putrefaction'.

RHUBARB WINE

5 lb. rhubarb	1 lemon
3 lb. sugar	1 oz. ginger (optional)
	1 gallon water

Wipe the rhubarb, which must be perfectly ripe, with a damp cloth, and cut into short lengths. Place in a crock or wooden tub, and crush well with a wooden mallet. Pour the boiling water over it, cover, and let it stand for a week, stirring occasionally. Strain, and add the sugar, stirring until it is dissolved. Add the ginger with the juice and yellow rind (no pith) of the lemon. Let it stand for six days longer, stirring every day. Strain and bottle, but cork very lightly until fermentation has ceased. It is advisable to leave this wine for about six months, though it is drinkable after three.

ROSE PETAL WINE

(This recipe is based on that of Mrs Catherine McLennan, Port Appin. She describes it as a modern version of a very old recipe.)

1 gallon rose petals	2 lb. sugar
2 quarts water	½ oz. yeast

Gather only two quarts of fresh rose petals to begin with. Put them into a crock or basin and pour over them the boiling water. Leave until the water has become thoroughly impregnated with the scent of the roses, then strain into another vessel through a muslin bag. (A three-pound flour bag that has been boiled and bleached will do very well.) Wring all the liquid out of the petals, and throw them away. Gather another two quarts of petals and repeat the straining and wringing until you think the liquid is sufficiently scented. Add the sugar (using the best quality white) and boil gently for ten minutes, removing any scum that arises. Turn into a crock, and when the liquid has cooled to lukewarm, stir a little into the yeast and pour the creaming yeast into the crock. Keep closely covered until fermentation has ceased. When bottled, keep the wine as long as possible, as the perfume becomes richer with keeping.

According to another recipe, white wine may be added to the rose petal wine, pint for pint.

ROWAN WINE

Ripe red rowanberries	1 lb. loaf sugar to each
Water to cover	gallon of rowan liquor

The berries should be gathered on a dry day. They should be quite ripe, but not over-ripe. Put them in a crock, mash them well, and pour over them just enough boiling water to cover. Place a cloth over the crock and leave for three days; then drain off the liquid (without disturbing the scum that has formed),

s

measure it, and put it into a pan with sugar in proportion. Stir over heat until the sugar is quite dissolved. Pour into a small cask or into brown stone gallon jars,[1] which must be kept full while the wine is working. Leave for seven days, or till the working ceases; then fasten down tightly. Leave for six months before bottling.

SKEACHAN or TREACLE ALE

'The earliest recollections I have of Christmas', writes a native of Aberdeenshire, 'are associated with "sids" being brought from the meal-mill to be "steepit" for sowens, and with my being dispatched to Burnie's chop (shop) for hops, ginger, and a big flagon of treacle, with which ingredients and malt from the "Canal Heid" my mother brewed the Yule Ale. . . . When it was brewed with honey when the skeps (bee-hives) were "smokit" in the autumn, it was nectar fit for the gods.'[2]

Another name for Treacle Ale is *Brown Robin*.

Skeachan
(Meg Dods's Recipe)

Treacle (molasses), hops or gentian or dry ginger,
yeast, soft water

Boil for twenty minutes four pounds of molasses in from six to eight gallons of soft water, with a handful of hops tied in a muslin rag, or a little extract of gentian. When cooled in the tub to 80°, add a pint of fresh beer-yeast, or from four to six quarts of fresh worts from the brewer's vat. Cover the beer (and all fermenting liquids) with blankets or coarse cloths. Pour it from the lees and bottle it. You may use sugar for molasses, which is lighter.

N.B. This is a cheap and very wholesome beverage. A little ginger may be boiled in it a half-hour, if the flavour is liked, instead of hops.

An old cottage recipe says: 'Let it stand over one day, when you must cork it tightly.'

1. These are suitable for small quantities.
2. William Watson: *Glimpses o Auld Lang Syne* (1905).

Skeachan
A Perthshire Recipe)

> 2 lb. black treacle   2 oz. yeast
> 5 quarts water

Put the treacle in a crock and pour the boiling water over it. When lukewarm, add the yeast spread on toast. Cover closely and leave for three days. Then bottle, cork tightly and wire the corks, as this ale becomes very lively.

Treacle Peerie is a yeastless variety of skeachan.

SLOE WINE

> 1 gallon sloes   4 lb. sugar
> 1 gallon water   2 small lemons

The sloe is the blue-black fruit of the blackthorn. The fruit should be perfectly clean and ripe and dry when gathered. Prick each berry with a needle, place them all in a crock, and pour the boiling water over them. When the water is tepid, crush them well, using either a wooden spoon or the hands. Cover and allow to stand for a week, stirring every day. Put the sugar and thinly sliced lemon into another crock and strain the sloe liquor over it. Stir occasionally till the sugar is melted. Pour all into a small spirit or wine cask. Leave loosely corked for a few days, then fasten down tightly.

After twelve months sloe wine, it is said, is 'almost as good as port'.

SPRUCE BEER

Spruce beer appears to have been made from very early times, and was particularly popular in the Highlands. An unknown poet writes:

Gur a milse do phog	Sweeter is thy kiss
Na mil agus beoir,	Than honey and spruce,
Ge robhas ga'n ol	Though we were drinking them
A gloineachan.	From glasses.

Spruce Beer
(Mrs Dalgairns's Recipe)

2 lb. outer sprigs of the spruce fir	6 lb. black treacle
	1 teacupful yeast
3 oz. bruised ginger	10 gallons water

Boil the water, treacle and ginger together for half an hour; then add the sprigs of spruce and boil for five minutes. Strain through a hair sieve. When milk-warm, put it into the cask and stir the yeast well into it. Cover lightly. When it has fermented for a day or two (i.e. until fermentation ceases), it should be bunged up, and on the following day bottled. It will be fit for use in a week.

Spruce Beer
(Another Recipe, using Essence of Spruce)

2 lb. black treacle, molasses or essence of malt	2 tablespoonfuls essence of spruce
1 oz. yeast	2 gallons spring water

Dissolve the treacle in a gallon of warm water. Put it into a cask and add a gallon of cold water. Then add the essence of spruce, and when the mixture is tepid, stir in the yeast. Leave the cask, closely covered, in a warm place for a day or two, until the fermentation subsides; then bung it firmly. It will be ready for use in a week.

If a spicy flavour is desired, boil a few hops with some ginger or allspice in a little of the beer and add it to the cask.

The above recipe makes 'black beer'. 'White beer' is made in the same way, except that honey or sugar is substituted for treacle.

Essence of spruce should be procurable from a good herbalist, but it can also be made at home if there are trees within reach. The usual practice is to make a supply in the spring and use it all the year round. It will keep indefinitely. The young shoots should be gathered as soon as they appear in the spring. Put them into a preserving pan, cover with water, and boil until the resinous flavour is extracted and the water is coloured brown. Strain, and return the liquor to the pan. Boil again until it is reduced to half the original amount; then bottle and store.

Spruce beer is reputed to be one of the most wholesome of drinks—cleansing and healing, stimulating and strengthening, and a great purifier of the blood. As a powerful anti-scorbutic, the essence used to be carried by sailors setting out on long arduous voyages, the beer being brewed as required. Its virtues may have been somewhat exaggerated, but undoubtedly it is a wholesome and antiseptic drink, and, over and above, its effects are mild.

WHEAT WINE

1½ lb. wheat	5 lb. Demerara sugar
1½ lb. potatoes	1 oz. yeast
1½ lb. raisins	1 gallon water

Peel and slice the potatoes and put them into a pan with the wheat, raisins, sugar and water. Heat slowly, but remove just before boiling-point is reached. Turn into a crock, and when the liquor has cooled to tepid, add the yeast. Cover lightly and leave for three weeks, stirring daily. When fermentation has ceased, strain into clean, dry bottles, and leave lightly corked for a few days; then cork tightly. Keep for at least six months, and preferably for twelve, before drinking.

8: *Simple Country Beverages*

OATMEAL POSSET

(Mrs Cleland's Recipe)

Flour of oatmeal, sugar, nutmeg, cinnamon, milk, ale, sack

Take a mutchkin (pint) of milk, put in two spoonfuls of flour of oatmeal and boil it with nutmeg and cinnamon till the rawness is off the oatmeal; then take three spoonfuls of sack and three spoonfuls of ale and two spoonfuls of sugar; set it over the fire till it is scalding hot, then put it to the milk, give it one stir, and let it stand on the fire for a minute or two, and pour it into your bowl; cover it and let it stand a little, then send it up.

STOORUM

Said to be splendid for nursing mothers.

Oatmeal, salt, milk, water

Put a heaped teaspoonful of oatmeal into a tumbler; add a little cold water and stir well. Fill up half-way with boiling water, then to the top with boiling milk. Season with salt, and serve.

BLENSHAW

A wholesome and nutritious beverage.

Oatmeal, sugar, nutmeg, milk, water

Put a heaped teaspoonful of oatmeal into a tumbler with the same quantity or less of sugar. Pour in half a gill of good milk, stir to the thickness of cream and then pour in boiling water, stirring till the tumbler is full. Lastly grate a very little nutmeg over it. Do not drink it too hot. It should be the temperature of milk from the cow.

N.B.—The names *blenshaw* (Fr. *blanche eau,* whitish water) and *stoorum* seem to be used arbitrarily for any of the many varieties of oatmeal drinks.

WHITE CAUDLE

2 large tablespoonfuls finely ground oatmeal	Strip of lemon rind White wine (optional)
1 quart water	Sugar

Pour the water over the oatmeal, mix and allow to stand for two hours. Strain through a sieve and boil the liquid gently with the lemon rind for half an hour, stirring frequently. Sweeten and add wine and seasoning to taste. Pour into a heated jug and serve hot, with or without thin slips of toast or rusks.

BROWN CAUDLE or SCOTS ALEBERRY

Make as above, substituting a pint of good mild ale for the wine, and adding, if desired, a glass of brandy.

OATMEAL NOG

1 tablespoonful oatmeal	1 teaspoonful honey
1 tablespoonful whisky	or sugar
Pinch of salt	½ pint milk

Put the oatmeal into a small bowl; heat the milk and pour over the oatmeal. Cover and leave for an hour; then strain, squeezing the meal dry. Return the mealy milk to the pan, add the salt and honey, bring to the boil and simmer for ten minutes. Pour into a tumbler, add the whisky, and drink hot.

A HARVEST DRINK

This drink, which is reputed to be strengthening, used to be popular with the workers in the harvest-field.

4 oz. oatmeal	Pinch of ground ginger
6 oz. sugar	(optional)
Juice of 1 lemon	1 gallon water

Put the oatmeal and sugar into a pan, and mix it with a little warm water and lemon juice; then pour over it, stirring all the time, a gallon of boiling water. Boil (still stirring) for three minutes. Add (or omit) ground ginger to taste. Strain and use when cold.

GREEN WHEY

(Mrs McEwen's Recipe)

Have a stew-pan on the fire half full of boiling water; have a quart of new milk in a jug that has a stroup, set it in the stew-pan on the fire, put a tablespoonful of rennet or yearning to it, take it from the fire and let it stand in hot water; if the yearning is good it will be curds in a few minutes; this you will know by leaving a spoon in the jug. If you find that it does not fasten in five minutes put a little more to it; take care that you do not make it too salt; when it is fastened, draw the spoon through it two or three times; let it stand; the whey will rise to the top, the curd fall to the bottom. It is now fit for use.

In former days ailing folk often resorted to the Highlands to drink goat's whey.

Stroup, spout

SACK OR WINE WHEY

Mrs McEwen's Recipe

     1 pint new milk   ½ pint wine

Put the milk in a saucepan on the fire; when it boils, take it from the fire, put the wine into it—Sherry, Madeira, or mountain; stir it, cover it up; in a little the curd will fall to the bottom; strain it off; it is now ready.

BLAAND *or* SPARKLING WHEY

This traditional Shetland beverage is simply the whey of buttermilk left to ferment in an oak cask, and used at the proper stage. To make the whey, pour enough hot water on to the buttermilk to make it separate, and drain the whey off the curd. (The latter may be pressed and eaten with cream.) Pour the whey into the cask and leave it undisturbed until it reaches the fermenting, sparkling stage.

It is a delicious and most quenching drink, and sparkles in the glass like champagne. After the sparkle goes off, it becomes flat and vinegary, but may be kept at the perfection stage by the regular addition of fresh whey.

Blaand used to be in common use in every Shetland cottage, and was at one time given by fashionable doctors to consumptive patients under the name of the Sour Whey Cure.

BRAWARDINE'S DRINK

'A silver jug, which held an equal mixture of cream and buttermilk, was placed for the Baron's share of this repast (breakfast).'

                                         Scott: *Waverley*

KIRN MILK AN' SOOROCKS

'Drink off this wersh brew, sir—it was my mither's way to caller the blood—just kirn milk boiled wi' soorocks.'

Kirn-milk, buttermilk; *soorocks*, sorrel; *wersh*, insipid, unsalted; *caller*, freshen

CARAGEEN DRINK

½ oz. carageen (dried)	1 egg (optional)
3 pints milk	Sugar to taste
Flavouring if desired	

Wash the carageen and steep for half an hour. Put it into a saucepan with the milk, bring slowly to the boil, and let it simmer very gently for four or five hours. Add sugar to taste, and if the sea-flavour is disliked, flavour with a bit of lemon rind, a bay leaf, or a pinch of dried elder flowers. A beaten egg may be added, but must not reach boiling point.

Carageen contains iodine and sulphur, and is often recommended for chest troubles.

GENERAL INDEX

INDEX OF AUTHORS

SONGS AND POEMS

INDEX TO TITLES

INDEX OF FIRST LINES

INDEX OF RECIPES

289